# LADY ANNE BLUNT

## *A Biography*

For my mother,
Beatrice Mary

**Lady Anne Blunt**
**A Biography**

Copyright © HVF Winstone 2003

Barzan Publishing
128 Kensington Church Street
London W8 4BH
Tel: 020 7221 7166 Fax: 020 7792 9288
website: www.barzanpress.com


ISBN: 1900988 577

CIP Data: A catalogue record for this book is available from the British Library

*Design*: Sam Crooks

*Printing & Binding*: Biddles Ltd.

# LADY ANNE BLUNT

*A Biography*

---

## H V F Winstone

**BARZAN PUBLISHING**

# CONTENTS

# Illustrations

Unless otherwise indicated, all illustrations are taken from the Wentworth Collection in the British Library and are reproduced here by kind permission of Lord Lytton and the British Library. The engravings at the head of chapters were made by Molony from Lady Anne Blunt's drawings and published in *Pilgrimage to Nejd* (1881). They are reproduced here by kind permission of John Murray, Publishers. The publishers have made every effort to trace the owners of copyright, but will be happy to correct any errors or omissions in further editions.

Jacket pictures:

*Front:* Lady Anne Blunt in a wicker chair from a photograph album entitled 'Egypt 1907' BL. ADD MSS 54085

*Back:* 'The Citadel at Aleppo, Syria, 1878', watercolour by Lady Anne Blunt, BL. ADD MSS 54061.

*Spine (and page 8)*: Lady Anne Blunt as a girl, from a drawing by G.F. Watts.

*Between pages 96 and 97:*

1. Lady Anne Blunt with her Arab mare Kasida. By permission of the Fitzwilliam Museum, University of Cambridge.

2. Photograph of a portrait of Lady Anne Blunt, 1893. BL. ADD MSS54085.

3. George Gordon, Lord Byron. By permission of the Bridgeman Art Library and the National Portrait Gallery, London.

4. Anne Isabella Milbanke, Lady Byron. By permission of the Bridgeman Art Library.

5. William, Earl of Lovelace, 1874. BL. ADD MSS 54085.

6. Ada, Countess of Lovelace. By permission of the Bridgeman Art Library and the *Illustrated London News* Picture Library.

7. Lady Anne painting Wilfrid Blunt on a horse at Crabbet Park.

8. Lady Anne in the drawing room of Crabbet (photograph by Mrs. Pollen, 1884). BL. ADD MSS 75270.

9. Wilfrid Blunt in Paris, 1873. BL. ADD MSS 54085.

10. Lady Anne with her daughter Judith, undated. BL. ADD MSS 54085.

11. Lady Anne sitting at her easel, with Judith as a young girl holding a puppy, undated. BL. ADD MSS 54085.

12. Lady Anne in Dublin, 1888. BL. ADD MSS 75270.

13. Judith after her marriage to Neville Lytton (photograph by Lafayette, undated). BL. ADD MSS 75270.

14. Lady Anne in Arab dress (photograph by T. Ellis, undated). BL. ADD MSS 54085.

15. Wilfrid Blunt in Arab dress with Sherifa (photograph by T. Ellis, 1883) BL. ADD MSS 54085.

16. From Lady Anne's watercolour of the 'ghazzu', the desert battle.

17. Lady Anne on her mare Fasiha (photograph by Gertrude Bell, Egypt, 1907). BL. ADD MSS 54085.

18. Lady Anne and Wilfrid Blunt outside their tent. BL. ADD MSS 54085.


*On page 122*: Lady Anne Blunt in 1872 with one of her celebrated Stradivarius violins. Drawing by Wilfrid Blunt.


*Between pages 256 and 257*:
19. 'Hamid's mare, Kihefet Ajouz', undated watercolour by Lady Anne. BL. ADD MSS 54048.

20. Drawing of 'Faris', March 16, 1878 by Lady Anne. BL. ADD MSS 54048

21. 'House at Hail', January 29, 1879, watercolour by Lady Anne. BL. ADD MSS 54048.

22. 'Haj Camp at Birket Jamourah', undated watercolour by Lady Anne. BL. ADD MSS 54048.

23. 'A View from the Residency at Baghdad', March 16, 1879, watercolour by Lady Anne. BL. ADD MSS 54049.

24. 'Persian Pilgrimage seen in mirage', undated watercolour by Lady Anne. BL. ADD MSS 54048.

25. The 'Pink House', Egypt, 1900, watercolour by Lady Anne. BL. ADD MSS 54055.

26. 'Desert Days', January 31, 1900, watercolour by Lady Anne. BL. ADD MSS 54055.

27. 'Esmafiha', undated coloured drawing by Lady Anne. BL. ADD MSS 53856.

# Introduction

The circumstances of Lady Anne Blunt's childhood and adult life have been set out in some outstanding biographical studies. First, and of seminal importance, came Malcolm Elwin's trilogy; *Lord Byron's Wife*, *The Noels and the Milbankes*, and *Lord Byron's Family*, published between 1962 and 1975. Then came a second generation of studies which owed much to the first, chief among them Doris Langley Moore's *Ada Countess of Lovelace*, and Elizabeth Longford's *A Pilgrimage of Passion: The Life of Wilfrid Scawen Blunt*.

It was tempting in the light of those full and excellent accounts to suppose that the reader of my book would be familiar with the background and social connections of the Byrons and Blunts which influenced so profoundly the life of Lady Anne. But I have taken the course, always open to criticism by those who subscribe to the 'head-on' approach to biography, of dealing with my subject's years at length in the context of historical events that may be seen by those who are familiar with them as superfluous. Lady Anne's exceptional qualities of tolerance and forbearance, as well as her modesty – and in later years her eccentricity – pass all understanding unless they are related in the telling to prior events which would be barely credible if they were presented as fiction. Lady Anne Blunt was born into a family whose capacity for engendering hatred has been described by one of its best informed students as 'exquisite'. The man she married, Wilfrid Scawen Blunt, augmented that reputation and carried it to astonishing depths of indulgence. The need for a biography is suggested by the strictures of the Blunts' own daughter Judith, Lady Wentworth. Writing some thirty years after the death of her mother, Lady Wentworth had this to say of her parents:

> Her devotion to this brilliant but wayward being is a record of self-sacrifice and self-effacement which will be dealt with one day... Hitler and Mussolini were amateurs compared to him! His tyranny and spirit of discord eventually alienated him from his family, from most of his friends and from several countries... his temper was not improved by hashish and morphia... utterly ruthless in love or war, loving no one beyond the 'mad minute', hating most people and ready to fight with a feather, life with him was a series of earthquakes and thunderstorms with the one compensation that no one could complain of its monotony.[1]

Lady Wentworth found apt comparison between her father and her maternal great-grandfather, Lord Byron. And she saw irony in the public's response to the rejected wives. 'But the public wants romance and can forgive anything in a woman except good works, which are traditionally the monopoly of prudes and pedants! Morality is such a bore! And good Samaritans so desperately dowdy!'

The daughter had a great deal more to say, which Elizabeth Longford found 'extremely biased and unfair' in so far as it related to W. S. Blunt, and which must take its due place in the narrative that follows. It is enough by way of preface to say that the immense collections of papers inherited by Lady Wentworth from her brilliant and errant forebears eventually found their way to the British Library in London and the Bodleian at Oxford.

Thus I was able to take up the task which the daughter predicted, a biography of Lady Anne which would tell her side of an unequal story, and perhaps at last free her reputation and her very real achievements from dependence on her husband's claims to public attention.

Until now she has always figured as a footnote to his life; in reference books and encyclopedias her works and attainments are seen as mere appendages. In everything, she is overshadowed by his exultant and tempestuous personality, by his pride and vanity, his vainglorious challenge to a world that he despised in proportion to the privileges it heaped on him. Her victories were won without fuss or din, but they are no less deserving of recognition.

Lady Anne Blunt was the granddaughter of Lord Byron, born in the shadow of the cause célèbre of the age, though it would be thirty years or more before she became fully aware of the scandal portended by the whispered asides of childhood.

Byron had died at the age of 36 in 1824 while supporting the nationalist movement in Greece, 13 years before Anne's birth. The public saw in his heroic self-sacrifice a romantic message which they carried forward into the Victorian age and beyond.

Greece, the very heart and lungs of European culture, remained under the yoke of the Turks, and within three years of the poet's death the Royal Navy took sides against the 'infidel' Ottoman power and, together with its French and Russian allies, blew the Turkish fleet out of the water at Navarino Bay.[2] Britain would yet need Turkey as an ally. But Greece would always encompass the spirit of Europe, and long after his own death, Byron was honoured as its modern muse, a passionate advocate in the days of its bondage.[3]

That reputation would lie side by side with domestic rumour, whispered at first, then unfolding until it became a ferocious gale of innuendo and slander, with barely-concealed hints of an incestuous relationship with his half-sister Augusta Leigh, and other sins – including sodomy.

The essential facts are better set out here and now, so that the reader who is not familiar with them – or has forgotten them – is saved the confusions of parallel history. On 2 January 1815, the 26 year-old 6th Lord Byron (1788-1824) had married Anne Isabella Milbanke, the only daughter of Sir Ralph and Lady (Judith) Milbanke (née Noel).[4] By that time Byron had published *Childe Harold*, *The Bride of Abydos*, *The Corsair*, and other lesser works, and had made a distinguished maiden speech in the House of Lords; English society was at his feet. Ada, his only legitimate daughter and Lady Anne's mother-to-be, was born the following year. Soon afterwards, her parents separated. Byron left England in 1816, never to return.

The poet's scandalous bachelor affair with Lady Caroline Lamb, daughter-in-law of the eminent Melbournes and wife of the future Prime Minister, had been trumpeted from the rooftops by the lady herself. And before his engagement to Miss Milbanke, he had admitted to a more than platonic devotion to his half-sister Augusta, who was married to a spendthrift dolt by the name of Colonel George Leigh. Their passion, so it was rumoured, had led to the birth of a child, Elizabeth Medora, in 1814.

If Ada was 'sole daughter' of the poet's 'house and heart' it was the illegitimate Elizabeth Medora who reminded the world of the romantic young woman of *The Corsair*, who bore the same name.

The word 'incest' was on the tip of many a tongue, but few uttered it. In those days such accusations were not spoken aloud in polite circles. But that 'darkest of all secrets' was confided by Lady Byron to her wide circle of friends in the years that followed her separation from the poet. Following Byron's death at Missolonghi in 1824, whispered rumour turned to scandal. Medora, encouraged by Lady Byron, brought her mother Augusta, lady-in-waiting to the Queen, to disgrace and ruin.

Ada first learned of the 'most strange and dreadful history' of the alleged union of her father and aunt and its destructive aftermath when her own daughter was four. Anne was in her thirties, and on the verge of her own marriage, when conspiratorial chatter overheard in childhood became public property with the publication by Harriet Beecher Stowe of her apologia *Lady Byron Vindicated,* which contained 'indisputable evidence' of that crime for which there could be no atonement, 'no salvation in this world'. The venomous family testament which Anne would inherit is amply illustrated by a sentence or two from a letter written by the supposedly illegitimate Medora (some contemporaries thought she resembled her legal father, Colonel Leigh) to her aunt Lady Byron, on encountering her estranged mother Augusta, in 1842:

> Her large eyes are ever & indeed unchanged, her walk is most altered she shuffles along as if she tried to carry the ground she walks on with her & looks WICKED. Oh were there a thing I had hoped to be spared it was this... Oh how dearly fondly I loved her & had she only stifled the existence her sin gave me – but God is there – & I will do my best to bear as I have ever done but it is so long & so constant – God forgive her – Oh how horrible she looked – so wicked – so hyena like... If for my good or that of Marie [her own daughter], intimidate her! – she will grovel on the ground, fawn, lick the dust – all – all that is despicable – & bad... Now we will try & never mention her name – she will live for years – Oh could I only have loved the memory of my mother but had death passed over me – the chill – the horror – could not have been so great.[5]

Not for ten years or more had the 28 year-old daughter as much as set eyes on the mother she so despised and cursed with those words. But time was no healer in her baleful family. In the long unfolding of that most public of domestic dramas, discord among family and friends would grow in malevolence and intensity as it spread from one generation to another, from one century to the next.

# Acknowledgments

In thanking the many people who have helped and guided me, I must place first in priority the present Lord Lytton, senior surviving member of the family, and his literary agents, Laurence Pollinger Ltd.

The impetus and initial encouragement came from the late Doris Langley Moore who held court with aplomb when I first plied her with questions about the Byron and Lovelace family histories, matters on which she had strong views and an incomparable store of knowledge.

Afterwards came the paperwork. I acknowledge most gratefully the keepers of those collections already mentioned, especially the Wentworth Bequest in the British Library and the Lovelace Byron Papers in the Bodleian Library. Those archives, containing the papers of both Wilfrid Blunt and Lady Anne, as well as those of Lady Byron and the Earl and Countess of Lovelace, have been my retreat for many long months. I have sifted through thousands of letters, as well as diaries, notebooks and sketchbooks, kept up – in the case of my subject – from the age of four until her death at 80. In addition, over a period of four years, I have examined the Wilfrid Blunt correspondence in the Cambridge University Library, and the Lovelace, Somerville, Babbage, Ruskin, Nightingale and other papers in universities and public collections which I acknowledge in my notes at the end of the book.

I am particularly grateful to the late governor of the Saudi Arabian province of Al Jauf, His Highness the Amir Abdur Rahman al Sudairy. Through the offices of the British Council I was able to visit the Amir's territory and tread the paths of the Blunts, enter the castles in which they were received, and make an aeroplane survey of their route to the remote desert region of Jabal Shammar and its capital Hail, where my subject experienced the happiest and most hazardous days of her life. The Amir's hospitality and courtesy were augmented by his son, the Prince Ziad, whose knowledge of the history and qualities of the Arab horse, a subject inseparable from the life of Lady Anne, would not readily find its equal. Also I must thank Ali al-Rashid of the Al Sudairy Foundation at Jauf, who cleared up mysteries of geography and ancient castles which were as confusing to the Blunts as to their biographers and who so patiently dealt with my ceaseless enquiries about old tribal allegiances and Jauf governorships.

In the same connection, my friend and colleague of past enterprises, Zahra Freeth, contributed to our joint work, 'Explorers of Arabia', a carefully researched essay on the Blunts' journey to Nejd which saved me a great deal of labour. Mrs Freeth also read my manuscript with her customary thoroughness and made several useful suggestions. And I owe a particular debt to Helen Ryan, distinguished actress, whose own interest in my subject was reinforced by her playing the part of Gertrude Bell, Lady Anne's predecessor in Arab lands, in a film made in Baghdad at the behest of former President Saddam Hussein. She read my text with a practised eye and I appreciate her sensitive observations. My friend Peter Scott read and made valuable suggestions. They cannot of course be held responsible for any defects, but between them they removed many an incongruity and quite a few literary wrinkles from my story.

In the specialist areas of horse breeding and equine history, I have made extensive reference to the works of Rosemary Archer and James Fleming, especially their *Journals and Correspondence of Lady Anne Blunt, 1878-1917*, and *The Crabbet Arabian Stud*. Mrs Langley Moore and Lady Longford between them delved very thoroughly into the papers of my subject's mother and husband, and I have leaned heavily on their works too. Though I do not necessarily share their judgements in matters which have divided bitterly the loyalties of Byrons, Lovelaces, Blunts and Lyttons, and their friends and protagonists, I hope I represent them without distortion. The two institutions whose names are synonymous with literary research in England, the Bodleian and British Libraries, as ever made light of the most onerous demands; I thank especially Dr Judith Priestman of the former and Ms J M Backhouse and Ms C M Hall of the latter's Department of Manuscripts.

Others to whom I am indebted for favours large and small: Bromley (Kent) Library; Devon County Libraries (in particular the Barnstaple and Bideford branches); Wandsworth Library; Mrs Henrietta McCall; Mr William Dewhurst; Mr John Edwards; the late Marghanita Laski; Ms Margaret Pringle and Polly Scott. My wife Joan and my daughter Ruth read and re-read as ever, while the rest of my family fetched and carried with varying degrees of enthusiasm. I thank them all.

Lastly and most importantly, I express my gratitude to my publisher, Dr Mohammad Al Rashid, member of the distinguished Arab family that ruled over Hail and the territory of Shammar from 1834 to 1921, whose publishing company Barzan reflects in its name the remote palace in which Lady Anne and Wilfrid Blunt were entertained by Muhammad Al Rashid, most famous of the princes of that house. The Barzan company is destined to become an important force in Anglo-Arab publishing, and it has been a pleasant experience to have my latest book pass through its hands. I have been greatly helped by the company's editor Lionel Kelly, its British associate Stacey International and my friend Peter Harrigan, who lives in Saudi Arabia and writes with distinction on Arabic and other matters.

On the vexed question of Arabic transliteration, I confess to the small liberty, even in some quotations, of opting for consistency in the spelling of common words such as sheikh, amir not emir, Iraq not Irak, wadi not wady, etc. It makes life easier for the reader and I seek no other justification. A list of common Arabic words is given at the end of the book with alternative renderings.

# Part One

---

# Family
# &
# Childhood

---

# *Chapter One*

# Shadows of Genius

It was confidently expected that the child would be a boy, and when a girl appeared the parents took a detached view.

All the same, the infant was assured immortality from the outset, for her mother, Ada Countess of Lovelace, was the child of Lord Byron, his only legitimate offspring. Annabella, or to be precise Lady Ann Isabella Noel King, was born on 22 September 1837 at 10 St James's Square, the London home of her parents, Lord and Lady King, the Earl and Countess of Lovelace.[1]

The child assumed the name Anne in later years and so the name of her choice will be used henceforth, except in quotation. Her brother Byron, a year old at her birth, mercifully succeeded to the peerage of Ockham when three years old so we are spared a further hurdle in a family history as noted for its confusion of names as for its animosities. Nearly two years after Anne, there arrived the third and last child of the Lovelaces, Ralph Gordon.

Her mother's behaviour in and out of marriage suggested much of the eccentricity which would dominate Anne's adult life; something too of her father's wilfulness. Ada was ill-suited to motherhood. Her interests and talents lay elsewhere. She was an enthusiastic horsewoman and devoted to all animals, she was an accomplished musician who played several instruments, a brilliant mathematician and an inveterate gambler.

Soon after giving birth to Anne, and before lapsing into a severe but medically unexplained post-natal illness, she wrote:

> You cannot think how charmed I am with the metaphysical child, & how I have thought of her. If she will only be kind enough to be a metaphysician & a mathematician instead of a silly minikin dangling Miss in leading strings I shall love her mind too much to care whether her body is male, female or neuter.

The life that lay ahead of the infant was foretold by what followed:

> But really, all joking apart, I feel there is that in her which I shall delight to commune with as she comes to maturity (& which has nothing to do with her sex either way). William too begins to feel her superiority. He says he hopes she will marry a man whose position & circumstances may be such as to place his wife above the necessities of giving her intellect and energies to the mere daily affairs of life.[2]

Ada's attitude to motherhood was, to say the least, unusual. On one occasion she wrote: 'If A[nnabella]'s mind is capacious & superior, it would be a shame that it were not free to follow out its own bent & studies.' She was an altogether *rara avis* as mother and wife. She adopted the habit, soon after her marriage to Lord King (later Earl of Lovelace) in 1835, of using bird names as tokens of affection. Since her mother Lady Byron was close to both, so close in fact, that the marriage could be described with some justice as a *ménage à trois*, she too was admitted to the aviary. Thus, Lady Byron was Hen, and Ada herself Chick, Thrush, or sometimes Avis or Ucellina, and William King, the brooding, dark-complexioned husband, Crow.

The children were not part of this homely circle. They were placed in the care of nannies and governesses appointed, rewarded and dismissed by Lady Byron with almost total disregard of the parents' wishes, the interests of the children or the competence of the employees concerned. And since their wealthy grandmother bought and rented houses as the fancy took her, much time in the children's early years was spent in bouncing, windswept carriages as they careered between one home and another; Esher and East Horsley in Surrey, Mayfair and Belgravia in London, Brighton and Southampton, suburban Ealing and Porlock on the Somerset-Devon border; to say nothing of the residences of her ladyship's legion of sympathisers.

Grandmamma's influence seems to have extended to the nursery. 'When Annabella is washed', Lady Byron told the first of many nannies, 'she is to stand upon a flannel instead of in the tub. The tub should be wood so that she may sit over the edge without danger to have the water stream down her back, &c. The feet to be washed separately in warm water.'

Evidently the father was just as demanding in his way as mother and grandmother. As the infant Anne lay in her cot, Ada wrote of William's belief that she 'might be tolerably happy at home until 20, provided she liked to study & had pursuits.' What he dreaded, his wife noted, was 'a purposeless, desultory Miss whose interests merely consist in flirting, embroidering or perhaps (as a great God-send) the piano & miniature painting.' So the far-fetched list of 'dawning anticipations' was laid out by way of convincing the parents themselves, if no one else, that the birth of a female child in a family where there was already a son was not an unmitigated disaster. 'You will be vastly amused at this letter; and at our dawning anticipation that the female misfortune may turn out not quite overwhelming.'

Anne's own recollections of early childhood were unreliable. In later life she would insist that she spent 'many happy hours with Grandmamma',[3] yet of the nursery she would recall only the joyous bedtime stories related by her aunt Hester Stanhope, the eccentric explorer of Syria and the Levant who, in her early years, kept house for Pitt the Younger. In fact, Anne probably remembered stories passed on by her mother, for she was only two years old when her aunt died. The child who listened in wonderment, however, would one day make her aunt's travels seem ordinary. Aunt Hester aside, nothing stayed in her memory so poignantly as the favouritism shown towards her brothers, even with food, so that she often felt hungry and hoped, usually in vain, that one of them might spare her a morsel.

On one of the rare occasions when Anne was in the care of mother and grandmother, Lady Byron scolded her own daughter for slapping the child, telling her she should have used 'moral influence'. Ada usually allowed her mother the last word but on this occasion she launched a spirited counter-attack. Why had there been no objection when she slapped young Ockham? she asked. 'She is far more naughty, when she is naughty, than he ever was.' Ada went on to insist that her only regret was that she had not administered harder punishment to Anne at other times. But that was an isolated example of parental interest. By the girl's third birthday, Ada had renounced the everyday world for the academic life she craved, and Lady Byron and 'moral influence' had taken a firm grip on all three children.[4]

In June 1833, Ada had come into contact with the work of Charles Babbage, Lucasian Professor of Mathematics at Cambridge. He was working on a revolutionary calculating machine, a mechanical device for which Ada immediately saw an 'electrical' future. The device was called by its inventor the 'Difference Machine', but it would eventually be known as a computer.[5] She bided her time for a year and then attended a lecture by Dr Dionysius Lardner on the principles of the new machine. Afterwards she was introduced to the great man himself. Babbage was enchanted by the extraordinary Ada, daughter of the finest of romantic poets and clearly an exceptional mathematician. For the next year Ada combined science with the essentials of motherhood, though her letters began to contain Newtonian asides which suggest that the scales were tipping in the direction of science. When young Ockham was three, she wrote: 'Little B. is more attracted I think by motion than by anything. I think he has an experimental disposition... He knows me well.'

'Little B' was Ada's favourite, but even he was soon cast aside in a family life circumscribed by Ada's scientific interests and her husband's almost complete disregard of the children. Their mother had found a divinely inspired mission and she set out to fulfil 'God's will' in collaboration with Babbage, ever on the move between academics of one cast and another and between one Lovelace estate and another, while Lady Byron took charge of the children's upbringing.

Governesses came and went in quick succession. Lady Byron's immediate instrument was Miss Lamont,[6] an Irish woman who had been appointed Ada's governess in 1820 when her charge was five, and had been dismissed three years later because she was 'quite unable to gain the necessary ascendancy over so masterly a mind.' Nevertheless, Lady Byron had granted that the governess was 'humble' and 'a good teacher', even if 'unfitted to so uncommon a situation as that of Governess here'. She had paid off Miss Lamont and sent her packing; but now the lady was back in the fold as governess to the next generation, as was nurse Grimes, dismissed in Ada's second year because of 'cruel opposition to maternal wishes'.

Governess and nurse doubtless recalled Lady Byron's earlier instructions on 'the rational order of education from the cradle':

> I shall consider the best means of rendering the study of History as subservient to moral cultivation. The memory will retain most tenably such combinations and transitions as are suggested by the natural desire to know more of what is already known...[7]

Lovelace kept a discreet distance from this world of female hegemony. Having in 1835 entered into marriage with Ada and, for all practical purposes, with her mother, in a state of mind close to delirium – of happiness 'too excessive to be enjoyed otherwise than in a dream' – he relied entirely on his mother-in-law's judgement in matters of child rearing and even of property. It was three years after their marriage, in June 1838, that as the eighth Lord King he was elevated to the earldom. He was the direct descendant of a distinguished Lord Chancellor, was collaterally related to John Locke, whose *Life and Letters* was published by his father the seventh Lord King, and was widely thought of, not least by Prime Minister Lord Melbourne, as a man of scholarly mind who, like Ada's father, was never so much at home as in Greece and the Ionian islands. It was Lord Melbourne, Lady Byron's cousin, who secured Lovelace's appointment as Lord Lieutenant of his home county, Surrey, an office which brought a lifetime's dispensation to drive on Constitution Hill. Lady Byron encouraged him in one of the first enterprises of his married life, the establishment at Ockham Park of an industrial training school along Owenite lines, similar to an institution which she had set up in 1834 at her then home in Ealing, west London. Both were based on the Pestalozzi system of teaching founded by Emmanuel de Fellenberg in Switzerland, which was much admired by educational progressives. Lovelace's aim was to 'help deal with the many troubles of the working classes and the

insufficiency of all efforts made to improve their condition.'
Nothing could have commended her son-in-law more
surely to Lady Byron with her penchant for helping and
educating her 'inferiors'. If she execrated the husband
whose name she bore, she still found a perverse pleasure in
the nickname 'Princess of Parallelograms', which he had
given her in their courting days. Lovelace consulted her on
every point of detail concerning the school and she called
him 'the comfort of my life'. Approbation rubbed off on
Ada, too – 'dear happy wife'.

From the time of her daughter's marriage Lady Byron
had lived chiefly at Esher in Surrey, where she maintained
two large, unlovely houses, one for guests and the other for
herself. As often as not the Lovelace children found
themselves in the cheerless rooms of one or the other.
Passing through was a constant procession of imposing
middle-class intellectuals who, if they could not heal the
wounded pride of the rejected wife or stem the flow of that
famous 'bleeding heart', were ready to recommend
anything from conventional leeching to phrenology and
mesmerism in an attempt to ameliorate her ladyship's
condition. It was a mixed bag of friends and confidants and
it contained some distinguished people. Elizabeth Fry, with
her Quaker dress and manner, was a frequent visitor, along
with her own grandchild. And there were the Somervilles:
Mary, the most famous of women writers on scientific
matters in Victorian times, and her husband Dr William
Somerville, inspector of the army medical board. The
Unitarian Dr William King, Lady Byron's medical adviser
and closest confidant, and his wife, who had been Ada's
first governess, were almost always present to moralise
when any member of the family stepped over the
boundaries of that carefully regulated regime.

The most attractive member of the Esher circle, before
she went to America to marry, was the enchanting actress
Fanny Kemble, who had just given up reading the 'naughty'

poems of Lord Byron that had sustained her at boarding school when she was introduced to the poet's widow. Then there was Mrs De Morgan, matriarch of a most brilliant and eccentric family. Before her marriage she was Sophia Frend, and in the year of Anne's birth she became the wife of Augustus De Morgan, the first professor of mathematics at the University of London. Of their seven children, the first daughter Alice became Anne's most intimate childhood companion.[8] The eldest boy William was to become a leading member of the Arts and Crafts movement and the outstanding potter of his day. Sophia's father William Frend had been tutor to Lady Byron when, as Annabella Milbanke, she had proved a most able mathematical and philosophical scholar under his private tuition. It was almost certainly through Frend's influence that she turned to Nonconformism and gained a first insight into the Unitarian version of the Christian faith which rejected the Trinity and the divinity of Christ. Opposition to 'priestcraft' and rejection of the 'Scarlet Woman of Rome' were at the heart of an austere view of the world and its creation. Politically speaking, that view embraced vigorous support for the new co-operative movement and viewed with equanimity the revolution which was confidently expected to follow the passing of the Reform Bill.

Other forceful personalities came and went at Esher, some of whose views and prejudices were to prove significant in the lives of the Lovelace children. There was the popular Mrs Jameson, essayist and critic, passionate friend of Italy and Greece and all things classical, drawn by the name Byron to live at Esher where she could be within earshot of the 'angelic' widow. The ever flattering Miss Montgomery (nobody ever seemed to use her first name) and her brother, Colonel Hugh Montgomery (the man Lady Byron had pretended to love in maidenhood so as to excite Byron's interest), paid frequent homage, as did others who had known Augusta Leigh and Medora and would yet be ready to intervene in the ongoing drama of the illegitimate daughter's pathetic attempts at survival through extortion – people such as the Hon Mrs Theresa Villiers, Sir Robert and Lady Wilmot Horton, and the lugubrious family lawyer Dr Stephen Lushington.[9]

It was a fraternity which, by virtue of early marriage and longevity, embraced three generations and became familiar to Anne and her brothers. But the older generations seem not to have made much of an impression on Anne. Lady Byron's mathematical and other abilities had been inherited in good measure by her daughter, but Ada was too high-spirited, too much given to the physical delights of horseriding and the ballroom, too much embroiled in the application of higher mathematics to Babbage's calculating machine, to concern herself with her mother's outlandish philosophical and religious notions. Anne, for her part, was destined hardly to know her obsessive mother, or indeed her father; her grandmother's power over her, however, was to prove almost absolute. It says something for the child's strength of character that attitudes and precepts which dominated the lives of her parents and grandmother seem not to have troubled her unduly. Self-awareness and self-interest were manifest in her family. From the outset, she exhibited a refreshing disdain for those qualities. In later life, as in the nursery, she showed a tendency to self-denial.

Sophia De Morgan, a contemporary of Ada's, brings this extraordinary coterie to life. She had first set eyes on Lady Byron when the latter was 24, in 1816; she herself was seven at the time, and Ada was a year old. It was the year of Byron's final flight from England. A nurse carried Ada, 'the beautiful baby', to the threshold of the De Morgan home on Clapham Common. Then Lady Byron stepped from the carriage. 'I can only say, as Mr Carlyle said to me many years after, hers was a face never to be forgotten... the great charm of her face was its sweet and intellectual, but rather mournful, expression...' Then again, as the child had its 'bumps' examined while the ladies discussed her responses to the minor poems of her father: 'But the head showed imagination, wonder, constructiveness and harmony, with very high intellectual powers. How could these fail of making a poet? [But] music and mathematics – often found to go together – were both strong elements of character.'

And we have a picture of Anne in her first year, in Lady Byron's arms, while Elizabeth Fry embraced her own grandchild of about the same age. The proud grandmothers talked of health and the efficacy of direct oral teaching on the minds of the morally diseased, and of the de Fellenberg system of education, each quite certain that her baby far outshone the other in promise and beauty.

(Mrs Fry to Lady Byron) 'Dost thou not find it a very pleasant relation?'

'Of course', Lady Byron answered, 'with cordial assent'.[10]

In a letter written when Anne was four years old, Ada compared her children with each other, contrasting the 'gentlemanlike & noble' appearance of Ockham with the somewhat wild aspect of Anne. Ockham's masters were delighted with his progress and everyone who met him was impressed by his manners, the 'goodness of his disposition' and, significantly, by his docility. Anne on the other hand, was a positive firebrand. She rode fearlessly and danced with vigour.

Ada was not unaware of her daughter's merits. Indeed, Anne's early vitality seemed to owe as much to her mother as to anyone – the mother who, before each of her confinements, alarmed her doctors by riding and dancing almost to the moment of delivery.

The world, she said, was just as charmed with Anne as with Ockham, 'but they tell me that in a boy (at that age), this obedient temper & pliability are far more remarkable than in a girl; unless in a child so stupid as to have no animation or intellect.'

Ada had been brought up in strict accordance with the moral, religious and academic precepts of her mother, and now her own children were being subjected to the same regime. It suited Lovelace, a strict disciplinarian by nature, to allow Lady Byron a free hand, and since she was financing his ambitious house and school building schemes at Ockham Park and Ashley Combe, it is unlikely that he would have objected anyway. Schools, even Eton where Lovelace was educated, were out of the question for her grandchildren. Schoolmasters were notoriously apt to indoctrinate children with the insidious poison of the Trinity and to dull their intellects and senses with mischievous theories.

Lady Byron's approach to education had two basic props: Nonconformism and de Fellenberg's concept of teaching by natural example and moral precept, raising the lower orders and training the higher by direct contact with nature and agriculture. When she first met de Fellenberg, Lady Byron was so enchanted with his notion of educating the children of the rich alongside those of the proletariat that she began a sonnet extolling his ideas. Unfortunately, she did not finish it. Her own principles had a great deal in common with de Fellenberg's, though less with those of Pestalozzi. She saw the need for an arm's-length approach to the poor, and had a strict sense of social priority: 'I trust to the principles with which I have always treated my inferiors.'[11]

In Anne's case, the injunction to commune with nature needed no pleading. From the beginning of her life to the end, the flowers of the garden, the creatures of the wild and her dogs and horses were paramount influences. But people also mattered to her. If Lady Byron's world was one of cold houses and sparseness amid wealth and privilege, Anne kept a heart that was, by the consent of all who knew her, warm and loyal. Considering the nature of her childhood, such qualities must have derived more from inner strength than from example.

Her concern for animals, reflected the attitudes of both parents, to say nothing of her grandfather's, which was manifested in his famous stories of the goose and the eaglet he thoughtlessly shot; 'the first and the last'. Remarkably for his day and age, Lovelace had been a vegetarian since the age of 19. He and Ada shared at least one common conviction, a strong disapproval of Queen Victoria's alleged pleasure in the suffering of the animals which her consort shot and left to die agonisingly on the royal estates. Lady Byron, on the other hand, had no time for the non-human creatures of the earth, insisting that the absence of soul rendered them incapable of feeling. She never spared her own or Lovelace's steeds and her treatment of her son-in-law's horses would prove the first cause of dissent between them. For the moment, though, all was harmony.

Singing, riding, drawing, arithmetic, the playing of every kind of musical instrument, speaking French and German: all were carried on from the unheated, bare nursery rooms under the supervision of an imposing array of teachers.

'All their masters indeed seem to grow very fond of these children', Ada wrote. An Italian master, Signor Chisso, was said to have taken a particular liking to Ockham and to have devised studies which would, it was hoped, help him overcome the defects of 'slowness, dawdle and absence'.

Involvement with Babbage and the Difference Machine was now the core of Ada's existence, but every now and again she took time off from the calls of numerical science to care for the children. Occasionally the joy of young motherhood would break through:

> 'Mr Knoff is to teach the children a little singing... I will tell you a funny thing. Today, when their dancing master (in my presence), made the two children join hands together in a most graceful attitude, & chasseur round the room in that way (which they did in beautiful measure), the tears rushed to my foolish eyes. There was something irresistibly touching in the picture, & in the playful affectionate look which Annabella kept beaming forth on her little brother partner. I shall not forget it. They are beginning to learn the waltz.'

The first of Anne's surviving letters was written soon

after her sixth birthday. Dated 16 October 1843, it was addressed to her mother from Ashley Combe, where the children had spent the summer and autumn months playing and riding amid the scenic splendours of the Somerset-Devon border, joined at intervals by their parents.

> My dear Mama, If it is fine we are going to Lynmouth tomorrow. We went on Sunday a very pleasant expedition and on Saturday we took a very nice long drive. Ralph and Byron send their love to Mama and Grandmamma and I send my love to them as well. Your Affectionate Annabella.[12]

A week or so later she wrote again, keeping her parents informed of her academic work, sending Ada some compositions in a very confident and careful hand, and a little Latin: 'I read very much in the natural history. Yesterday evening Byron and I went down to Papa and did draw on some paper which Papa gave us. Byron, I and Ralph send our love to you and Grandmamma.'

The summer vacation of that year was spent in Germany but only Anne's sketches survive to testify to the child's joy at her first sight of Rhineland forests and castles. Lessons under the supervision of father, governesses and the ordinary run of tutors were coming to an end by the time the vacation was over. Grandmamma had more ambitious plans.

'Both B & A told me they were delighted in the lessons & that it made them less regret Ashley. I think Dr C. is on the right track.' Lady Byron conveyed to the Lovelaces her satisfaction at her latest educational appointment in November 1844. Byron and Anne were in their ninth and eighth years respectively. Their new tutor, Dr William Carpenter, was no ordinary choice for so menial an educational task; he was one of the country's leading academic physicians, lecturer in physiology at the London Hospital Medical School, visiting lecturer at University College and about to be appointed Fullerian Professor of the Royal Institution. Only 30 years old, kindly and serious, and possessing the highest medical qualifications, he was also – and much to the point as far as Lady Byron was concerned – a Unitarian, and could thus be trusted to mould the minds of her grandchildren.[13]

Why so eminent a medical teacher accepted the appointment, it is hard to imagine. Lady Byron had visited him at his Bristol home, making a contract with him 'subject to her son-in-law's approval', and offering him a house, to be built at East Horsley, plus a stipend of £400 a year and £1,000 in compensation for giving up other sources of income. Ada at this time was showing alarming signs of physical ill health and mental unbalance. There were signs too, in the midst of mathematical studies which would have taxed any mind severely, of a compelling emotional interest in more than one of her collaborators, an interest which she readily confided to Babbage. But the eminent scientists with whom she was now on the most familiar terms were social inferiors and must not be allowed too much latitude. A gentleman was another matter, and at about the time of Carpenter's appointment she had discovered a very suitable candidate for her attention while riding in the vicinity of Ashley Combe – Mr Frederick Knight – an 'excellent creature' who deserved 'a nice lady-love'. A gossip columnist of the day wrote:

> The resemblance of Lady Lovelace to her renowned father, beyond some parental likeness, has as yet been confined to a certain amount of eccentricity. Her ladyship from her whimsical notions is thought a little daft.

And with a withering combination of innuendo and guesswork:

> Lady Lovelace thinks so highly of the opinion of Mr Frederick Knight... that she does not fancy even her costume complete until it has received the sanction of his acknowledged taste. The address of the gentleman may be inferred to be at least as remarkable as the dress of the lady.[14]

Ada admitted to one of her mother's closest friends, the

lawyer Woronzow Greig, that rumours of her affair with Mr Knight had spread. The cat-and-mouse game the flirtatious Ada proceeded to play with Dr Carpenter was more serious in its implications.

Knight was a gentleman, and the flirtation was between equals. Carpenter was but a doctor of medicine and a university lecturer, and she treated him with a mixture of cold command and coquettishness, while he tried to deal with the educational conundrums set out by Lady Byron. At the same time, Ockham showed dangerous signs of rebelliousness and was inclined to imitate the speech and mannerisms of the workers on his father's estates. Anne, though she tended to copy her brother's 'coarse servant-like way of talking', at least attended to her lessons and maintained a ladylike demeanour. Lady Byron attributed Anne's better behaviour to her independence from the latest governess, Miss Cooper, who was said to be terrified by her own 'conscious insufficiency'. Dr Carpenter tried to reassure the parents: 'I need scarcely say, dear Lady L., that I have felt much pained by the communication you have made respecting Byron. Yet I wd not have you feel discouraged by it; for you and I need not go beyond ourselves, for instance of the same want of regard for veracity in childhood... I can quite understand your depression, from the action and reaction between your bodily & mental state of discomfort; each aggravating the other'.

Ada had obviously consulted him about her condition and he unwisely responded as friend rather than doctor. After reminding him of his proper place, that of a servant, Ada had suggested that she should meet him alone at the St James's Square house. Whatever was said or done at that meeting, Carpenter felt emboldened to write her a long, rambling letter in which he set out his conditions for acting as tutor to her children and adviser to her. Miss Cooper – recently appointed governess in succession to a German lady by the name of Kramer who, according to Lady Byron, 'encouraged unruliness' – would be under his supervision. He would assume medical care of the children which would be 'overriding'. He proposed that two boy boarders should be accommodated in his house as companions and pace-setters for Ockham. Then came a dangerous thrust. 'That your children are above average in many points I have no doubt; but that they have many peculiarities, hereditary and acquired, which it will be difficult to control and direct... I think you must also be well aware.'

From the outset, Carpenter was faced with the father's unbending belief in incessant, unrelieved study, and the mother's conviction of genius running like a river in full flood through her family. On one occasion Carpenter wanted to take the children on a riverboat excursion to Richmond, combining learning with amusement. Lovelace, when he heard of the suggestion, was as humourless and unbending as ever. He accused the doctor of trying to evade the proper discharge of his duties. Meanwhile Ada had not finished her equivocal game. She had spoken to the 'dear doctor' of her inability to digest any but the smallest portions of food, and of drinking two or three medicinal glasses of claret at meals. Most significantly, she indicated that she had developed a 'distaste' for the company of her children, and an indifference to her husband, and men in general. Dr Carpenter might have been forgiven for believing that he had entered into a close and confidential relationship. His voluminous letter ended with the words: 'And now, my dear Lady Lovelace, shall you be angry or pleased with me if, recalling our last conversation in your sanctum, I ask your permission to sign myself – as I feel – Your affectionate friend.'

In her reply Ada wrote of 'impassable barriers'. Capriciously, she then reopened the door. 'I suspect it is a sense and an instinct of this being the case, which makes you venture and myself permit certain little familiarities, and I feel them not only harmless but even beneficial on appropriate occasions.'

The preposterous affair dragged on for a few months while Carpenter tried to come to terms with Ada and her irascible husband and the children's grandmother whose promises had started it all. The luckless tutor, inexperienced and maladroit in his dealings with women, floundered hopelessly, constantly referring to his wife's opinions and his marital fidelity. Mischievously, Ada had threatened to tell Mrs Carpenter of his 'naughtiness' and his 'state of very considerable excitement' when they were together. More rebuffs were followed by apology. 'I perceive that I have gone too far, and regret my error and presumption; but it was with good intention and in consequence of the encouragements you had given me. I shall endeavour not again to forget that you are the Countess of Lovelace and I am the tutor to your children.'

After nearly a year of this untenable tutorship, Carpenter was driven by guilt and confusion to put Lovelace in the picture. His lordship promptly terminated the contract with an *ex gratia* payment and Carpenter returned to tasks for which he was better equipped, never afterwards losing an opportunity to broadcast the details of his ill-usage by the Lovelaces. They in turn wrote to each other, commiserating over his ingratitude. 'What a villainous incendiary we have been harbouring,' Lovelace wrote, when it came to light that Carpenter had engaged in similar folly with another young lady. 'The sex will ruin him.'

Whether the children were aware of what was going on around them is uncertain, but it is significant that Dr Carpenter retained his link with Lady Byron and returned to the scene nearly 20 years later as a friend and adviser to Anne when the influence of her parents was no more.

Anne made good progress under the supervision of Miss Cooper, who surprisingly survived the Carpenter crisis. However, Lovelace left his door open in the morning so that he could hear the domestic servants and staff descend the stairs. Miss Cooper was sometimes not on duty until 7.30, a quarter of an hour past the appointed time. He wrote to Ada in August 1845 to tell her that he was 'tired' of Miss Cooper's 'idleness'.

A more serious crisis was in the making, involving Ada's new-found scientific colleagues. In November 1844 Ada had taken herself off to Broomfield in Somerset, no great distance from Ashley Combe, to the home of the physicist Andrew Crosse, a friend of Babbage and Charles Wheatstone. She had been told of Crosse's untidy existence, and Wheatstone had burst out laughing when she told him that she intended to stay in his house.[15]

Crosse's son John, also a scientist, with a penchant for horse racing and the betting shop, took an instant liking to the attractive, clever and slightly eccentric lady visitor. The lady was soon sharing the young man's bed. And with the connivance of both Crosses, she set out to construct that classic absurdity, a foolproof system of betting, based on her mathematical knowledge and perhaps, though of this there is no proof, using the Difference Machine to make the necessary calculations. Her symptoms of sickness had also begun to increase in intensity. They were at first thought to be due to a fourth pregnancy, but that turned out to be a false alarm. In letters to Woronzow Greig, Sophia De Morgan and others she wrote of 'strange sensations' about the head and of the need for laudanum, morphine and alcohol. Yet at other times she was the most balanced of people, and never more so than in her scientific dealings with Babbage. Throughout the previous year there had been a spate of correspondence in which he congratulated his 'dear Lady Lovelace' on her clear and precise mathematical calculations, especially in connection with the sorting of cards by which the first computers worked. 'The more I read your notes the more surprised I am and regret not having earlier explored so rich a vein of the noblest

metal', he wrote in July 1843. By September, just before
Carpenter came on the scene, a more personal note had
crept in. 'I will leave all other things undone & set out for
Ashley taking with me papers enough to enable me to forget
this world and all its troubles... everything in short but the
Enchantress of Number... Farewell my dear much admired
Interpreter.' At about the same time, Wheatstone asked if he
might call on her. Faraday, another of her scientist admirers,
expressed his amazement at her 'elasticity of intellect'. By
the summer of 1844, the balanced woman who had
declared a few months before that the computer would
prove a tool of inestimable value to mankind 'so long as its
limitations were understood', who had appreciated more
readily than its inventor the importance of its development
along electrical rather than mechanical lines, showed real
signs of insanity. She proclaimed messianically, 'I am the
instrument for the divine purpose... Like the Prophets of old
I shall speak the voice I am inspired with. I may be the
Deborah, the Elijah of Science.' And for good measure:
'However intensely I may love some mortals, there is One
above whom I must ever love & adore a million-fold as
intensely; the great All-knowing integral!'

Anne and her brothers were engaged in the innocent
pastimes of youth at their retreat in England's west country
when their mother entered the inferno.

## Chapter Two

# Sins of the Parents

$A$nne began to keep a diary in 1847, her tenth year, and she maintained the habit for the rest of her life with only a few short intervals which usually marked moments of crisis.

> 1st July. Thursday. I began my journal. I went to the town to receive some lessons in Music, in Drawing, in Riding, in Dancing. In the morning I read some of 'England and its People', in the afternoon, some of Miss Edgworth's Rosamond, which I thought very entertaining. So I think that day was pleasantly spent.[1]

She was staying at Moore House, Lady Byron's Esher home, in the care of Miss Lamont. She dutifully kept her mother informed about the family pets, particularly Birroch the black and white mongrel bitch that had a habit of producing puppies and then running away. Anne and her governess were constantly being called on to collect her from the local police station.

Ada's dogs were a constant source of pleasure and amusement to her daughter, but Anne longed nonetheless for a human companion of her own age. Walks with Miss Lamont in nearby Claremont Park, Queen Victoria's haven for the dispossessed crowned heads of Europe, was one of her favourite pastimes; riding at East Horsley and, during the holidays, at Ashley Combe in Somerset, was another, but there are unmistakable signs of loneliness in letters to her mother. At Christmas the previous year she had been sent to Esher to look after the youngest child of Lady Byron's legal adviser, Dr Lushington, whose family usually descended on Ockham Park for the festive season. On this occasion one of the children, Hugh, had proved tiresome to the adults and so was packed off to Esher with Anne and Miss Lamont. On Boxing Day Anne wrote:

> Dear Mama I am glad that you are pleased with my music, and I still continue to try to do it better.... At Esher I have not anyone to play with, except Birroch and the baby; Birroch is not a person or a child so she cannot speak or read, and Hugh is not so near my age as Ralph is so he cannot talk about the same things...[2]

Diary and correspondence began to reveal more of the girl's thoughts and aspirations, but there was still the untarnished innocence of childhood. A diary entry referred to a meeting with a poor Irishman while out walking with Miss Lamont. 'He really seemed to be in want,' she wrote, 'and thanked Miss Lamont even for answering him. He really was a sort of person to whom I should be glad to give something. I wished that I had happened to have a few pence, or halfpence, in my pocket, and so did Miss Lamont.'

Lady Millicent Jones, a friend of Lady Byron and Miss Montgomery, was staying with her children in the guest house at Esher during Christmas 1846.

> Sunday 4th. I was awake a little before six, & that time I consecrated to writing some of my journal. After breakfast I

went for a run in the garden; I heard Lady Millicent's children in the other garden... such a play with the children... Then Miss Lamont gave me the story of Lazy Lawrence to read, which interested me very much... In the evening we walked up the Oxshott Road went over the stiles where Ralph and I were steamers\*, and came up the Claygate Road which leads out of Oxshott...³

She explained the asterisk. 'I allude to when we were little children.' Occasional lapses of spelling, the unsophisticated utterances of the child, and – in vivid contrast – precocious words and grown-up expressions and opinions, mark the letters of the growing girl. They seem to suggest a conflict of personality and upbringing; the competing influences on a child of tender years and unambitious nature, of genetic inheritance and eccentric parenthood.

Lady Byron reasserted her guardian's role in 1847. It was time that Anne's education was taken in hand and suitably qualified tutors found for her. Never one to make do with second best she asked John Ruskin to become Anne's art teacher.

It was, like the Carpenter appointment before it, a remarkable choice of tutor for a ten-year-old child. But Ruskin may have had reasons for accepting that were not entirely charitable. The man who was to become Slade Professor of Art at Oxford, the acknowledged international authority in his subject and an abject failure in marriage and affairs of the heart, had a good deal in common with Lady Byron, not least his approach to education. In his youth his father had taken him to Hofwyl Farm, the site of the Fellenberg Institute, and he had become a devotee of that same system of education which Lady Byron espoused. A qualification unlikely to have swayed Lady Byron in his favour was his devotion to her late husband. On reading the later cantos of *Don Juan* he had vowed that Byron would be his 'master in verse' as 'Turner is my master in colour'.

He also had a well-known liking for young females, and Anne was not the only daughter of his wealthy acquaintances to be given private lessons. But 1847 was the year of his ill-fated marriage to Effie Gray, and also his appointment as critic to the *Quarterly Review*. Thus, he arranged for his friend and colleague Mr Tom Boys, one of the finest engravers of the day, to stand in for him when he was too occupied with other matters to attend his private pupils. Boys's concern for line and detail rather than imaginative composition suited Anne's temperament well. The line drawings and watercolours which began to fill her sketchbooks owed more to the down-to-earth Boys than to the great art philosopher whose pantheon was headed by Turner. Drawing confidently and expertly, and with the good sense of colour which she soon acquired, she became an indefatigable recorder of the things that engaged her attention: landscapes, buildings, people or animals, and most of all horses.[4]

Her first surviving drawing is of an orange tree, appearing on the day of Mr Boys's advent, 30 July 1847. On 22 September – 'My birthday,' she noted – Miss Lamont gave her the *Adventures of Ulysses*, and Grandmamma 'a little wee box with both chess and draughts in it, and a nice board.'[5]

She also attended a lecture by one of Lady Byron's Unitarian friends, Mr Scott, entitled, 'Because of Iniquity the love of many shall wax cold'. 'I could understand very little of what Mr Scott said,'[6] she told Lady Byron whom, whenever she sought a change from 'Grandmamma' in correspondence, she was now allowed to address as 'Hen'.

Miss Lamont's governorship of the children had been in the balance for two years, during which time Ada found every possible excuse to divest herself of parental responsibility. In April 1848 she wrote to Hen, who was on a 'health mission' to Tunbridge Wells, to explain that she had given the governess a good dressing down and that all was well.

I have said to her point blank <u>for myself</u> that I hoped she clearly understood how entirely I had accepted your kind superintendence of Annabella, which I considered to be from various circumstances of the <u>greatest importance to the child</u>. Any difference must be due to my being so much apart from A. as to render my knowledge of the facts about her habits and state of mind somewhat imperfect; and that on all such occasions she must understand that I consider <u>you</u> as the only competent judge.[7]

Ada always used underlining to make her point abundantly clear, especially when writing to Hen.

Miss Lamont returned to her native Ireland at the end of 1848 and a new governess was appointed.[8] Lady Byron's cousin Robert Noel had married a German lady, the Countess Henniger. That connection was strengthened by Ada's growing reputation in German academic circles and it was no surprise to anyone except Lady Byron when Fräulein Waechter appeared. Grandmamma insisted that the lady had been 'set up', not a good omen for Miss Waechter's future.

Increasingly, Ada fell back on ill health, which was becoming a problem of very real dimensions.[9] In August she told Lady Byron that she was so unwell that she was almost unable to speak: 'it is absolute cruelty for people to expect me to see them.' She was able to grapple with Anne's education, however. 'I hope that Annabella will be sufficiently advanced to commence next year a really proper course of (elementary) mathematics and natural philosophy', she told Hen from Ashley Combe in August.

I am sure she will be otherwise a very presumptuous & dogmatic person. Besides, I think if her faculties are well worked & occupied upon matters laid down for her, there will be less likelihood of her expending her wits upon manoeuvring and managing. More can be done for her indirectly than directly. Plenty of riding, & plenty of study, may greatly aid in keeping her out of mischief – But I see that she is very artful indeed. She is not the better at present for B[yron]'s company. Miss W[aechter] sees this; & says it unsettles A. very much indeed.[10]

On the other hand Byron was developing as 'a very sincere & guileless little boy, which is a great merit'. She did not think that Byron suffered as much harm as Anne from their spending long holiday periods together at Ashley Combe. Anne, according to her mother, was disappointed at not being allowed to ramble across the country, 'to which I put a peremptory stop by saying it was useless even to mention the subject again... She is headstrong about everything – unless she sees that the matter is entirely hopeless... I have made her understand that she is to exert herself to ride well, steadily, & to observe proper rules on horseback, – or else no riding at all.'[11]

In November, still at Ashley Combe, Anne wrote to Lady Byron in her best hand:

Dear Grandmamma, Ralph and I both thank you very much for your letter. Mamma desired me to say that you spoke of having sent her a Daily News, but she says she has only received a Spectator and Observer, and she mentioned this because she thought the Daily News might have been forgotten. I was also to say from Mama that she was very glad to have the Spectator and Observer.[12]

Lady Byron had obviously written the children one of the more light-hearted letters that she was eminently capable of composing when in the mood. 'I shall be very sorry to make you scratch,' Anne told Lady Byron, 'besides, Ralph and I are lame mice, and cannot run out of reach of your claws.' Ralph would have written a note had he 'not been just going to ride with Papa'. She concluded, 'I forgot to say in the beginning of my letter, that Mama would like to see the second No. of the Chemist.'[13] Anne was learning at a tender age the virtues of tact and the price her elders frequently put on a sense of responsibility.

Even by the standards of the Victorian upper class, the Lovelaces were remarkable in their determination to mould their children according to parental precepts, while keeping sufficient distance from them to ensure that sentiment was not allowed to cloud judgement. 'Family ties' were important for Byron, Ada told Lady Byron in September, but Lovelace was more and more inclined to send the boy to sea. Ralph, it seems, showed increasing signs of being jealous of his brother. He had refused to read a letter composed for him by Byron on Christmas day in 1849. Mrs Kinsett, the temporary governess (Miss Waechter had gone home to Germany for the festival), sent the boy to his room.

Anne's own letters and diaries did not altogether bear out the picture of life as it appeared in the exchange of letters between her mother and grandmother.[14] She was delighted by the new arrangements; especially, she wrote, with her art teacher Mr Boys. Life with her grandmother at Esher and her parents at East Horsley began to brighten with the prospect of enjoyable lessons and agreeable conversation, interspersed with visits to musical events and galleries. She had acquired from her mother a Stradivarius violin which was destined to become one of the world's most coveted musical instruments.[15] And the young girl's happiness was almost unconfined when Mrs Woronzow Greig suggested that she and Miss Waechter should accompany her on a journey to Germany.

Mrs Greig might have known better than to suggest such a thing without consulting Lady Byron; 'as if you would let your daughter go to a Stranger abroad on her authority!' she exclaimed to Lovelace in a letter signed 'GM', another of her familiar signatures, when he told her of the plan. Lady Byron used the proposed journey as an excuse for a long letter about Anne's upbringing, in a mood of disapproval that was becoming ever more apparent in her dealings with the son-in-law who once could do no wrong. There were even references to the unsuitable nature of the girl's 'intellectual companionship'. Lovelace replied that he would be glad of any suggestions she, Lady Byron, might care to make about Anne's future. 'It must be recollected however that Miss Waechter... is not the only intellectual leader the girl has – from our mode of life & the frequentation of friends of much cultivation of mind.' The snub was transparent, and for good measure he added that Babbage – whom Lady Byron heartily detested – was one of those cultivated friends. He was even bold enough to defend Miss Waechter, whose 'general deportment, temper & morals' were superior to those of most governesses.

The growing rift between grandmother and father had another more serious cause. Ada's sickness was becoming worse, but her determination to fulfil her scientific mission was as strong as ever. Collaboration with the Crosses, father and son, had led to a sinister involvement with gentlemen of the turf, and to the inevitable consequences of debt and blackmail.[16] How much Lovelace knew is uncertain, but he was a worried man whose dependence on the financial and moral support of Lady Byron left him in a most invidious position. Ada gave the impression of being above or outside it all. When the family physician Dr Locock was attending her, Ada referred to Anne and her brothers as 'Lady Byron's grandchildren'. The doctor corrected her: 'Your children'. Another time she observed: 'Unfortunately every year adds to my utter want of pleasure in my children. They are to me irksome duties and nothing more. Poor things! I am sorry for them. They will at least find me a harmless and inoffensive parent if nothing more.' She was no more sanguine about her marriage: 'No one would suit me as a husband; tho' some might be a shade or two less personally repugnant to me than others.'

Despite this outbreak of family disunity, the trip to Germany went ahead eventually and proved a happy, inconsequential holiday.[17] There was plenty of opportunity to practise the German language and draw Rhineland scenes as their riverboat made its journey from Liège via Cologne to Coblenz, and on to Wiesbaden where they stayed with Miss Waechter's family. 'The Rhine is so very beautiful... I made twelve sketches.' Aboard the boat the captain's cabin was full of birds and Anne impressed her governess with a discussion about the antics of her own starling, which she had tamed and taught to bathe. The captain told Anne that he admired her German.

She tasted the spring water of Nassau – 'nasty!' – and read *The Taming of the Shrew* and *The Merchant of Venice* as they travelled. 'I like Portia very much.' On her 13th birthday, 22 September 1850, Anne wrote to GM from Munich:

> I cannot be written to, any more, for we are moving about so fast that no letter could catch me anywhere. I hope I shall soon see you and Ralph... I am having a very happy birthday, I have had a great many congratulations and such beautiful presents. Mrs Greig gave me a ring with a garnet in it, on which I am to have A engraved. Mr Greig gave me a beautiful brooch in the shape of an angel with its wings spread out, and Miss Graham gave me a statue of Albrecht Dürer, 3 inches high, in bronze... When I see you and Ralph I have a great many sketches to show you, they are some of them very rough as sometimes I had only a very few minutes.[18]

There was a description of a visit to Frankfurt to buy a clasp for a favourite bracelet in the same letter, and a reference to a young friend she had met at Basle on her previous visit to the Continent, Emma Vischen.

The return to Esher was accompanied by an intensification of the battle between Lady Byron and Lovelace, this time sparked off by the treatment of Lovelace's horses. 'I have been appalled at the Hen's arrangements which have fallen on our poor horses,' he told Ada. Grandmamma insisted in the course of the ensuing dispute that she should have charge of all three children, but her wish to have the children under her wing was conditional. She was determined to hold on to the youngest, Ralph, and to be rid of Miss Waechter, who had been appointed without her consent. Anne would be with her 'only till a suitable governess is found.'

The girl was becoming difficult, a verdict that was confirmed by Dr Combe, one of Lady Byron's phrenologist friends, who was asked to feel her bumps. As for poor Ockham, once Ada's and Lady Byron's favourite, his 'nonchalant and disrespectful' tone was beyond the pale. Rejected by his mother and father, fearing his grandmother and constrained to say 'I feel déclassé', he was packed off to a cadetship in the Royal Navy before his 14th birthday.

Arrangements for the children's accommodation were complicated by the fact that Ada had returned from London to Esher to seek refuge from her creditors, accompanied by Babbage's maid Mary Wilson who had been transferred to her household and acted as her 'runner', placing bets for her and keeping her in touch with John Crosse and other friends of the turf.

In November 1850, Lovelace had written to Lady Byron about her daughter in unconsciously apt terms: 'The bird is in an immense flutter & likes being on the wing.' Lady Byron was busy with her latest scheme to set up reformatory homes for fallen and delinquent women and, despite her recent claim to Anne and Ralph, had dispatched the children to Horsley Tower with Miss Waechter.

At the time, Anne was trying to interest her parents in the fate of her brother. 'I suppose you have received Ockham's letter, and I am so glad we have heard at last, but I fancy there must have been one letter between this and the last, from the way he began it.'[19] She recounted a day of domestic disasters, and wrote that she could imagine Mamma 'tut-tutting'.

As Christmas approached, Ada decided to stay at East Horsley Tower (to give the house its full title) where she could be 'under expert medical care'. She was too unwell to join the family as it assembled with the Lushingtons at Ockham Park. Anne wrote to her almost daily, praying that her health would return, enclosing drawings of birds and horses, and discussing the welfare of Midshipman Ockham, whose ship, the *Daphne*, had run aground in a storm. On Christmas Eve Anne received a somewhat sour note from her mother, now confined to bed at Horsley: 'I hope your Xmas is as happy as some recent circumstances have conspired to make mine. I suppose I need not make my meaning more clear.' Next day there was an air of conspiracy in Ada's communication: 'Dear Annabella, show this letter to Miss Waechter directly – I shall write again tomorrow to say if you can come here on Wednesday.' It was apparent that the governess had become some kind of go-between in Ada's betting activities.

On 7 January Ada was taken to Brighton for sea air and she wrote to Anne, who was at East Horsley, thanking her for 'a nice little letter' composed in her daughter's best handwriting, and observing that it contained no 'little horseshoe' as promised:

> I had no idea you meant to give me one, and I assure you I shall value it very much from you – & so am a little disappointed that none could be found. It was a nice thought of yours. Will you look after my birds and say a word to Nelson? Most affectly A.A.L.[20]

Derby Day 1851 marked a low water mark in Ada's ebbing fortunes. She lost £3,200, an enormous sum at the time, on an unidentified horse. Meanwhile, Lovelace was trying to institute legal proceedings against the several bookmakers and blackmailers already pursuing her.[21] Lady Byron, aware of her daughter's serious ill health if not of her financial problems, took herself off to Leamington Spa, convinced that hers was the more urgent plight and that the hand of death was upon her.

By the onset of summer 1851 there were distinct signs of Ada's brain being affected. A letter to GM of 17 May was headed, after the date, 'DOOMSDAY' and began, 'I scarcely like to recollect or allude to today, with my views of life & death etc., etc.' The letter itself was incoherent, with its repeated references to 'Armageddon' and 'extinction'. Inevitably, death came to alarm her and consume her mind. As her condition worsened, three doctors were called to examine her, including Sir James Clark, physician-in-ordinary to the Queen, the same Sir James who had caused a stir at the beginning of Victoria's reign by diagnosing pregnancy in an unmarried woman at Court when she was subsequently discovered to be suffering from cancer. In Ada's case he diagnosed cancer correctly, without hesitation. Lovelace rushed off to Leamington to inform Lady Byron and to make a full confession of Ada's and his own problems. The mother-in-law who had once found him the 'consolation of her life' turned on him contemptuously, blaming him for Ada's activities and telling him, 'I cannot mask the truth and give up my principles.' She spoke of the degradation of the children and the loss of their respect, but offered neither sympathy nor help.[22]

Believing that his family might be brought closer together by these cumulative disasters, Lovelace decided to regain custody of Ralph, but his nerve failed him when it came to asking his mother-in-law. Ockham was away at sea. Anne, whom he confessed 'not to understand well', was the only one within reach, and Ada wanted her at her sickbed, feeling that she had come to know her daughter better after her 'so happy' return from Germany. As for the unhappy Ockham, undergoing his cadetship as Midshipman Lord Ockham despite a loathing of the upper deck and a desire to serve with his friends below, Ada in her intense discomfort had found the strength to draft a letter to her son's senior officer, Commander Aldham, not for her husband's consideration but for GM's. She sent it from the Lovelace's latest London house, 6 Great Cumberland Place, opposite Green Park, which Lovelace had recently leased after selling the house in St James's. In it she explained that when her son left England 'we begged you [Commander Aldham] to spare no expense which could conduce to Lord Ockham's instruction & reasonable gratification.' She went on to say that 'we', by which she presumably meant Lovelace and herself, had thought of having the boy transferred to Portland naval barracks when his present ship, the *Daphne*, returned to England, since the senior naval officer at that station was Admiral Morsby, 'an old friend of ours'. She added, uncharacteristically, 'with the sanction of the Admiralty, of course.' Meanwhile, she hoped that everything possible would be done to make Ockham a credit to his profession.

Poor Lovelace was reduced to a mere cipher as the women in his family played out a malign drama with several eminent physicians and much of London society coming and going as the dying Ada was transported between one home and another. Ada's writing became almost unintelligible. 4 July 1851, to GM from Great Cumberland Place:

> Sometimes I am too ill in the morning (?) to take a journey (?)... I saw Ralph yesterday for a few minutes... Dr Locock gave me over to Dr Cope yesterday morning – & his account in my presence to Dr Cope of what my state had been, really made me shudder retrospectively... Dr L. said there was more death than life in my face, and that my hands were like bird claws.[23]

On 10 August she was at Horsley Tower writing to GM to say how pleased she was with Dr Cope. 'They say coming events cast their shadows before. May they not sometimes cast their light before?' The question doubtless referred to the possibility of her latest medical adviser performing the miracle for which she prayed. There were constant references to drops and the words 'crystalline' and 'prismatic' kept appearing, with reference to their effect on her mind.

A journey to France with Mrs Greig and Miss Waechter was planned for Anne, but it was delayed by Ada's sickness.[24] In the interval, fate struck another blow. Miss Waechter, whom Anne adored, though Lady Byron was still trying to find a 'suitable' replacement for her, was found to have breast cancer. Ada, who had not been told of the seriousness of her own condition, wrote poignantly to Mrs Somerville in August 1851, 'It is most afflicting to hear her speak of her future just as usual, unconscious of her horrible doom... Annabella must be prepared for this sad misfortune.' By then Anne had left for France with Mr and Mrs Greig, having been told by her mother and Lady Byron that Miss Waechter was too unwell to travel.

Anne threw herself into the brief holiday with muted enthusiasm. The awful illnesses that surrounded her had brought an unaccustomed sense of responsibility to her young life and left her with a natural desire to escape the sickroom, and with an equally natural sense of unease. Most of the time on the short visit to France was spent with Mrs Greig in Paris. She noted the fine collection of Egyptian and Mesopotamian antiquities in the Louvre, acquired by France when Bonaparte occupied Egypt and Botta began to dig at Khorsabad and Nineveh. She knew about such things, having heard Sir Henry Layard talking to her father and mother at Ashley Combe about the Assyrian treasures he had brought home from Nimrud. 'There was an entire side of a room pasted over with Papyrus, which had been unrolled in the most beautiful manner possible. We saw also two immense winged bulls from Nineveh.' Soon after the party returned to England, Anne was told the nature of Miss Waechter's illness. The young German woman had been her companion for two years, sharing her games in the garden with Birroch, walking with her and tending the animals at Horsley, Esher and Ashley Combe, worrying with her about her morose father, to whom they gave the nickname 'Somebody'.

'Poor Somebody is very dull without you, he will be vastly pleased when he sees you again', Anne had written to her mother at the height of the Crosse affair. Surrounded as she was by so much agitation and instability, Anne barely noticed the departure in September of her friend and governess, who was sent home without ceremony to Wiesbaden to die.[25] She noted, simply, 'Miss Waechter left today.' Ada's spirits had been raised in her daughter's absence by the appearance of Ralph at East Horsley. Her letter to GM thanking her for permitting the visit – Ralph liked his grandmother and spent much of his time with her – suggested an enhancement of those delusions of grandeur which Lady Byron had so successfully instilled in her daughter:

> He is like a gush of warm rays from the rising sun... I begin to find that I am and can be of use to Ralph... No one can be so fit to awaken his mind to certain truths which are hard to learn, as myself... Set a thief to catch a thief! Set a comet to catch a comet. Set a genius to catch a genius. And set a Byron to rule a Byron! For Ralph is a Byron... There is a curious sympathy growing up between him and me.[26]

Even as they learned that their mother and their governess were both dying, a ghost from the past came to haunt Anne and her brothers.[27] Ten years had gone by since Lady Byron had first disclosed to her daughter the story of Aunt Augusta's alleged incest with Byron, that 'shocking' story with its 'strange and dreadful' aftermath, the birth of Elizabeth Medora in 1813, just a year before Ada was born, and the subsequent seduction of Medora by her brother-in-law Henry Trevanion with the issue of a daughter, Marie. At the time, Ada had responded sensibly, suggesting to her mother that since Augusta was married at the time to Colonel Leigh, it might not be easy to prove adultery, or at any rate for there to be any degree of certainty about Byron's paternity.

Following the disclosure, Lady Byron had induced Ada to drop the work she was engaged on at the time with Babbage and go to Paris to meet Medora and 'hold out the hand of sisterhood', thus setting in motion a train of events which led to her, Lady Byron, taking Medora into temporary custody and financing an action in Chancery against her mother Augusta over a deed of settlement, before abandoning her protégé with ruthless finality. By 1851, as Ada lay dying, Medora's daughter Marie began to follow in her mother's tragic steps. Having tried in vain to obtain help from the impoverished Augusta, she wrote to Lady Byron from the French convent which had given her shelter, asking to be rescued from 'starvation' and the 'attentions of undesirable men'. Like her mother before her, she was rejected. If Anne was aware of this new element in the nightmarish scene unfolding around her, she gave no hint of it in her diary. But of her mother's alarming decline there could be no doubt, and that was enough for a child to cope with almost single-handedly.

On 28 October Ada wrote a note to GM to tell her that Babbage's maid had given '£1 to William', suggesting a continuance of the betting saga of which Lady Byron was now fully aware. She told her mother that she was left with about five shillings in her purse. Then: 'a thousand fatigues and worries tear my wretched nervous system to pieces. I never have peace... Those eternal arrangements without which life cannot go on in any way crowd in on me... I wish I could rest on my perch, in solitude... I wish I could disappear & have rest... I am much better today.'

The next day, Wednesday 29, 'Afternoon', after seeing GM in the morning, the floodgates of dementia opened: 'Some of the conversation between us this morning on general topics has been like a genial maturing to a certain seed which is sprouting (but as yet has not reached the surface of the soil!)' Then a large smudge, as though medicine had spilled onto the page; and the word 'Music'.

Then: 'iron rulers of the earth may even have to give way... harmoniously disciplined troops marching in irresistible formation to the sound of music.'[28]

By mid November, Ada had recovered her wits sufficiently to plead with GM to honour a pledge by Mrs Margaretta Burr, one of Lady Byron's Brighton set, to take Anne to a new year's ball with the family of Sir John Gardner Wilkinson, the distinguished Egyptologist, on 8 January. 'It is an old promise that A. is to go, but they [the Burrs] reckon on you most particularly, & Mrs B. has begged me to use all my persuasion. Annabella is to be a Spanish Lady with Montella, etc. This is Wilkinson's wish, who thinks she will look irresistibly sparkling in that costume, which will particularly suit her. If you have refused Mrs B. (which however I can scarcely believe possible) may I repeat it wd also be a pleasure to you to see how handsome & admired your granddaughter will be!'[29]

Ada had presumably got wind of GM's refusal. There is no evidence of Anne's going to the ball. Neither, characteristically, does Anne appear to have complained. The barrage of letters which Ada was sending to her mother at this time of 'pain too excruciating to bear' – sometimes there were two or three missives a day – were addressed baldly to 'The Lady Noel Byron, Esher', as if the Post Office placed her in much the same category as the Queen.

In the same letter that conveyed her wish for Anne to go to the ball there was news of Ockham. It seemed the *Daphne* had been engaged in intercepting 'Indians' (possibly Sinhalese or Indonesians as the ship was attached to the Indies station). 'Two to three hundred' of the unfortunate natives had been killed in the engagement. 'What a very odd mind Byron's is', wrote his mother. 'He is delighted with the scalps, & wanted to get some to bring home!' Within weeks, Ada's condition suffered another jolt. The *Daphne* had nearly been lost in a hurricane and was only saved by the 'falling of all the masts'. One sailor had been killed and several injured. 'The officers are all safe. It makes me shudder', she told GM. Meanwhile, the pain had become intolerable and Ada turned for a moment against her mother's insistent regime of treatment. 'My suffering is indescribable. I do hope there will be no more proposals of leeches.' Pathetically, she concluded a letter of 11 December, 'If I scramble through this I shall consider that I have, as they say cats have, nine lives.'

Augusta had died three months earlier in the poverty and disgrace that her unforgiving sister-in-law had brought her to, her last letter to Lady Byron returned unopened. Ada, whenever she was out of bed, wore black respectfully, as did Anne as she dashed from sickroom to concert halls and galleries, and to Denmark Hill where Ruskin had resumed direct supervision of her drawing lessons. Even from a distance, Lady Byron insisted on cultural fulfilment.

Anne was at her mother's side for much of the time now, happy that the opiates prescribed by the doctors lessened the pain and reduced the intensity of her intermittent screams of agony. But when Lady Byron arrived from Brighton to take charge in the last agonizing stages of the sickness, mesmerists were brought to the house and the doctors' prescriptions banished.

Surrounded by scientific friends and her less salubrious colleagues of the turf, Ada summoned the assistance of Mary Wilson to secretly pawn the family jewels to pay off some of her most pressing debts. And with the knowledge of encroaching death she dragged herself from her bed, when she was able to summon the strength, to play the piano and have her portrait painted by Henry Phillips, son of the artist who had painted her father. Anne played duets with her mother and, to complete an almost hallucinatory scene, Mrs Sartoris, Fanny Kemble's sister, arrived to sing one of Ada's favourite arias from the doorway of an adjoining room while Phillips painted the invalid.

In July the doctors pronounced that she had two more

months of life. She recalled that her father had died at 36, her present age. When Lady Byron gave Lushington a draft for £800 to redeem the pawned jewels, which had been worn by her own forebears, the lawyer commented, 'the scene is to me most melancholy.'

Anne, according to her father, 'commanded herself much'. By his account, Ada told the daughter who sat beside her for long hours that she could give her 'but a poor welcome'; that she had always tried to do her best for her though she might not have accomplished all she wished for her. Babbage was another staunch companion, and though Lovelace had little time for him, he recalled the philosophical discussions 'begetting only an increased esteem & mutual liking' between his wife and the famous scientist and inventor.

As the agony of the sickroom became unendurable, Ralph was sent away to Switzerland to further his neglected education, while Anne was sent to the Gardner Wilkinsons, a stone's throw away from Lady Byron's friend Mrs Burr.

In August, Lovelace was for once alone with his wife and he started to record her rambling requests in his journal:

[She] spoke to me of her wishes about Anabella, her hope that Lady Byron would direct supremely – that Annabella should be 6 weeks of the year with her – next to Lady Byron that our dear & excellent friends Mrs Burr & Mrs Greig should be cultivated & consulted – I told her that her wishes should all be sacred, but that they only anticipated & confirmed my expectations & hopes.[30]

Anne was packed off to the Wilkinsons[31] with Miss Chadwell, the governess chosen with great care by GM to take Miss Waechter's place, while her brother Ockham arrived home unexpectedly after docking at Plymouth.[32] When the young midshipman arrived at Great Cumberland Place, his mother told him that she was dying. Some idea of the scene which greeted the eldest son may be gained from Lovelace's journal: 'Alas when I witness the agony I am almost tempted to ask "Is this necessary – Cannot her slight & delicate organs be spared this excess of aggravation?"[33]

Anne wrote to her mother: 'I cannot help thinking of you and Byron, and Papa, all day (tho' my thoughts always return to you) and at nights too it seems, for I woke with a start this morning, and the last thing in my dream was something about Byron, though I do not recollect what.' Ockham's situation seemed to cause her some concern. 'I cannot help comparing what he was – I am going to write to Miss Waechter to let her know, for she was so sorry that she could not see him.' Mrs Burr came down to London with Anne and was more concerned with the salvation of Ada's soul than the preservation of Ockham's reputation, pleading with the patient to acquire 'a moral sense of sin'. Anne was more earthly: 'I am so glad that Mama is suffering less pain for it is painful for me to think that while I am here to enjoy myself she should be suffering at the same time.'

On the last day of August, Lovelace and his unrelenting mother-in-law each held one of Ada's hands in their own. Her life seemed to be ebbing and haltingly she discussed her funeral arrangements with them. She kept insisting that she should lie alongside her father. Lovelace constantly reassured her.

To complete the agonizing farce, John Crosse appeared on the scene to orchestrate a final conspiracy. Somehow, Ada secreted with that foolish and dishonest son of a respected scientist the jewels which Lady Byron had recently redeemed, so that he could pay off £800 being demanded by one of his blackmailing acquaintances. In the wake of this second pawning of the jewels, Lady Byron took the offensive. She referred to her daughter as 'Lady Lovelace', turned her back on Lovelace whenever he came into the room and accused him of conniving with Ada in the jewellery affair, lacerated Dr Lushington with assertions of his guilt and professional incompetence, denied Babbage entrance to the house and dismissed all Ada's servants, retrieving from Mary Wilson before she left a packet of letters that revealed a great deal of what had gone on between Crosse and Ada. Lady Byron remarked that 'the greatest of all the mercies shown her [Ada] has been the disease – weaning her from temptation, & turning her thoughts to higher & better things.'

Charles Dickens called on the invalid and was 'wonderfully struck' by her courage and calmness. In the chaotic days that followed, Lovelace and Anne sat by the bedside, to be joined by Ockham on compassionate leave from Plymouth, and they sponged their mother's face and hands: 'The water gurgled a little... we went back to some of the scenes of our tour of the Lakes... on which she dwelt with great pleasure and interest – telling me that I must take Annabella.' On 26 August Ralph arrived from Switzerland and at last the family was together. Convulsions and epileptic fits set in. But the agony was not over yet. Lady Byron chose this moment of togetherness to predict the next hostile step – to divide the children from her. 'It will not be well for those who take it,' she said. She called on the Reverend Robertson from Brighton, he himself dying from consumption, to prepare Ada for the next world.

Ada's saga of agony had three more months to run and there was still time for bitterness. The cancer had spread throughout her body and was almost certainly affecting her central nervous system. On 21 September, she began suddenly to confess to sins of the flesh to add to those of gambling and financial deception. Without warning she blurted out the names of several men with whom she claimed intimacy. Lady Byron responded by attacking the husband who now could do no right: 'God be merciful to him! – Pharisee as he is, from whom his poor penitent wife could draw no kinder expression by her complete submission & humility for such was her spirit – I know.' Dr Locock, who had been given the questionable *nom de guerre* 'Arab Horse' by Ada and her betting friends and who, it must be supposed, was familiar with the racing fraternity, pleaded with Lovelace not to keep John Crosse from the bedside. Knowledge of Ada's admission of guilt seemed to spur Lady Byron to magnanimity. She sent Greig a draft for £825 to redeem the Lovelace diamonds once more.

Ockham said goodbye to his mother for what he thought would be the last time, his contempt for the aristocratic world in which he had been reared complete. He decided to desert the Navy and seek passage to America from Bristol or Liverpool. But the family suspected he might do something of the kind and the police were warned. At the request of uncle Robert Noel, detectives intercepted him at Liverpool, where he was found using an assumed name. He was returned to the Royal Navy to serve aboard the new *HMS Victory*, but was able to see his mother once more.

'She was awake but unconscious of that last look,' he told Anne.

In an ultimate act of kindness the doctors prescribed belladonna. Lady Byron's circle gathered like vultures at the bedside. Ada died on 27 November 1852 and was buried as promised in the village church of Hucknall Torkard, her coffin touching that of the father who had written:

*Is thy face like thy mother's, my fair*
*child!*
*ADA! sole daughter of my house and heart?*
*When last I saw thy young blue eyes they*
*smiled,*
*And then we parted, – not as now we part,*
*But with a hope.*

# Chapter Three

# Coming Out

Ashley Combe, where Lovelace and Ada had found some of their rare moments of happiness with the children, offered the immediate prospect of quiet after the tempest. It was from there that Anne wrote to Grandmamma in December 1852.

> Ralph and I have been for a ride today with Papa, which I enjoyed very much... You are right that Papa talks about Mama and he seems to feel pleasure in recollecting and thinking of those spots where she has walked, and what she liked and thought. I do not like to talk of her much, but I don't mind if it gives Papa pleasure.

Almost daily letters showed an even closer attachment than hitherto to the woman who had caused so much sorrow in the critical year past, and whom she always addressed now by the familiar 'GM': 'I think a great deal of you, but I shall think more of you tomorrow, for it is Mama's birthday.' On 10 December:

Perhaps this is the happiest birthday Mama ever passed. I
hope it is – It seems so natural to me, to think of her as being
very happy now – I could not imagine her otherwise – I am
putting together all her letters to me which are very precious
– and I shall arrange them in the order in which they were
written, for though they are not all dated with the years, I can
pretty well tell when they were written by the contents...[1]

She mentioned a long letter from Miss Waechter, who
recalled her mother's rambling words at their parting. In
effect, she said, 'We shall meet again shortly.' Anne could not
be sure from her ex-governess' French whether Ada had
meant in this world or the next. Anne went on, 'She [Miss
Waechter] says she often thinks how strong Mama was in
suffering and how patient, and she seems to look up to her as
an example (which she is so truly) of fortitude in suffering.'

Lady Byron now communicated with Lovelace only
through her solicitor, while Anne kept her informed about
the family with a spate of affectionate and detailed letters.

The new year was not three months old before that
correspondence took on a sardonic edge. Anne had
complimented her father on his 'resolution' during the past
few months, and his 'concern' for her welfare during their
brief visit to the Somerset paradise of her childhood years.
Criticism of her father became bitter in a way that was out
of character. Letters contained coded passages and
pseudonyms which, if Lady Byron's penchant for using
family and friends alike to grind down her opponents was
not so well documented, might be considered no more than
a young girl's trifling imagery. In contrast to the matter-of-
fact but always generous tone of her earlier letters, she
suddenly launched into a pretentious, Latinised lampooning
of her father in which he took on names such as 'It' and
'Future-in-Bus', and the influence of GM was all too
evident.

'The Future-in-Bus has already formed I don't know how
many plans for disposing of the first quarter of your kind

provision for books... It (i.e. the above mentioned Future-in-Bus) will have a great deal to arrange with As-in-proesenti concerning the plans, As-in-proesenti being the medium of communication with booksellers etc.'[2]

Lovelace – the villain of all that had gone before in Lady Byron's eyes – had resumed his official duties as Lord Lieutenant of Surrey and was inspecting troops garrisoned at Guildford. Anne promised GM that as she would almost certainly have to go to Guildford she would call at Esher and sleep there overnight. She signed herself 'A. King-in-Bus', offering in a postscript the German rendering 'Ein Koenig auf dem Lande', presumably referring to the family surname.

The nonsense language went on through the year. The new governess, Miss Chadwell, had been appointed by Lovelace after Ada's death, like her predecessor, without reference to Lady Byron so that she too was under a cloud from the outset. Anne seemed to get on with her, however, and other matters began to occupy a correspondence that veered between the playfully innocent and the sinister. On one occasion when she had been indisposed for a few days, Anne assured GM that she 'need not be anxious'. Father had put off a journey to 'the West' until he was satisfied that she had recovered, a far remove from the indifference suggested in other letters to her grandmother.

Ada's embers still smouldered. The dying woman had left the family coachman a silver tankard which was sent away to be engraved. When it came back, Lady Byron refused the coachman's entreaties to hand it over. Ada had pleaded with the same servant to take care of her favourite dog Nelson, and left him five pounds a year for that purpose. 'I will not part with him for the regard I had for my dear mistress', said the coachman when Lady Byron refused him the bequest. In the same way, Mary Wilson the very confidential maid, and her namesake the butler, were refused bequests made in the will intercepted by Lady Byron.

Weary of a battle he could not win and had only inadvertently joined, Lovelace held out many an olive branch. 'I will lay my whole heart open to you in the interview even if it is to be the last – if you will but be patient & listen... Do not treat lightly a request which is so important for the recovery of my peace of mind', he wrote. That request too – the desperate request of a man whose crime was that he had blurted out in his anguish the deeds revealed by his wife on her deathbed – went unanswered.[3]

Together again at Ashley Combe in the summer of 1853, father and daughter seemed content in their shared devotion to the animals and plants of the estate and its surroundings. But news of Ockham overshadowed the holiday. He seemed to be in deeper water than usual. The Crimean War had brought his latest ship *Inflexible* to the Dardanelles and rumour was that he had deserted.

> Papa does not think anything can be done at present about Byron. He says he does not know the circumstances – Besides which he is quite in despair – and does not hope for anything. So I shall not be astonished. I even expect a court martial. Perhaps that might save Ockham – in the way that it might awaken in time a sense of what he has done...[4]

That letter was written on 3 June 1853. The crime was nothing like as serious as the rumours had suggested. It transpired that Midshipman Lord Ockham had been guilty, not for the first time, of offending senior officers and showing a marked preference for the company of the lower deck. Anne told GM that her brother was still in Turkish waters and had been in the Dardanelles on and off. It was clear, all the same, that Ockham was not enjoying his naval service.

In early July Lovelace took himself off on a walking tour of Wales but only got as far as Minehead, an hour's journey from Lynmouth, when he was struck down with the quinsy. He rested up before proceeding. GM, to whom Anne confided details of life at Ashley Combe, had gone off to

Germany. While the rest of the family went on holiday, Anne and Miss Chadwell were left together in the idyllic surroundings of Ashley, riding to their hearts' content. Before leaving them for his walking tour, Lovelace had spoken of taking Anne abroad in the autumn. Telling Grandmamma of the prospect, she stated her own preference for Italy: 'those lakes in Northern Italy must be magnificent.'

She confessed to wanting to see her brother Ralph, who after the funeral had been sent back to Switzerland at GM's instigation. 'Could it be arranged?' she asked gingerly. Anne had to be careful in her dealings with Grandmamma. While at Ashley she had commented on the Lushington daughters who had spent a few days with her, remarking 'they never seem to get into any adventures, at least what I mean is... the course of their life is like the course of a smooth river through a flat plain.' Anne admitted that she preferred 'the course of a rocky torrent descending from the mountains.' Realising that such thoughts might cause alarm, she added that she was drawing a good deal and not neglecting other tasks. Lady Byron kept the letter and appended a note: 'There is a fate in this letter – the persuasion that life cannot be "interesting" unless it be tempestuous, full of vicissitudes.'

Lady Byron allowed Ralph to return home in the autumn. He brought his sister a gift of a chamois and its young, welcome additions to the menagerie at Ashley Combe.

Lovelace and family were joined as usual at Christmas by the Lushingtons and by another of the families that had flitted on the edge of Lady Byron's circle, the Nightingales of Derbyshire. Fanny Nightingale and her daughter Parthe had been especially fond of Ada, and in 1833 Ada had sent them a long and amusing account of her own and her mother's presentation at the court of Queen Adelaide, Lady Byron wearing a 'blonde hat & feathers on her head...Mama did not know a single gentleman... C'est divine! C'est un ange.'⁵

Florence Nightingale was still at Scutari, and Anne quickly took Ada's place in the affections of Florence's sister Parthe, though the latter was considerably older than Anne (34 at the time).

In one of her letters to GM, Anne wrote of the 'melancholy dreariness' of life at Horsley. She admitted that her father was being kind and considerate, and life was comfortable for her and Miss Chadwell. But, 'I wonder Papa is not tired of always, always, making alterations and always residing in the same place... Do you know, Papa will never talk about anything but lodges and building and art in general.' Her fingers were so cold, she said, that she could hardly write. Re-reading one of her letters she became aware of a note of self-pity that Lady Byron might have thought unbecoming. It was, 'full of I I I, nothing but No.1. I am very sorry.'

There were complaints about her tuition. Since Ada's death, Lovelace had paid little attention to her education, or Ralph's, and Grandmamma was thoroughly wrapped up in the sermonising milieu of the Reverend Robertson and the Kings at Brighton. 'Miss Chadwell is endeavouring to induce Papa to take me to London this Spring, that I might have the benefit of good masters, but it is no use, he will not hear of it, and says the idea of London is intolerable to him.' A week later, 'Papa suggests Guildford for a dancing master!... Papa's ideas are curious... None so deaf as those who will not hear.'

Lady Byron egged on the young girl; and the response obviously pleased her:

I hope dear Grandmamma that I have expressed myself clearly but if I do make a mistake you must not wonder at it – for whenever Papa states any arrangement there always seems to be such a want of distinctness – such a confusion.

Ockham reappeared in the spring of 1854. On 16 April Anne wrote to say that her (Lady Byron's) lawyer, Dr Lushington, still occupying Lovelace's house at Ockham Park, had written an urgent note to their father who refused to divulge its contents. Lady Byron already knew what was in the letter and indeed had proposed 'a plan' for Dr Lushington's consideration. Next day, Anne learned that her brother was in London in the care of uncle George Craufurd, looking pale and sick.

The role of Lady Byron in augmenting an impressionable young girl's disapproval of her father became more and more transparent. 'Papa is not at all delighted or glad to have found his son again.' The 'Stern Earl' was gloomy and, she said, spoke constantly of what a sad thing it was that his son had worked as a 'common sailor.'

> I can't conceive how Papa can talk & think so. I am so glad he [Ockham] has been found, that I can think of nothing else... The most strange, extraordinary, odd thing to me is this: how Papa can go on talking of walls, and coolly superintending them, because he cannot have seen Byron yet... Wall & Building Worship!

Lady Byron was understanding personified. She had just met a charming young naval officer, Lieutenant Arnold, the son of Rugby's Dr Arnold, who had agreed to undertake the tutorship of the boys.[6] But Ockham was not keen on the new arrangement. In July, two months after his arrival in England, he escaped from the clutches of his grandmother and Lieutenant Arnold and went to work as a colliery labourer at Sunderland on the north-east coast of England.

Ralph, who unlike his brother was conscious of his aristocratic heritage and anxious to preserve its privileges, found the young Arnold most congenial.

Anne returned to Horsley in June to find her father entertaining the 'Singing Birds'. The Nightingales were always welcome at Lovelace's home – he and the lanky William Nightingale, who never sat down, got on famously.

Florence was home from the Crimea and Anne found her just as agreeable as her sister Parthe. The visitors invited Anne to stay with them at Lea Hurst, their Derbyshire home. Perhaps she could persuade Ralph and Lieutenant Arnold to join her? In the event, Anne went with Miss Chadwell and made a sketch of Florence's famous ride round the camp at Sevastopol, with landscape detail from one of 'Crimea' Simpson's lithographs. She also forged a new bond of friendship with Hilary Bonham Carter, cousin of the Nightingale girls and Florence's devoted companion.[7]

In a letter to Lady Byron describing the Nightingales' visit, there was an aside which provided oblique evidence of her elder brother's dispute with the Royal Navy. She referred to a letter from one of the officers serving with the Balkans fleet, and observed: 'If nothing worse was said in the letters to Byron than that "all the officers in the navy were good for nothing", as he told me when he wrote, I should not think it would do much harm.' It seems that Ockham had been discharged from the service for spurning his own kind in favour of the lower deck. On 2 July she told GM: 'I am glad you have heard from Byron... I am glad he has got work of some sort, whether the quantity be large or small.'[8] The grand tour had taken a long time to materialise, but on Monday 3 October, 1854, at the age of 17, Anne set out on her first major European journey, accompanied by her father, Miss Chadwell and several volumes of Shakespeare.[9]

*Macbeth* kept her company on the cross-channel steamer. She wore her mother's wristwatch, the single bequest to her in a memorandum in Lady Byron's hand which, it seems, superseded Ada's last will and testament. Dated 7 September 1852, it stated that 'today or within the last 2 or 3 days' Lady Lovelace had noted that Annabella should have her watch, Mrs Greig her leather inkstand, Sir Gardner Wilkinson the 'Penny Cyclopoedia', and Babbage 'A book'. Babbage declined the gift.

They took a route described to father and daughter by Ruskin, taking them to Switzerland and Italy. Ralph and the Arnolds joined them at Bonn, and at Basle the enlarged party stayed with the Vischens, friends of the Waechter family and of the Robert Noels, about whom Anne had written on her previous visit to Switzerland. Anne resumed her earlier accord with Emma Vischen, who was about her own age and who played a Chopin mazurka 'charmingly'.

Anne had been keeping sketchbooks for four years, but not until now was she able to demonstrate the progress she had made in drawing technique. Watercolours began to show the strength of the immaculate Boys's tuition, and of Ruskin's Turneresque approach to the use of colour.[10] The diaries began to adopt a gentler quality than of late. There was even a sense of fun indulged in at the expense of the students of Bonn and English gentlefolk met with on the way: 'Bye the bye, I forgot to mention an absurd anecdote told me by an English gentleman.'

Ralph and the Arnolds went their separate ways, and Anne expressed her approval of her brother's tutor. Lovelace too, merged into the benign scene. 'Papa purchased a carriage for the journey, much more comfortable than the diligence,' she noted as they galloped on to Lucerne, through the snowy St Gothard Pass into Italy, complimenting their driver on his sensible handling of the horses. Most of Italy was under Austrian rule in the post-Napoleonic dispensation. Anne wasn't altogether sure whose side she was on. 'I fear much as I like & admire the Italians, they are inclined to be dirty.' The itinerary was marked by copious sketches and cryptic diary notes – Lugano, Lake Maggiore, Milan and the Duomo. She found the outside architecture of the cathedral 'imperfect' but its interior 'unforgettable'.

She was welcomed everywhere. Her grandfather's reputation still pervaded the continent, and her mother had left her mark a generation after. The British communities came out in force wherever they went. So did the native intelligentsia. In Switzerland they had met Professor Schoenbein, the inventor of guncotton and one of Ada's admirers: 'a queer-looking little man, but with a most intelligent countenance.' There too was the consumptive Scot George Macdonald, who years before had introduced Lady Byron to Ruskin. And in Rome there was high mass in the Sistine Chapel, the Pope 'majestic' and 'venerable', the unaccompanied choral voices 'heavenly'.

A feast of Raphaels and Leonardo cartoons, opera and Austrian military bands, awaited them. As they made their way to Pavia, through the Po valley to Cremona and Parma, Anne found the Correggios of the cathedral dome too high for comfort and the Virgin's countenance 'most lovely'.

At Venice they stayed with the Rawdon Browns, whom Lovelace and Ada had met on past visits. Mr Rawdon Brown had helped Ruskin with his Italian researches over the past few years and was prominent in the sizeable British colony. And in Venice there was also Charles Eliot Norton, the Unitarian American devoted to art and literature, first professor of art at Harvard, who charmed everyone with his silvery tongue. They reached the Rawdon Brown palazzo by gondola, experiencing the 'strange magic of gliding at ease' in the still of night.

Anne took drawing lessons en route from Signor Molmente, while Miss Chadwell, an accomplished singer, took charge of her voice. The governess was proving a good companion on their daily walks and gondola journeys, and being a lady of good family was well received in Venetian society. The social calendar, headed by the Hohenlohes and Esterhazys, included Count Stuermer, former Prussian ambassador in Constantinople, the French consul-general Baron Denois, the Princess Jablonowska, the Countesses Nietzabitowska and Balbi-Elsdorff – 'the Silvio Jellico woman with her hair scratched up' – 'Baronne de Something', and 'Chevalier de Scarella (l'inevitable).'

Lord and Lady Vane were their hosts in Rome. At Florence the Somervilles awaited them at their villa, Casa Capponi. Anne was saturated with Italian art and the cultural enthusiasms of the alien aristocrats who occupied the country's best hotels and villas, but there was more to come: Etruscan tombs; a recital by John Thomas, the young Welsh harpist whose musical education Ada had contributed to; the stained-glass windows of the duomo; the Uffizi's Venus de Medici; Raphael's Madonna; the singer Madame Piccolomini, 'of noble family and weak voice'; Michelangelo's sculpture; and the 80-year-old Mrs Somerville, civilised and spritely despite her age.

They left Florence on 2 April 1855, galloping on to Pisa and Carrara, across the river Magra by moonlight, reunited with her father in spirit and in their concern for the horses which were fevered but still kept to their task: 'Poor things, they cannot eat and cannot therefore go fast, and the road is very steep in places.' At Genoa, Anne sketched the waterside from her bedroom. Marseille was crowded with troops on their way to the Crimea.

The Lovelaces were accompanied by a horde of English and American tourists on the road to Paris, where the Emperor Napoleon III, whom Anne and Miss Lamont had seen catching a train at Esher station during his exile some ten years before, was expected for the opening of the Grand Exposition.

Arriving home in late April, Anne went to stay with Grandmamma, who had taken up yet another residence at 4 Cavendish Square. Ockham returned from the north with grimy hands and in labourer's dress to greet her. Ralph followed a few days later. Lovelace returned to the solitude of Horsley; 'Glum Castle' Anne called it. In July she went to Derbyshire to stay with the Nightingales, and from there visited Newstead Abbey.[11] Her mother had been there only five years earlier, an experience which is said to have reduced her to silence. Anne was no more communicative.

She noted nothing of the place of her grandfather's birth or its associations in her diary. Perhaps her mind was full of concern for her brother Byron at the time. She wrote to GM to thank her for passing on news of him.

Anne was 18 now, and time for her 'coming out' and presentation at court had arrived. She was presented by the other Lady Byron, wife of the seventh Lord Byron, the poet's cousin, an inveterate gossip who had presented Ada in 1833. The tone of Anne's diary entry was not ecstatic: 'I thought it a charming night and I should enjoy going again. The Queen looked very nice I thought.' Prince Albert and the Grand Duchess of Mecklenburg Strelitz were the only other members of the royal family present.[12]

Social life was now severely restricted by Lady Byron's cultivated ill health. She had enjoyed a lifetime of hypochondria and for at least the past 20 years had been surrounded by doctors and quacks, cupped and leeched almost daily. 'Grandmamma very ill,' was a constant indication in Anne's diaries that she at any rate believed the old lady when she claimed to be at death's door. Miss Boutell, Ralph's nursery governess, had returned after Ada's death and now looked after GM, while Anne rushed from concert to gallery, often in the company of Parthe Nightingale and Lady Cranworth, the wife of the Lord Chancellor, in the customary flurry of cultural entertainment. Her father went with her to the 1855 Royal Academy. He was still designated by the mocking 'It'. Anne's account of the exhibition was reserved. 'Good on the whole, nothing either bad or superlatively beautiful.' Ockham had returned from Sunderland to take another labourer's job, this time with Brunel's team on the Isle of Dogs, where he was known to fellow workmen as Jack Oakey. He still visited Lady Byron however, exchanging temporarily the grime and sweat of his daytime employment for the relative comfort of her London home.

Another member of Lady Byron's set, Harriet Beecher Stowe, gives us a description of Lady Byron at home with the ill-at-ease Ockham in the mid 1850s:

> His bodily frame was of the order of the Farnese Hercules – a wonderful development of physical and muscular strength. His hands were those of a blacksmith. He was broadly and squarely made, with finely-shapen head and eyes of surpassing brilliancy... When all were engaged in talking, Lady Byron came and sat down by me, and glancing across to Lord Ockham... she looked at me, and smiled.[13]

Although the American writer admired the young man's eyes and his 'intelligent intellectual expression', and was obviously impressed by his muscular frame, Lady Byron thought his body accounted for his eccentricities, requiring a more 'vigorous animal life' than his social background gave scope for. He was working on the ironwork for the Great Eastern Railway, and Mrs Beecher Stowe complimented him on laying aside his title to go in daily with the other workmen, adding: 'I said there was something to my mind very fine about this, even though it might show a want of proper balance.' Lady Byron said she thought Ockham might yet accomplish something worthy of himself. 'The great difficulty of our nobility is apt to be, that they do not understand the working-classes, so as to feel for them properly... I am trying to influence him to do good among the workmen, and to interest himself in their children... I think I have great influence over Ockham.'

Mrs Beecher Stowe thought the conversation very characteristic of Lady Byron, 'showing her benevolent analysis of character.'

The death in 1856 of Lord Scarsdale, Lady Byron's co-heir, enabled her to petition for the Wentworth title left vacant since her uncle Thomas Noel's death. She did not intend to use the title, but wanted to keep it in the family. It would eventually go to Ockham and Ralph and thence, by way of Ralph's daughter Ada Mary, to Anne. It was one of the few English titles which could be inherited through the female line. Anne wrote a letter of wry sympathy to her grandmother, referring to the pain which Lord Scarsdale's death had caused, 'it vexes and grieves and annoys me'. The father's ambition for his son Ralph, now that Ockham was given up as a lost cause, perhaps lay behind that confidence.

The undercurrent of hostility was never allowed to diminish. Lady Byron gave Anne a new pony and trap. Tax would be chargeable and Lovelace wanted to meet the bill. GM maintained that as Anne was now her responsibility so were the horse and carriage; she would pay. Lovelace asserted his role by purchasing a horse for his daughter, a brown one which she called Zephyr, but though it was 'beautiful' she had, she told her grandmother, 'dreamed of a black one.'

Sometimes father and daughter would walk in the grounds when they were together at Horsley or Ashley Combe, and he often talked of 'Norrels', which Anne took to be a plant of some sort.[14] She wrote a few disjointed stanzas when she returned from such walks, one verse of which ran:[14]

> *Yesterday for 3 hours I*
> *was walked*
> *Of every pleasure baulked.*
> *I thought, Papa, you did not*
> *want me.*
> *You ought my dear on such*
> *occasions to enquire*
> *You might more eagerness*
> *have shown me.*
> *Norrels to see and to admire.*

The influence of GM had become all-consuming, but it had almost run its course.

# Part Two

---

# Marriage
# &
# Adventure

---

## Chapter Four

# A Labyrinth of Troubles

In the summer of 1856, Lovelace allowed his daughter to throw a 'trial' ball at Horsley. The rambling Georgian house, lit by gas lanterns and hundreds of candles, resembled a fairy-tale castle.[1] Anne danced all night, making a note of her favourite partners: her cousin Robert Noel, Hilary Bonham Carter's brother Henry, an eligible young man by the name of Gerard Smith, and Captain Douglas Galton, a young sapper on the War Office staff whom Hilary found both clever and gentlemanly. He later married the flirtatious Marianne Nicholson, cousin of the Nightingales.

Ardent in friendship, a lively conversationalist, attractive in looks and manner, and an heiress of no small means, Anne must have represented a tempting challenge to many a young man. Yet, though she was in her 20th year, an age at which most young women of the day were at the very least contemplating marriage, there is no hint in her letters or diaries of communion with the opposite sex beyond the ordinary calls of the social round.[2]

Nevertheless, as GM took increasingly to her sickbed, Anne's social life blossomed.

The other Lady Byron and the 7th Earl took her in hand, introducing her to the more socially active members of the royal circle and London's political acolytes: Foreign Office dynasties and the inevitable sprinkling of social gadflies and academic dignitaries; Cranworths, Curzons (the Zouches of Parham), Drummonds, Lambtons, Hardinges, Palmerstons and Monteagles; Mr Townley and Dean Milman ('whose appearance I did not like').

Hilary Bonham Carter shared Anne's enthusiasm for drawing. She too had taken lessons from Ruskin and both girls looked forward to his visits. Ruskin had spent Christmas at Horsley in 1856 in the aftermath of his separation from Effie, which rivalled the Byron split in its appeal to the popular imagination. Sometimes though, Anne wished that she could get on with drawing horses, her favourite subject, and not have to worry so much about landscapes. Another of Anne's friends at this time was Anne Thackeray, Mrs Richmond Ritchie as she later became, who testified in *Harper's* magazine to Ruskin's penchant for young ladies. After listening to Ruskin, Anne decided that he should have been a novelist rather than an art historian. Whatever its cause, his interest in young girls was innocent enough. Failure to consummate his marriage suggested a lack of sexual drive if not impotence.

Music was the dominant force at this time. Minnie Cranworth, the Lord Chancellor's daughter, was a good amateur pianist, and Charles Hallé was a frequent visitor at their London home. It was there in June 1855 that Hallé heard Anne play the piano for the first time and he subsequently gave her a course of nine lessons, along with Minnie.[3] Afternoons were often devoted to the Houses of Parliament as guests of the Cranworths, sometimes with Hallé, before going off to Willis's Rooms or a drawing room for more musical entertainment. Outside Lady

Byron's narrow circle of Nonconformist clergy and do-gooders, there was stimulation to be found also in such radical spirits as Charles Lyell, the Lubbocks, the Stanleys of Dover Street, the Wilkinsons and Henry Layard. After another visit to the Nightingales in Derbyshire, and a diversion to Newstead to see her mother's grave, Anne went on to Ashley Combe where her father was entertaining Gardner Wilkinson and Layard, the latter fresh from some of his most important discoveries at Nimrud and Nineveh.

She was often in the company of the Nightingale sisters, who had taken up residence with their parents at the Burlington Hotel in London. Florence held court there for the benefit of a chosen few, though by 1857 she had faded from the public eye. One of the 'special' visitors Anne met there was Sir Harry Verney, a widower of 56 who was reputedly the most handsome man in London. He fell in love with Florence and when she refused him, he married Parthe. Another member of this circle was Monckton Milne, a friend of Carlyle and Thackeray, and another of Florence's rejected suitors.[4] Anne took them all off to a lecture by Mr Scott, whom she had found unintelligible on a previous occasion. This time the subject was 'The Age of Dante', and there was all-round approval. Monckton Milne was unstinting in his praise. Anne's latest music tutor Mr Tansa, enticed Florence from the isolation of the Burlington to give her, a passable pianist, an afternoon lesson in which she, like Anne, struggled with Beethoven's 'Kreutzer' sonata. It was a joyful time for Anne, spoilt only by Lady Byron's failing health and the fact that she often had to go to Richmond after an evening in town, for GM was now staying with Miss Montgomery at Ham Common. There was constant commotion as evangelists, mesmerists, naturopaths, herbalists, physicians and other attendants fought for the attention of the two ladies, both habitual invalids. Anne turned away on one occasion, unable to face the pandemonium, and went for a walk in Richmond Park, recalling as she did so a descriptive phrase her father had uttered at the high point of Ada's financial difficulties, 'a labyrinth of troubles'. She began to resent the responsibilities which settled so readily on her young shoulders.

It was her elder brother's 21st birthday on 12 May 1857, and she underlined the date in her diary. But Ockham was not present to celebrate with her. She had earlier written to Lady Byron at the request of the Noels, who were anxious that she should 'say something about O'. The letter was in the mysterious tone that still characterised the correspondence. 'But I suppose the cause of his not coming here has been heard of since... Finally, many happy returns "for the sake of us poor little people."'[5]

GM let it be known to her friends that Ockham was working in the London docks as a kind of missionary, on behalf of downtrodden shipyard workers, and was conducting social research. A remote cousin, Henry Gratton, had asked Lady Byron if he could take Ockham to Ireland, but that rescue attempt failed. In June, Anne went to the London docks to meet her brother at another moment of unexplained crisis. Two months later the Greigs proposed to Lovelace that they should take Anne to Europe with them, to enjoy a brief rest and take the waters, along with Charles Noel whose wife had recently died, and the Robert Noels. They would join up with their younger brother Edward Noel in Switzerland where he was living with his daughter, a beautiful blue-eyed child named Alice.

Anne met Charles Noel at London Bridge station on 3 August. As they went to catch their train Lady Byron's man Grieves appeared, with a 'message' concerning Ockham. Whatever the import of that message, there was nothing Anne could do about it. She and her companions arrived in Dresden nine days later following a brief stop at Cologne to pick up Emma Vischen. At Lille, the two servant girls with the party had to follow on a later train 'on account of the second-class.'

Anne's attachment to Emma became intense. The Vischen family were friends of Miss Waechter, who had died before the visit. Anne invented for Emma the nickname 'Nobody', and the German girl assumed a sudden and crucial importance in her life. One moment she is there in reality; another there is the familiar glimmer of a young girl's attachment to a companion of the mind with elaborate and unsubstantiated outings to concerts and dinner parties, fond greetings and reluctant farewells. Anne shared her only with Grandmamma in her correspondence, and of course with the pages of her diary. It was a friendship strangely reminiscent of Florence Nightingale's affair of the mind with the 'tall, stately, intellectual and irresistible' Salina Bracebridge, to whom Florence gave the pseudonym 'Sigma'.[6]

Cologne, on to Dresden, then Bohemia with Emma and Miss Chadwell, in a breathless series of invitations from the famous as befitted Byron's granddaughter. Then back to Dresden. There was music with Madame Schubert and Madame Schumann, calls on Mozart's surviving son Karl and on Johann Strauss, and a visit on her 20th birthday to that porcelain extravaganza the Japonische Palais with its fine collection of oriental art. They also went to the zoo established by August the Strong, its exotic creatures copied by the great modellers of Meissen a hundred years before. They stayed with Ottolie von Goethe in Dresden, where Mrs Jameson, Lady Byron's bosom companion, had once reigned as the grande dame of the English community. 'Der Freischutz at theatre built by Semper. Enjoyed it unendlich.' Even Anne's diary leaves the reader gasping. 'Gallery, many of Titian, Giorgione, Francia (magi)'. Frau von Goethe again and again, General von Engel, Madame Labinsky, Strauss waltzes, Figaro, 'my 4th lesson (singing) with Mme Schubert', synagogue for more music.[7]

'Nobody' appeared obsessively in Anne's notes. 'Nobody and I went to church', 'Nobody and I to bankers',

'Nameday of Nobody', 'Nobody took me to the opera.' In October they were in Leipzig, Berlin, Dusseldorf. She said a reluctant goodbye to Nobody and her sister Minzia at Leipzig. As for all the illustrious people they had met on the way, Anne merely listed the majority.

On the way home through Paris they stayed with Hilary Bonham Carter and her host Madame Mohl, 'Clarkey', in the Rue du Bas. Like Mrs Gaskell, who had been introduced in 1854, and countless other visitors to Paris, Anne was captivated by the extraordinary Clarkey for whom men fell with blind devotion, despite the mountain of tangled hair on a diminutive body which caused Guizot to remark that she and his Yorkshire terrier shared the same coiffeur.

At the end of the year, Anne was at Ashley Combe with her father. Near the end of November her diary contained a cross and the legend, 'The day of Mama's death, 10pm Saturday, November 27th, 1852.' Anne was in her 21st year. Girlhood had flown and the problems of adulthood gathered.[8]

She went off to Hurstbourne for a pre-Christmas union with the Portsmouths. Anne had visited them briefly in November 1856, when Lady Portsmouth had suddenly and unexpectedly produced a baby daughter. During this visit Anne was able to meet her hosts' eccentric nephew Auberon Herbert, younger brother of the 4th Earl of Carnarvon, agnostic, vegetarian, republican and pacifist.[9] Anne found him fascinating. Brown's Hotel and the London Library with Miss Chadwell led her back to the Lovelace home. Somewhere along the way she met up with her 'beloved Nobody'.

The family was united at Horsley for Christmas 1857, except for Ockham, whose absence was accepted without question. The tree at the end of the hall was lit and Anne ensured that there was a present for everyone. 'Beautiful!' she wrote before retiring to bed on the eve. As snow came in the aftermath of Christmas, she was visited by Mary Currie, a childhood companion whose banker father owned the estate on the west side of Horsley which, here and there, abutted Lovelace territory. Legions of cousins from both families appeared. Mary came into contact with one such cousin on her side, who read poetry to her and confessed his devotion. He was about the same age as her, perhaps a little younger, and his pale face flushed red when he was roused. His name was Wilfrid Scawen Blunt.

During the holiday Anne was thrown in the snow by her horse Zephyr. 'A beautiful horse all the same', she wrote. In the thick snow after Christmas, dog carts were being used to get people to the railway station, and Anne had to make hurried use of one in February when she was called urgently to GM's bedside. She found Lady Byron sitting in her room in an armchair, 'suffering much'. Lady Byron had cried wolf often enough over her health; now she was truly sick and had moved yet again, this time from Richmond to St George's Terrace by Primrose Hill, and few, except her intimates and her faithful granddaughter, took her seriously.[10] Ralph, too, was called to St George's Terrace, to give relief to Anne while she took her violin lessons with Mr Tansa, attended a drawing room at St James's Palace with the other Lady Byron, and ate with the Cranworths. She also heard Sir Henry Rawlinson describe to fellows of the Royal Geographical Society the discovery of Ashurbanipal's palace at Nineveh. In a new flurry of activity she helped Hilary Bonham Carter and Douglas Galton organize fund-raising concerts for Florence Nightingale's scheme to improve hospital administration and record keeping. In between, she went back to Horsley every now and again, where GM's morally elevated friends Miss Montgomery, Mrs De Morgan and Miss Fitzhugh had taken up temporary residence on the pretext of keeping Lovelace company. On one occasion she was delighted to find that Fanny Lushington and William De Morgan, the potter son of the maths professor and the saintly mother, had also taken up residence. 'So we had as it were a party,' read the opening of the day's diary entry. While at St George's Terrace she spent much of her time playing chess with GM and 'attacking' Tacitus together with Ralph, who had been permitted by his grandmother, with his father's consent, to attend University College; 'not fashionable enough', his protector thought, to invite the kind of temptation his grandfather had found irresistible at Trinity College, Cambridge.

Miss Chadwell, the devoted governess of good family, had become Anne's regular companion and chaperone. She had proved a staunch supporter of unity when father and children were being prised apart by Lady Byron, but she had been noticeably absent for much of the year, when Lovelace was taken ill and Emma Vischen had appeared in the flesh. Anne and 'dearest Nobody' went to stay with the Wilkinsons at Aldermaston in August. Miss Chadwell seems to have sensed that the attachment of the two young women was not altogether healthy, and Emma's father was summoned from Germany to take his daughter home before the girls went together to Aldermaston. 'Still here,' Anne told GM on 12 August. She added that Miss Chadwell had returned to her duties 'a martyr, and she shows it in little things.' She wrote too of 'a series of feminine squabbles – but on Tuesday it will all be over, a good thing for Emma as well as for me.' Herr Vischen eventually arrived to take Nobody home.

If Lady Byron's decline was not as painful or dramatic as her daughter's, it was just as protracted. She was confined to her home almost entirely from 1858 to 1860, and Anne was with her for most of the time. But whenever she was away from GM the clandestine letters continued, discussing Lovelace's attempt to purchase a smaller and less expensive home, bringing the dowager Lady King, Lovelace's estranged mother, into the argument about suitable properties. The nomenclature of the aviary returned. Anne was now 'dear little chick' or 'bird' or 'canary'. Father, it appeared, had met another, and the title which Lady Byron once applied to herself was now given to the future Lady Lovelace. 'The Hen has not said whether she will use the house [Horsley Tower] – I suppose not if she is looking or rather he is looking for a house,' wrote Anne to GM. Then, cryptically: 'I have much to tell but as the time draws near for speaking, I wait for that [as] for most things instead of writing. Your own A.I.N.K.'

Lovelace had written many letters to Anne in the six years of suspicion and alienation which followed his submission to the will of Lady Byron. Few of them survive, but there is a batch of letters preserved, dating from 1858, which conveys the tone of their correspondence. The letters were nearly always matter-of-fact and seldom betrayed a personal or affectionate touch. They usually began 'Dear A' and were signed just 'Lovelace'. Occasionally he would summon enough feeling to add 'Affectionately'.[11]

As Lady Byron's breathing became alarmingly spasmodic early in 1860, the indefatigable invalid began yet again to contest the father's right to have a say in the lives of his children. Ockham became the subject of another battle: 'he should be chiefly with me during the year... When he dined here on Sunday he showed off his Greek – which was better than showing off slang.'

On 21 April 1860, GM enclosed a message for Ralph within a letter to Anne, 'Tell Ralph I hope he may know again what it is to be loved as by me for his better self.'

Less than a month later, on 16 May, with Anne at her bedside, propped up with pillows so that she could breathe however fitfully, she departed the world quietly.[12] Many members of that wide circle of sympathetic admirers who had stood by her from the first months of the famous separation were dead or had abandoned the unbending moralist she had become, who expected so much and who gave so bountifully yet so selfishly. A few remained to the end: Miss Montgomery, Lady Wilmot Horton, Mrs George Lamb, the Lushingtons, Miss Fitzhugh, and Mary Carpenter, the last and most determined of the maiden ladies who succoured and paraded that famously wounded heart. And Anne, ever the faithful granddaughter.[13] The doctors decided that ossification of the lungs was the cause of death on the day before her 68th birthday. Anne wrote immediately to GM's solicitor and confidant Lushington: 'You will have heard that Grandmamma died at 4 this morning. I know that you will do what is necessary – & I leave you to inform my Father. Ever yours truly A.N.K.'

A few days after the death of the old lady, Anne wrote typically to GM's close friend the Hon. Mrs George Lamb: 'My darling suffered very much except the few hours before the end – the end was in sleep, which passed into the sleep of death – gently & calmly – Yours most truly A. Noel King.' On 4 June, Anne wrote briefly to her father: 'Dear Papa, I wish very much to have a photograph taken of the picture of Grandmamma by Hoppner which hangs in the hall at Horsley.'

Despite Lady Byron's efforts to retain a hold over the 24-year old Ockham in the last months of her life, the young man had more or less thrown off all family ties. Even Anne, in whom he confided most, was kept in the dark as he toiled happily among the boilermakers and labourers of Brunel's yard. But his physique had all along belied the incurable consumption that condemned him to early death. In the last year or two of his life he took accommodation in Woolwich, where dockyard slums came into visual collision with the fine Georgian houses occupied by the Royal Military Academy and the dockyard authority. While there he had fallen in love with a working girl, but she had suspected that the name Jack Oakey concealed another identity and refused his proposal of marriage. On Lady Byron's death his father had persuaded him to apply for the

Wentworth title, and though he did not use it, he died the 12th Baron Wentworth in the arms of his sister Anne in September 1862. He was 26. Lung haemorrhage was the stated cause.[14]

Anne was wealthy now in her own right, an heiress with a large fortune left her by Lady Byron and an entitlement to the Wentworth barony and estate after her brother Ralph. Her income amounted to £3,000 a year, and the only condition of her grandmother's legacy was that she and her brothers should add her family name, Noel, to their own.[15]

Ralph was the first-named beneficiary, Ockham having protested that he wanted nothing to do with the inheritance, but Lady Byron's considerable estate, including extensive properties in Leicestershire and Surrey, was fairly divided between the grandchildren. The two executors, Dr Lushington and George Anson Lord Byron, the 7th Earl, were handsomely rewarded for their pains. In the last of several final wills and testaments, 17 densely packed and carefully worded pages, there were endless bequests and conditions. Within the immediate family, only Lovelace was excluded entirely.

With the death of Ockham just two years after Lady Byron's demise, Ralph took his brother's title and the residue of the inheritance. Increasingly eccentric in behaviour, conscious of his aristocratic position, indifferent to university life and study and devoted to mountaineering which became the hub of his existence, Ralph was happy to adopt the barony. In so doing, he helped to perpetuate the family tradition of animosity.

The relentless attacks on his father which Lady Byron had fostered were now taken up by the son, and Anne became embroiled in a conflict far more vitriolic than the one she had waged hitherto in order to please her grandmother.[16] In a show of dreadful implacability, Ralph and Anne had asked Woronzow Greig to inform their father that if he attended the funeral of Lady Byron, they would not. The greater influence must have been Ralph's, for Anne was corresponding with her father in respectful, indeed dutiful, terms while she attended to the tasks of clearing up GM's last home in St George's Terrace and writing sympathetic letters to her disparate friends. Dr Lushington was appalled by the attitude of son and daughter. It was left in the end to the 7th Lord Byron to persuade Lovelace that his presence could be the cause of 'publicity and scandal' and that he had best stay away.

Within a few years of her grandmother's death, Anne told Mrs Greig:

> In many things I do not understand her, & yet to me she was like a guardian angel... and I feel I must defend her memory, yet it would seem she must have been mistaken towards my father. Then as to my Mother, I must believe all that my Father tells me. Do you know, I think all mysteries are quite wrong & that however painful it would be better I and my brother should know exactly the truth as to my parents & my grandmother. My Father says he has been silent so long & that he has been treated unjustly.

The bitterness of the woman who once said her greatest desire was 'to love and be loved', whose intellect and features Carlyle admired equally, rubbed off on many of those closest to her, but Anne was untouched. Bitterness and recrimination were foreign to her. Yet the attractions of this accomplished, much travelled heiress with the melodious voice (said to have been inherited from her grandfather), the carefully educated society woman with 'beautiful, unvarnished features and trim figure', were accompanied by a reserve that kept most men at bay. It was not until 1866, as she approached 30, that an eligible male stepped forward. When a tentative approach came, it was as if a mischievous fate had ordained the man and the moment.

The 26-year-old poet Wilfrid Scawen Blunt was a man to whom the word 'beauty' was often applied. He had already accumulated experience and notoriety in the course of his travels. The most sought-after and concupiscent women of the beau monde competed for his favour. He saw himself in looks, – if not in literary skill, – as a Byronic figure; a cut above the general run of diplomats and Foreign Office slaves, to whose ranks financial pressures had consigned him.

At the time Anne seems to have been unaware of his existence, which is the more surprising since they had probably come within speaking distance at Horsley. They were introduced by Olympia Usedom, the Scottish-born wife of the liberal German aristocrat Count Usedom, who had worked at Bismarck's side during the making of the German empire.[17] Anne had gone to Europe in pursuit of music and had landed up in Florence almost by chance.

In the six years preceding this fateful visit, she had travelled widely in France, Germany, Switzerland and Italy and her command of the languages of those countries was complete. She had purchased a London house of her own in Hertford Street, and on her occupation of that establishment in 1863 she made one of the meticulous notes of expenditure that run through her diaries:

Gas bill for Hertford St. 12/9d – Soap for Emma 3 shillings – Music for Macbeth & Where the Bee Sucks 1/9d – Washing bill 2/1d – Doctor's fee 1 guinea – Carriage for day £1 – Violin by Ruzzini £50.[18]

This prosaic column of figures summarised her current priorities. She had met up with Emma again in Germany in 1861, and in 1863 in England. The Nobody of earlier fancy had vanished, and Emma appears in the diaries as a real and much loved friend.

Music remained an important part of Anne's life. On one day in January 1863 she recorded six lessons from Mr Tansa, and others from Madame Lainton. Two years later her diary noted a cheque paid to Mr Tansa for £92. 0s. 10d. But it was at a popular concert given by the Musical Union in March 1863 that she embarked on the most important musical friendship of her life; an event which led indirectly to the meeting with Blunt, which took place in Florence.

At that concert she was accompanied by Madame Schumann and Mrs Lehmann. The conductor was the great Hungarian composer and violinist Josef Joachim, Royal Concert Director at Hanover. For the next two years Anne was given lessons by the great man and she formed a close attachment to him and his soprano wife Amalie.[19]

In 1865 they went to Germany together for a concert tour which led to Joachim's appointment three years later as director of the Berlin Conservatoire.[20] They were accompanied by Fanny Kemble, whose long friendships with Mrs Jameson and Miss Fitzhugh had brought her close to Lady Byron's inner circle, though she had never been truly part of it. Anne had met her sister Adelaide and her husband, Edward Sartoris, in Rome in 1855, and again two years later in that 'musical maelstrom' which centred on the London homes of Fanny and her operatic sister. Concerts at Lübeck and Baden Baden were followed by civic receptions. The women of Anne's party included Marie and Fraülein Schumann, Fraülein Liszt, Frau von Pachen, Fanny Kemble and Amalie Joachim. 'Walk with Frau Schumann, such a beautiful walk.' Her diary offered a matter-of-fact record if ever there was one of a few days spent in the most illustrious company that 19th-century Europe could provide.

Anne and Mrs Kemble left the party to go off to Switzerland and Italy together, and by the end of October 1865 they were in Milan. Fanny was some 30 years Anne's senior, but they seemed to have an easy rapport. It was 20 years since the famous actress' much publicised divorce from her American slave-owning husband. At the end of the tour she went to Venice to join her sister Adelaide Sartoris and her brother-in-law, after a month of travel with Anne.

Anne returned to London, where she bought herself a

new Broadwood piano and noted her expenses for the year, £1805. 3s. 5d.

The next journey to Europe with the Joachims was in May 1866. The maestro had conducted a concert at the Crystal Palace in late April and afterwards Anne left with him and Amalie for what was to prove their final journey together. It was also to be the end of her musical intimacy with one of the great masters of an instrument she loved but of which, to her own frustration and regret, she would never be more than a good amateur exponent.

They parted in Paris. Anne went on to Milan, where her cousin Edward Noel, the 'sublimely handsome' younger brother of Charles and Robert, was waiting for her with his daughter Alice. They were joined by Woronzow Greig and they all spent the ensuing summer and autumn as guests of Count Trivulzio and his family at their mountain villa. In the last weeks of the year she arrived in Florence and went to stay at the Prussian legation.[21]

On 7 December she arrived at the Usedom holiday residence, the Villa Caproni at Castel Solcio on Lake Maggiore. The occasion was noted without comment in her diary, and she made no mention of the other guest of the Usedoms, the handsome poet Wilfrid Blunt, Olympia's 'Baby Boy'.

Sometime before this meeting, Olympia had told Blunt she would find him 'a nice rich wife'.[22] The candidate she had in mind, who now called herself Lady Anne Noel in deference to GM's last wish, had greatly impressed her at their previous encounters and she was able to give Blunt an enticing description of Anne before their carefully contrived meeting. Anne was, she said, suitable in every way for the ever-lovesick Wilfrid. She was 'quiet, distinguished, a good musician and an even better painter.' Blunt would be a fool to let pass this 'gift from heaven'.

The romantic suitor was duly attracted by Olympia's recommendation of Lady Anne, 'travelling about Italy, forlorn, rich, well-born'. To a far-from wealthy member of the diplomatic service, she was in his own words 'an Ark of salvation'.[23] By his report they danced together at Villa Caproni, though she made no mention of the fact, and according to him she showed him her pen-and-ink sketches of Italy. Anne's journals maintained a silence on the matter, and it was Blunt who told romantically of shared memories of summer days in Surrey when he had spent some of his holidays with his cousin Mary Currie at West Horsley, and Anne rode and walked nearby without being aware of him. Perhaps Anne had not been encouraged to see too much of the family on the other side of the fence, for it transpired after her mother's death that Ada had borrowed several hundred pounds from Mary's banker father at the time of her betting difficulties.

For Blunt, the meeting held out nothing more or less than 'pleasant possibility'. He had other arrows in his quiver at that moment and he was not to be rushed by Olympia's insistence on his need for a suitable partner. Indeed, the young man was of an age when he could hardly be blamed for succumbing to the avalanche of advances with which the most beautiful, witty and sought-after women of Europe showered him. Anne seems not to have noticed that the man who talked to her so amiably and interestedly at their first meeting almost failed to recognise her the next day.

True love had turned up unexpectedly – as it usually did for Blunt – while on his way to Florence. It bore the angelic shape of Mrs Robert Baird – Ella, or 'Juliet' as she quickly became. They met on a perfect summer's day at Bellerive, her home on Lake Geneva, and she was there to smooth his brow when he awakened from a snooze in a chestnut wood with Goethe's *Sorrows of Werther* on his mind. 'I have tasted a little honey and behold I die,' he quoted. He asked for the roses she wore in her dress before they parted. She gave him Madame de Staël's *Corinne* to read.

Another married woman also had him in her sights at the

time. After his first diplomatic postings at Athens and Constantinople, thinking of Byron and his 'brethren in arms' and embracing Anne's cousin, the 16-year-old Alice Noel, he was sent in 1861 to Frankfurt, where the ambassador was Sir Alexander Malet. Blunt, like most intellectuals of the time, was fascinated by reports of the recently published *Origin of Species*, but being a Roman Catholic was not permitted to read it. All the same, he acquired a copy and dipped into it – his 'first deliberate sin' – and soon found a very sympathetic ear when it came to discussing Darwin's work. Lady Malet, the stepdaughter of Lord Brougham (some insisted his actual daughter), was an incipient evolutionist and a most attractive woman. Like Madame Usedom, whose husband was his country's ambassador in Frankfurt at the time, she held tight to her young man, and needless to say the two women were not well disposed towards each other. Blunt's dilettante manner and his preoccupation with the opposite sex may have encouraged the ladies, but the ambassador was less indulgent, arranging his transfer to Madrid. Lady Malet sorrowed and warned him against following in the footsteps of some notorious live-wires of the diplomatic service, and against confiding in Madame Usedom. Olympia Usedom told him in her direct Scots way, 'I want your shaggy head and dreamy voice.'

To the chagrin of both wives, Blunt's new posting gave rise to a meeting with a woman of such experience as would command his devotion and colour his whole life.

He stopped at Paris on his way to Madrid and there met the lady dubbed 'Skittles' by her admirers, lovers and clients. She was otherwise Catherine Walters, paramour par excellence, daughter of a Liverpool sea captain and his Irish wife. She was born in 1839 and was, therefore, in her early 20s when Blunt met her, and two years younger than Anne's 29 years at the time of the Florentine gathering.[24] She described their meeting as a straightforward encounter with one of the 'young attachés', and spoke of the 'look of admiration' in his 'soft brown eyes', thinking he might be taken for a homosexual with his high quiet voice and almost feminine beauty. His account was more effusive.

In an 'absolutely truthful' memoir written in later life and called *Alms to Oblivion*, he recalled the meeting with Skittles outside a theatre advertising Mademoiselle Esther in *Manon Lescaut*. How she took him to her room, unbuttoned her dress and stood before him 'clothed the more in loveliness'. She gave rise to one of his best narrative poems, *Esther*. She took him to Biarritz to show him off to the Emperor Napoleon III who was pursuing his favourite pastimes under the glorious *nom de guerre* of Captain Jones, where she shared her favours impartially. In the three years between his first meeting with Skittles and the journey to Florence in 1866, Blunt made his way through Europe by relentless stages of seduction and diplomatic boredom.[25]

After Madrid there was a posting to Lisbon, then the embassy of the poet Robert Lytton whose wife, formerly Edith Villiers, did not approve of his philandering. 'Only fancy my just discovering that he's desperately in love with – whom do you suppose – Skittles?' her husband wrote her.

Then, in Florence, Blunt found Anne. Here was metal of a different kind, and he assessed the discovery retrospectively:

She thought herself plainer than she was, and had none of the ways of a pretty woman, though in truth she had that sort of prettiness that a bird has, a redbreast or a nightingale, agreeable to the eye if not aggressively attractive. Her colouring, indeed, I used to think was like a robin's, with its bright black eyes, its russet plumage and its tinge of crimson red. She had beautiful white teeth and a complexion rather brown than fair, of the short-skulled west of England type she represented so well. In stature less than tall, well poised and active, with a trim light figure set on a pair of small high-instepped feet... It is thus I see her in recollection, an

*1. Lady Anne Blunt with her Arab mare Kasida*

*2. Lady Anne Blunt in 1893*

3. George Gordon, Lord Byron

4. Anne Isabella Milbanke, Lady Byron

*5. William, Earl of Lovelace, 1874*

*6. Ada, Countess of Lovelace*

*7. Lady Anne painting Wilfrid on a horse in the grounds of Crabbet Park*

*8. Lady Anne in the drawing room at Crabbet (taken by Minnie Pollen, 1884)*

*9. Wilfrid Blunt in Paris, 1873*

*10. Lady Anne with her
daughter Judith (undated)*

*11. Lady Anne sitting at her easel with Judith as a young girl
holding a puppy (undated)*

*12. Lady Anne in Dublin, 1888*

*13. Judith after her marriage to Neville Lytton (undated photograph by Lafayette)*

14. Lady Anne in Arab dress
(undated photograph by T. Ellis)

15. Wilfrid Blunt in Arab dress
with Sherifa (photograph
by T. Ellis, 1883)

16. *Lady Anne's painting of the 'ghazzu', the desert battle*

17. *Lady Anne on her mare Fasiha (photograph by Gertrude Bell, Egypt, 1907)*

18. *Lady Anne and Wilfrid sitting outside their tent*

unobtrusive quiet figure in Mme d'Usedom's noisy drawing room, dressed in pale russet with a single crimson rose for ornament, rather than the fashion of the day, but dignified and bright.[26]

Ella Baird, his Juliet, had heard of Olympia Usedom's plan to marry off Wilfrid to Anne, and did not like it. She advised him in her maternal way never to do anything 'so dreadful' for his happiness as 'to marry simply for money'. She added that though she would pity him, she would 'pity the heiress still more'. Mercifully, decisions were postponed by a Foreign Office directive to Blunt to report to Buenos Aires to take up the post of second secretary. He departed from Anne after a few days at the Usedoms to winter in Rome and visit Shelley's grave, then went to Paris, still infatuated with Ella Baird but keen also to see Skittles. Deploring his devotion to Mrs Baird and anxious to promote her own plan for him to marry Anne, Madame Usedom wrote: 'Think a hundred times of my plan & your own folly. Be a man & break at once.'

In Paris he had discovered not only the enchanting Skittles but also his amiable good-for-nothing cousin Francis Gore Currie, 'Bitters' to his friends. Since his retirement from the army at the age of 25, Bitters had given himself up entirely to the pursuit of women. And there was Madeline Wyndham, wife of his cousin Percy Wyndham, another beauty and one of G. F. Watts's Pre-Raphaelite models (the portrait artist who had painted Anne in her 13th year).

Blunt was not finished with cupid's morsels. Juliet Baird arrived with her husband and daughter and promptly refused an assignation, saying their meetings must be accidental. Blunt was not averse to that. 'She was the first quite good woman to give me all her heart,' he said, and at a final meeting before his departure for South America they agreed that their love should be eternal.[27]

Before finally departing for Argentina in 1867 he

obtained Anne's London address from Olympia Usedom and in July wrote to her with enviable bravado: 'at the door of the Villa Caproni I had it on my lips to ask you to marry me... I have never done repenting.' Was it too late? She had indicated when they were together that she was half promised to the Count Trivulzio. Sister Alice delivered his letter to Anne at Hertford Street, where she had set up temporary residence during Lady Byron's last illness.

> I have gone through a sea of anxieties and troubles since we parted,' he wrote, 'and you are the only pleasant thing with your bright eyes and your brown gown which never changes in my recollection. Can you venture to make sail with me in what has been such troubled water? I know that I could make you happy and I know that you have need of happiness – but it is weary work looking for it alone.[28]

Anne, in reply, remarked that she was approaching her 31st year and was older than he, and she doubted whether he would like her 'doubting and hesitating character'. She blew hot and cold too. She said that she had broken off a previous semi-engagement [with Trivulzio] 'in a kind of terror'. All the same, she wished him bon voyage. 'You will often be in my thoughts.'

Blunt took his sister Alice with him to Buenos Aires and told her of his intention. 'A marriage... I was ready to make, but not to go out in chase of it.'[29] Brother and sister went on an 800-mile journey together in South America, wandering by two-wheel buggy between the Andes and the Atlantic. He did not take long to find 'good company' in the shape of the consulate's most famous son, Sir Richard Burton, 'Ruffian Dick' to his friends, and the latter's bosom friend Orton, otherwise known as the Tichborne Claimant.

Alice soon went home to nurse their brother Francis who was suffering from a perforated lung, leaving Wilfrid to the mercies of the scholarly and riotous Burton and the infamous Orton. Wilfrid wrote to Anne to tell her that he hoped to be home by the following Easter (1869) and looked forward to seeing her. In the meantime, Alice and the ailing Francis spent the Christmas of 1868 with her at San Remo. Francis took to his prospective sister-in-law with instant enthusiasm:

We have spent a very pleasant Christmas here, the pleasantest that I have spent for many years. Lady Annabella has been staying with us now for a month and adds very much to our happiness. I have never met anyone with whom it was so easy to live and who enters so thoroughly into all we do, riding and play-acting and the rest. I never met anyone half so clever. I live in hopes of having her someday as my sister. I really think she would suit you well.

The kindly Francis may have understood Anne, but did not know the brother he was writing to half so well. Alice became engaged to a young man she had met in South America, William Wheatley. Poor Francis, universally liked, was dying of the pulmonary disease that had killed their mother Mary ten years earlier at the age of 50.

In March 1869, Wilfrid was home and impatient for Anne to return to England from Florence, where she bided her time. Even as he asked Anne to come to him, he professed that his heart still belonged to Juliet. He was angry with his beloved sister Alice who, anxious to protect Anne, had told her brother he should not call on Mrs Baird.

He was egged on in his attempt to lure Anne into marriage by all his women friends except Ella Baird. They included Skittles, Madeline Wyndham and Minnie Pollen (whom Anne had known as the child Maria Laprimaudaye, and who later comforted Rossetti as well as Blunt). Anne returned home and asked her friend Emily à Court to invite Blunt to dinner, proceeding in her open and rather naïve way to tell Blunt that she had asked Emily to ask him. Never wanting in urbanity, Wilfrid affected surprise at finding Anne there.

When we were left together, the meal over, it was not I that gathered up the threads of our past history. Simply and honestly she told me that she had not said 'yes' at Castel Solcio and was prepared if I would forgive to say it now. It needed no more words; and so it was arranged between us.

The die was cast. He started to call her 'My darling Child', and assured her that there was no objection to their children not being baptised as Catholics, though they should perhaps talk about it. She began to sign herself 'Your old-fashioned Child'. Then he went off to Paris and Lisbon, savouring the prospect of love and marriage. Old Julie, Skittles' woman, thought Anne must be a princess from the *Arabian Nights* from the description of her.

'How strange it seems to me that the labyrinth of troubles I grew up in should have suddenly disappeared out of my life,' Anne wrote. He asked her not to judge him as she would judge others, and she replied with poignant truth that he was not like other people. She wrote: 'Dearest, I feel as if I had suddenly come into a great unknown world in which only you could guide me – and now you have gone away.' She recorded the wedding at the back of her diary:

We were married on Tuesday 8th June, 1869, at St George's Hanover Square. My uncle, Sir G. Craufurd was the chief clergyman on the occasion. Philip Currie was Wilfrid's best man, for which he was rewarded by receiving a gold-headed cane well suited to his tendency to become an old bachelor. My bridesmaids were Hester King, Mary Fortescue, Darea Curzon, Minnie Jenkins, Mary Chandler, Alice Noel. These embellished their gowns as the saying is, instead of being beautified by them, for the toilets, at Lady Burrell's instigation, were concocted on the premises of 'artistic society'... fools in the matter of fashion and elegance. Of course after the marriage service there was a ceremony of signing the names in the vestry & then we walked out of the church & there was the breakfast where there had been places marked for particular people & nobody obeyed their orders – Ralph suddenly gave me a great pear-shaped pearl in a little round card box, saying he had nothing else for me. It was just before the breakfast. In the middle of breakfast came a note from Lady Palmerston, who sent me a gold bracelet with a large ball of blue lapis like a lump of blue clay. Before the breakfast I particularly remember Alice [Blunt] in a brown silk gown – I remember that at the breakfast she sat down between Nep [Wheatley] & ----. At last the breakfast came to an end. I went down to change my dress – I believe it was 2 o'clock when we started in an open carriage and four horses with postillions...[30]

In her factual rather unimaginative commentary, Anne revealed a good many of her virtues and her faults, and hidden in its revelations and its omissions was much that would bring the sins of the past into present and future focus. Her embittered father, unmentioned by Anne, had married a sensible widow, Mrs Jane Jenkins. They played no part in the proceedings, and Anne was given away by Ralph. There were three children of Mrs Jenkins's previous marriage, two sons (the eldest, Boycott, living in Switzerland) and a daughter, Minnie, who was a bridesmaid. Daria Curzon was the sister of Robert Curzon, Lord Zouche. Alice Noel had already succumbed to Blunt's amorous advances. What Anne did not know was that Juliet, Ella Baird, was at the back of the congregation, weeping bitterly throughout the ceremony.[31]

Blunt had entered into the bargain torn between an 'accepted courtship' and 'the fevers of illicit love'. Up to now his inheritance had given him an income of £700 a year. From now on he was worth £3,000 a year, placing him 'almost in the rank of the world's sublimities'. In his own words, he had acquired 'a pearl of the greatest possible price, a heart entirely single in the devotion it was prepared to give.'

Others would describe her charm, the dark brown eyes captured in the girlhood portrait by Watts expressive of high intelligence and warmth of heart, the petite figure, the gentle manner and dignity of carriage, the soft melodious voice.

Wilfrid had found a loyal heiress and that was enough. Perhaps, as the couple set off on their honeymoon, another thought was maturing in his fertile mind; a thought which would find its way into verse:

*Room enough beneath the sun*
*For her, and thee and me...*

## Chapter Five

# Robin and the Tyrant

A day or two before the wedding, the literary bombshell of the nineteenth century was exploded by Harriet Beecher Stowe with the publication of her essay *Lady Byron Vindicated*.[1]

Before the couple could board their carriage for the honeymoon journey, the press had taken up the old scandal with relish.[2] In essence, the American writer affirmed that Lady Byron had told her that her husband had been guilty of incest with his half-sister Augusta, and that this had been the primary reason for her returning to her parents' home and seeking a separation. Journalists were far from convinced that Mrs Beecher Stowe's simple uncorroborated account was the full story, however. An Irish Protestant priest by the name of Francis Trench, who had been one of Lady Byron's most fervent supporters, wrote in *The Times* that it should not be supposed Mrs Beecher Stowe 'was anything like an exclusive or even rare depository of the statement which she has made.' Indeed, according to

Trench, Lady Byron had 'fully stated the cause of her separation to many of her relatives and intimate friends.'

More damningly, Thomas Smith, a solicitor to whom Medora had entrusted her essay on the tragic state to which she had been reduced by Lady Byron's intervention in her life, allowed the editor of the *Illustrated London News*, Dr Mackay, the father of the romantic novelist Marie Corelli, to publish it in 'a very limited edition'.

Anne came under increasing pressure to 'reveal the truth', while Lovelace kept his distance in the ensuing controversy. Ralph, recently engaged to Miss Fanny Heriot, took his grandmother's part, though when he studied the papers obtained from Lady Byron's trustees after the will had been proved, he became less inclined to take her word.[3] Wilfrid and Anne laboured for days and nights on end writing letters to the press based on her recollections of childhood hearsay and such documentary evidence as Ralph made available to them. But they were unable to stem the tide of well-informed criticism. Anne was surprised to find that her grandmother had revealed so much to her American friend and she spoke of 'the odious Stowe pamphlet'. Considering the sheltered life she had led under her grandmother's supervision, an outsider might equally have been surprised at the extent of Anne's knowledge of Lady Byron's accusations and of her grandfather's alleged misconduct.

Wilfrid wrote on Anne's behalf to Godfrey Lushington, son of the family lawyer, to find out if his father could throw any light on the revelations, but the son could not summon the courage to ask his father about so 'unspeakable' a subject.[4] The 'guilty man', Lord Byron, may not have been the hero in England that he was on the continent 40-odd years after his death – had not Goethe declared that Byron's was 'the greatest talent' of the nineteenth century? – but influential writers in the press knew that his wife had protested her own cause too vigorously; that Byron had yielded reluctantly to the demands of the Milbankes for a separation, that he had accepted alienation from his daughter Ada even less readily, and that considerable financial inducements were offered to him to stay away from England and from his family. Lady Byron had been less than frank, and unwise in her choice of confidantes.

Family scandal notwithstanding, Wilfrid and Anne were determined to begin their honeymoon as planned at Worth, the forest estate which was to be one of their three Sussex homes.[5] Locals had erected a floral arch to greet them at the entrance to the estate. They stayed there for a week, the inclement weather doing nothing to detract from the shared pleasure of drives, walks and fishing expeditions. On 16 June they went to London for the wedding of Wilfrid's sister Alice to Nep Wheatley.[6] As at their own wedding, the Burrells played host at their Berkeley Square home, but the ceremony took place at the Catholic church in Chelsea.

The couple returned to Worth for a few days before continuing the honeymoon at Ashley Combe, at the invitation of Anne's father. When they arrived the house was empty and no one was there to greet them. All the same they made the best of it and spent their days among the steep hills, green fields and sculptured coastline of her girlhood. They called on villagers she knew. One family gave the couple books from their shelves, bound in bright red leather. There were visits, too, to some of Anne's west country relations – Fortescues, Portsmouths, Devons and others of the landed gentry; and to Wilfrid's aunt and uncle, the Glanvilles of Catchfrench.

They were back in London in July to see Ralph and his fiancée Fanny Heriot. Anne had begun to sense that her brother had been unfair to their father and had helped to cause an unnecessary rift. There were distinct signs of tension between brother and sister, and it was decided not to wait for the hurriedly arranged wedding on 25 August but to proceed as they had planned to Switzerland. Ralph's wife-to-be was described by Anne as 'very beautiful', but she wondered if Fanny would suit her brother. She noted that the trials of their short engagement had been many. Ralph gave his sister a photograph of Fanny and her sister Mary, and Anne made a sketch of the new Lady Wentworth. On 22 July she noted, 'Stupid quarrel with Ralph.'[7]

But already Wilfrid was growing weary of the family dispute he had married into and impatient to return to familiar pastures. Even during the honeymoon at Worth Anne had complained of sickness, and he had found solace in fishing while leaving her to read and practise the violin, something he found quite excruciating. He had found his wife a new lady's maid, Isabella Cowie, in London during the visit to Ralph and Fanny. Blunt had seen the girl on the station platform and for once urbanity deserted him. He had it on the tip of his tongue to say platitudinously, 'You are far too pretty for this place,' but he refrained.

Anne was ill in Paris on the way to Berne. They were met at the Gare du Nord by Julie, Skittles's *bonne*. 'Walking too much,' Anne wrote. Next day they were aboard the Neufchatel express. She kept two diaries at this time, one more elaborate than the other and added to retrospectively. In one, for 6 August, she said simply, 'I was ill'. In the other, a note completed months later: 'Friday a.m. I was taken ill. And thus we lost the hope of having a child soon.' [Later] 'It was miserable – & then when we had the hope again – it was to have it fulfilled & then to lose our child.'[8] Already, the patriarchal husband was determined to fulfil his need for a son and heir, a quest that was to cost Anne dear, emotionally and physically.

On the 7th she recorded, 'Still ill. W. rode.' While being attended by the doctor she completed an aquatint which she called 'Vue de Neufchatel', and was greatly comforted by a visit from the effervescent Fanny Kemble. Fanny left on 17 August, Wilfrid's birthday. Anne gave him flowers and a 'silly little wooden screen'. They went on by road to Berne, stopping at Thun, where Wilfrid fished and carried her across the river in her weakened state. They were joined by an Englishman, Mr Hildyard, and as the path was too steep for the horses with a full carriage he – 'tenderhearted to all dumb things' – got out and walked. Were it not for her recent illness, Anne would almost certainly have joined him.

She acquired a St Bernard dog named Josephine, which quickly became her pride and joy, and the threesome found accommodation at the Hotel Bellevue, Interlaken, by Lake Thun. Blunt went to the Berne legation by train each day while she read and played the violin. She had given up singing since her last visit to Rome when she had decided after more tuition that she lacked 'the necessary ability'.

The pleasant interlude was disturbed early in September by a new outbreak of the Byron story in the press, resulting from the publication in *Macmillan's Magazine* of a potted version of Harriet Beecher Stowe's apologia.[9] This time Lady Byron's solicitors Messrs Wharton and Ford compounded the matter by writing a letter to the magazine in which they attempted to demonstrate that Mrs Beecher Stowe was wrong in her presumed knowledge. Wharton and Ford had been intimately concerned with the negotiations between Lady Byron and Medora Leigh back in the 1840s, when Medora had stood up to her supposed stepmother-in-law, refused her offer of an annuity and threatened her with dire consequences if she was left without an income. Their letter was taken up by the world's press, and to her consternation Anne saw it in a Swiss newspaper.

It might have occurred to Anne and her husband that Medora's daughter Marie was still alive and living in France, dependent on charity for survival, and probably only too willing to grant interviews had any journalist of the day had the sense to pursue her. Marie, like her mother, did not accept with equanimity the fact that one side of the family was able to live in great comfort, with honour and respect, while she was reduced to begging because of the doubt surrounding her mother's birth. She called herself Marie Leigh but believed herself to be a Byron, the grandchild of the incestuous relationship all Europe was talking about. Anne's diary for 3 September revealed her feelings: 'Today I saw Wharton & Ford's ill-judged letter on the disagreeable subject of Mrs Stowe's article. The letter was copied into Galignoni's newspaper.'

Wilfrid having written to Godfrey Lushington without avail, Anne tried the father, but Dr Lushington was no more willing than his son to enter the public controversy, though he of all people must have known the truth. She considered the possibility of Ralph approaching the Prime Minister Lord Russell who had known most of the interested parties. In the end she put the matter to her father, and then told Francis Blunt: 'My father, who would certainly know if any proofs [of incest] existed even if he had not seen them has replied that it rests as far as he knows with one witness's assertion or belief – that witness being my grandmother.'

Rather late in the day, Anne began to suspect her grandmother's confidences. 'Now her belief may, and must, I feel, have been a mistaken one. It is a great misfortune that she ever should have believed so dreadful a thing, or that believing it she should have told anyone.' Blunt let it be known he was more concerned for the poet's great-grandchildren, yet to be born.

By her 32nd birthday Anne was unwell again. The desire for the all-important great-grandchild – a boy – had begun to torment the marriage; already Blunt began to despair and to greet successive miscarriages as if it were entirely his wife's responsibility. Anne found comfort in Browning and Shelley and a visit by Edward and Alice Noel. Wilfrid gave her flowers and a white picture frame, and promptly went off to Berne, ostensibly to look for rooms. Anne played the violin while Josephine the St Bernard amused herself by chewing a picture of the lake at Neufchatel which Wilfrid had been painting from the hotel window. 'Spent all day pasting together the hundreds of tiny fragments of J's handiwork. At last more or less succeeded.'

At the beginning of October Ralph and his wife arrived at Ouchy. Wilfrid had already made contact with Ella Baird. 'It woke in me the passionate longing which has slumbered for the past three years, with all the romance that had possessed my soul and which had never really been supplanted,' he wrote. Anne and Wilfrid had been joined by the honeymooning Ralph and Fanny and had moved on to Beaurivage, within sight of Mont Blanc and the Baird residence at Bellerive.

If Wilfrid and Juliet had not quite resumed where they had left off, the spark was only waiting to be ignited. 'Wilfrid went to Bairds... returned and found me <u>fiddling</u>.' The word 'fiddling' was underlined. Wilfrid hated her violin playing. Croquet with Bairds, dinner party with Bairds... hardly a day went by without a visit to or from the Bairds. Sometimes Juliet joined Anne at the piano and they played duets.

'It was not quite love again between Juliet and me but a very near attachment which seemed to wait its time,' wrote Blunt. And then: 'Anne in her good contentment cared not where her tent with me was set and though I did not explain to her all the reason, rejoiced with me because she saw the change had made me happier.'

It was a honeymoon which he thought might be made to last into eternity, 'a new earthly Paradise,' with shades of the Shelleys and the Williamses at Lereci. But of course all the parties to that quartet of love shared in its pleasures, until the two men were tragically drowned.

On 6 October 1869, Anne had underlined another diary entry. 'Wrote to my sister A'. A month later there was bad news of her devoted sister-in-law: Alice Wheatley, as Blunt's sister now was, had contracted the consumption that seemed to afflict almost all the family, and was not expected to live. She had become pregnant soon after her marriage to Nep, and he had written to tell Wilfrid and Anne the tragically double-edged news.[10] The Wheatleys were at Caldwell in the north, close to his new job as commander of the Renfrew militia. Blunt rushed home to be with his beloved sister and left Anne in the care of the Bairds. 'I am in pain Dick and you must suffer it too because you love me,' he wrote. Bird nomenclature was back but now Anne was 'Robin', 'Dick' or 'Dicky'. He had become her 'Tyrant'.

The emotionally disjointed Blunt had another cause for concern. His devotion to his sister had always been intense. Now he realised that he was jealous of her husband Nep, who was good-looking and much taller than he. Alice looked at them together and exclaimed to her brother, 'How small you have become!'

On 15 November Anne recorded her seventh letter in as many days to Wilfrid and finally resorted to a telegram telling him she could bear the silence no longer. Two days later, she telegraphed to say she was on her way home via Paris. She was met at the station in Paris by old Julie and taken by her to the Hotel Mirabeau, where she whiled away the time reading Voltaire. Wilfrid arrived in the afternoon.

They left for London on 19 November after sending Julie to collect '100 bottles of Chateau Yquem, 80 of Cantonne, 100 clarets, 100 champagnes and 24 cognacs' at a cost of £198. On arrival in England, Anne was despatched to Torquay to find suitable accommodation for Alice to be moved to. Alice and Nep came down from Scotland with Wilfrid in early December. Unwell again, Anne penned a heartfelt diary note. 'Both of us sick and sorry.'

The house Anne found at Torquay was called Glan-y-mor.[11] Perched on a cliff top, the temporary home seemed to cast a spell over the assembled foursome. Alice lost her baby, though she herself survived. The two women shared the remote house in perfect harmony but relations between the men were strained to breaking point. Anne longed to see more of her husband and encouraged his wish to leave the diplomatic service after 11 unproductive years. The Foreign Office offered him a posting in St Petersburg but he turned it down. He eventually retired from the service with effect from 31 December 1869. Lord Lytton, under whose aegis he had served congratulated him on his escape from 'this wretched profession', hoping that he would find employment befitting his 'genius' and 'originality'.[12] Lytton also remarked that he was curious to hear about the trip to Paris and wondered whether Wilfrid did not find 'the beatifications of domestic life refreshed by a temporary suspension of them.' He added superfluously: 'you are very wise to give yourself occasional relaxation of the nuptial knot. Variety of sensation is the sole refuge from permanent insensibility.'

Anne and Wilfrid decided to make Blunt's home, Newbuildings, their residence in a new life freed from the commitments of work in government service. Anne ended the first year of married life with a letter to her father, in touch again but still licking his wounds. It came from Glan-y-mor: 'Dear Papa, I wish you a happy new year's day and many of them.' She had heard, she said, that the ball which he and 'Hen', the new Countess of Lovelace, had given at Horsley Towers had been a great success.[13]

A wet and gloomy entrance to the year 1870 found Anne and Wilfrid still at Glan-y-mor. Anne, fiddling between times and deeply immersed in the arcane delights of Goethe's *Unterhandlungen mit dem Kanzler Friedrich von Mueller*, hoped wistfully for another pregnancy, for the elusive son to cement their marriage.

By the end of the month they were at Neufchatel with the Lyttons and Malets. Anne was unwell again and the doctor ordered her to bed. A letter from Lovelace to Blunt suggested little cause for optimism: 'Dear Mr Blunt, It is a satisfaction & nice to hear of Annabella's safety although preoccupied with doubt about your child. Sincere wishes to Annabella.'[14]

Pregnancy was not confirmed until March, by which time Anne was dividing her time between Neufchatel and England while Wilfrid was in Paris, looking for 'a suitable apartment' – not too far removed from cousin Bitters. He eventually found a splendid address at 204 rue de Rivoli. Rumblings of the Franco-Prussian war accompanied their move.

Blunt travelled back and forth between England and France and Anne complained of his frequent absences. She looked forward with childlike anxiety to receiving his letters. Now and again she accompanied him. The Lytton home at Knebworth in Hertfordshire provided her with a rare opportunity to savour the company of the 'glorious being' she had married and to play the part of the devoted wife among friends. Unfortunately for her, the undemonstrative manner imparted by her upbringing in households where it was bad form to show emotion convinced Wilfrid that her love, like his for her, would become – indeed had already become – a 'sensible, practical' affair.[15]

Alice and Nep, devoted to Anne and openly critical of Wilfrid's neglect of her, were comforting companions when he was away from home. They were together at Worth in April. In May, Anne left for Paris, accompanied as ever by her enormous canine companion Josephine.

Tennis and riding on the Bois de Boulogne suggested that all was well with Anne's pregnancy.[16] On 15 July, the day of the Emperor Napoleon's declaration of war on Prussia, she met Wilfrid off the Calais train. The faithful Julie was with him, but there was no sign of her mistress.

In fact, Wilfrid had seen a good deal of Skittles[17] while in London and corresponded happily with her. She had deserted Paris with the threat of war. The famous paramour now spent much of her time at her London home in Chesterfield Street Mayfair, giving tea parties, entertaining 'Bertie', the Prince of Wales, and hunting with the country set at weekends. Blunt and the Prince developed a close understanding; later on Skittles wrote that she was often merely a 'go-between' for the two men, and it seems that she helped to advance her young lover's schemes by whispered bedroom confidences.

Wilfrid's letters to Anne during what was still supposed to be their honeymoon became more and more prosaic, usually beginning 'Dear Dick' and ending 'Your husband', sometimes with his initials.[18] Alice Noel came to stay with Anne and they were often in the company of Frank Lascelles, now first secretary at the Paris embassy, and of the Olliffe family into which Lascelles was shortly to marry. Sir Joseph Olliffe was honorary physician to the embassy and Lady Olliffe, to whom Anne was much attracted, was a great favourite of Charles Dickens, who had become a frequent visitor to the Olliffe home.[19]

By August Paris was under siege and Anne was sick again. As battle raged on the outskirts of the capital she was told by the doctor to 'stay quiet'. She was more concerned for her dog, however, than for her own health. Josephine had become 'pitiably ill'. Her doctor and Josephine's vet were both in regular attendance. Worse, as the siege developed, every animal was under threat as the population began to look for domestic pets and even eventually rats and sparrows to supplement their diet.

With diplomatic help, the Blunt party was able to leave, though movement in and out of the city was forbidden to ordinary citizens and was in any case risky. Wilfrid took Anne and Alice Noel to Deauville, where Sir Joseph Olliffe owned considerable property and was engaged with Count Mornay in a scheme of redevelopment. By the middle of the month they had moved on to Caen. The war news was bad and Blunt sent Anne and Alice to Rouen before going to church for the first time in seven years to 'pray for France', returning to Paris on 24 August. He gave £100 for the French wounded and wrote a letter to *The Times* protesting at its pro-Prussian stance.

Wilfrid left Paris two days after his return, his cousin Bitters remaining behind in his rooms at the Palais Royale, content to see out the siege and the Commune philosophically in the company of the ladies of pleasure who shared his own priorities.

They spent Anne's 33rd birthday in England with her cousins the Robert Curzons at Parham. By November there were more premature birth pangs. Her physician Dr Black was sent for by telegram. By the time the physician arrived by special train it was Wilfrid who was most sick. He was jaundiced and ordered to bed. Anne dined alone and for the next few days kept a meticulous record of events. On 14 November, she noted with suspicious lack of exaltation 'the boy was born'. Then: '15th. Wilfrid baptised the little child. Mrs Tullet held him. Cowie and Mrs Selwood were present. In my room he was baptised Wilfrid Scawen. 16th. Mrs Brown the nurse came. I hated the sight of her. 17th. Had the little child in bed with me. He died on Friday morning at half past 2'. Four days later, Wilfrid rose from his sick bed to bury the child in the monastery at Crawley, 'buried with my little ring'.[20]

The vicar of Worth parish church had refused to bury the child, which had been given only a lay baptism. Beside himself with anger, Wilfrid went to the Catholic friars of Crawley, who buried his child courteously with 'the pomp of moral chanting'. The ceremony took place at night by the light of tapers. 'I was the only mourner present,' he wrote, 'for this my only son. God rest his small soul.'

Perhaps Anne should have learned lessons from her mother's hazardous confinements, always put at risk by riding and high jinks up to the last moment. Perhaps travel and an unsettled lifestyle were the enemies of the daughter's frantic attempts at childbearing. Whatever the causes, the effect on Anne's morale was, for the time being at least, devastating. She understood and shared her husband's terrible sense of loss.

They had recovered much of their verve, however, by the spring of 1871 when they went to Portugal and Spain for a riding holiday, accompanied by Cowie their maid.[21]

It was a time of harmony. Wilfrid's new-found concern for Anne, influenced perhaps by the shared tragedy of the son who bore his name, was conspicuous even before they set out, and he described their brief idyll as 'one of the happiest moments' of his life. They went by way of Lisbon, through the Bay of Biscay, and Anne drew the tempestuous, 'splendid' sea. Anne was not a good sailor and joined most of the ship's complement in being 'disgustingly sick'. Portugal was a country familiar to Blunt from the days of Lytton's embassy, and they were warmly received by Mrs Lawrence, an English hotelier of Sintra, who found the golden boy of earlier visits so thin that he was almost unrecognisable.

Wilfrid had begun work on his *Romeo and Juliet*, and he sought inspiration in a walk along the Lisbon road with its view of the Lyttons' old house below the Pena. Anne bought herself a copy of *Les Misérables* and 'a Balzac for Wilfrid', and he read passages to her on the inadequacy of womanhood. They planned a 'Book of Birds' to be illustrated by Anne, and Wilfrid took to an orgy of bird shooting in order to create a reference menagerie of stuffed creatures. Anne hated the idea but went along with it loyally. A grey crow and a sparrowhawk were among the eleven birds lined up by the end of March.

By then Anne was pregnant again and was attended by a French doctor. It was decided that she should be carried in a hammock to prevent exhaustion.[22] Wilfrid danced around their caravan as they progressed through the Portuguese countryside taking potshots at every bird in sight.

Then there was a terrifying journey by horse buggy along mountain roads, Anne worried as ever about the horse's welfare, Blunt shooting madly and holding up a cockerel for his wife to sketch. Switching to amphibian subject matter, he collected a frog in a jar with a book over it to prevent its escape; 'the poor little throat kept heaving and panting convulsively, so I moved the book sideways & let in a chink of air.' They read Wallace's *Travels in the Malay Archipelago* and Wilfrid decided that they must follow the author's paths to catch butterflies and shoot birds of paradise. For the moment they made do with a bullfight. Wilfrid thought it a magnificent 'science', while a companion, Mr Duppa, insisted that it was barbarically cruel to the horses. Wilfrid had boasted to Skittles that during his time at the Madrid embassy he had taken up bullfighting and had been allowed to enter the arena where he 'played a bull with courage and dexterity', glorying in the performance and in his gold-embroidered jacket and red cloak. 'I expected to feel sick and horror struck... but I am sorry to say that I felt nothing of the kind,' said Anne.[23]

Whenever she was out of her carriage, she was carried in her hammock, a remarkable sight even by the standards of the eccentric English travellers of the time, especially since she sketched industriously, indifferent to the curious glances of passers-by.

There was another sudden cry of anguish. On 13 April, 1871, she wrote:

> Today is a dark day for me, a day on which all the world seems blank and every little thing gives me pain, no future seems at all hopeful – instead of a mirage, I see a dark deep hole – although the sun is blazing outside the house and there are flowers everywhere and a bright blue sea.

She had no need any more to confide the unhappy word to her diary.

Alice and Nep came to join them and they went on together to St Vincente, Cadiz and Seville, Malaga and

Pizarra, Córdoba and the Almadinejos. A puppy they had acquired was attacked by boys and its leg broken. They put the injured limb in a splint and carried the patient in a basket. Cowie presented Wilfrid with a blackcap which sang beautifully, and so it was given a cage and went with them. Outside Madrid Wilfrid shot and injured a hawk. Next day they found it with an eye missing 'squawking piteously' and rather belatedly tried to save it. A few days later in this staccato journey they rescued a dog dying for want of water. There was news from Paris of increasing civil disorder and Wilfrid began to pine for Ella Baird. On 19 July, in Madrid, he left Anne a note: 'Dick, do you know what is going to happen? I shall put you into the train & ride on myself... I did not tell you before so as not to spoil your pleasure.' But Madrid, with its Titians and Velázquezs, and a day's riding with Mrs Goschen, wife of the British ambassador, combined to change his mind. Anne was reprieved.

By late July they were back in France. On the 25th they arrived in Paris, where they marked time for almost two months. Wilfrid was impatient to see Ouchy and Juliet again and he left Anne, pregnant once more, in the now quiet capital of the Third Republic.

He arrived at the Bairds' in time for Ella's birthday in October, surprising her by his sudden appearance, but the lake was shrouded in mist and the red roses had faded. She had cherished the thought of her golden boy through long lonely months, but now thought discretion the better policy. She asked him to leave, protesting later that she repented nothing, expected no more happiness and hoped that he might someday find 'all you think you have lost now'.

All was not lost for the insatiable Blunt. While on his way from Worth to France he had met Rosalind Stanley, the fascinating, witty daughter of the Stanleys of Dover Street, now Rosalind Howard, Lady Carlisle to be, and they had reminisced fruitfully. But another crisis intervened before he could follow up that promising opportunity. Brother Francis and sister Alice were terminally sick at the Madeira home Francis had chosen for its air, and in November Wilfrid went to nurse them. He was to remain at their side for four months, but neither his wife's constant miscarriages nor the desperate illnesses of his beloved brother and sister long delayed his search for 'true love'.[24]

He managed to fall for another wife of a family friend, this time Georgie Sumner, one of the Bertie set, whom Rossetti had sketched. Her brother Nigel Kingscote had married Blunt's cousin Caroline Wyndham. Wilfrid became her 'brown-eyed boy'. In Madeira he had bought a carved Spanish-style bed for Newbuildings, and he wrote to Anne describing the purchase. He christened the bed ceremonially with Georgie, sending Anne a jocular batch of 'poems without words', including one entitled 'love scene'. He also suggested to her a new small house in London, 'just for us'.

Anne was again in the agony of premature labour, dosed with laudanum.[25] In March 1872 she felt she could put off the birth no longer, though the pregnancy was only six months advanced. Two days later, the Catholic physician attending her, described in her diary as the 'hateful Dr Campbell', delivered the baby, Elizabeth Cordelia Catherine. Then he told Anne that she had been carrying twins and that another was about to be born. At 8.20 p.m., less than half an hour after the first birth, Alice Maria was delivered. Two hours later she died. The two babies had been placed side by side on a chair, propped up with hot-water bottles. By 7 March the surviving girl was too weak to take milk. Anne asked for the infant to be given to her.

> It is better my own child should die in my arms if it must die. I feel as if I could not bear anyone else to touch it. Oh, it was so lovely to me, it had feet and hands like its father and its voice went to my heart, and it opened its eyes and looked at me, how many times and the last time the eyes were open they

saw me and I kissed the lids to shut them forever and I kissed my child's hands and feet and head. I kissed the mouth.[26]

Wilfrid remarked that Anne at least 'was doing well'. He added that there was the 'dismal satisfaction that the children were not boys.' The two babies were buried at Crawley alongside the boy Wilfrid Scawen.

Francis died on 21st April as his brother read to him from Newman's *Dream of Gerontius*. Alice died in August and was buried in the same monastery grave on Wilfrid's 32nd birthday, 17 August.[27] Death and disaster seemed to Anne to hang over her marriage like an omnipresent cloud. Her husband's response to a two-year period of almost unmitigated tragedy was to seek consolation once more in extra marital attention. Rosalind Howard encouraged his advances and then rebuffed him. Minnie Pollen came to the rescue in an atmosphere of Pre-Raphaelite passion in which her love ignited like 'a perverse flame'. As that passion waned, Madeline Wyndham filled the void, and then Georgie Sumner returned to England, already pregnant, to engage his clandestine attention at Stafford House, the London home of the Duchess of Sutherland. Georgie soon fell for others, however, including John Brown of Balmoral ('and almost made Her Majesty jealous'), and the Reverend Norman Mcleod, the Presbyterian preacher who was another royal favourite.

With Francis's death, Wilfrid became the squire of the family estates. He and Anne worked feverishly at their other ancestral Sussex home, Crabbet Park, using much skill and imagination to rebuild the old Tudor house with Portland stone and new heavy slates. The attached farms were in good order. Tapestries picked up in Paris lined the hall.

By early 1873, Anne was expecting again. They took a house in London's Lower Brook Street for the confinement, and the pious Minnie Pollen came every morning to see Anne and take Wilfrid to mass. His new love for Minnie had, he wrote, 'softened him'. The baby, a girl, was born at 3.30 on the morning of 6 February 1873, at 45 Lower Brook Street. She was a month premature but she lived. Judith Anne Dorothea – the names were drawn out of a hat – was baptised by Monsignor Talbot, and Wilfrid noted that Dorothea meant 'gift of God'.[28]

There were more European journeys in the immediate aftermath of Judith's birth.[29] There was disappointment of course. A boy would have been preferred, but after so many abortive confinements a girl was better than nothing. Anne's own pleasure was unspoken, muted by her husband's undisguised disappointment.

Shadows of family scandal lurked where Anne and Wilfrid and their daughter now travelled. Marie Leigh also wandered on the continent and played the only trump card she held – that she too was the granddaughter of the 'heroic' Lord Byron. In October 1872, as Wilfrid and Anne returned to England, George Eliot was taking the waters at Bad Homburg in Germany. She wrote to her publisher John Blackwood: 'The saddest thing to be witnessed is the play of Miss Leigh, Byron's grand niece, who is only 26 years old, and is completely in the grasp of this mean, money-raking demon. It made me cry to see her young fresh face among the hags and brutally stupid men around her.'[30]

George Eliot's *de facto* husband, George Henry Lewes, was with her and he too mentioned the encounter at the gaming tables. 'Miss Leigh (Byron's granddaughter) having lost 500£, looking feverish and excited. Painful sight!'

Uncertainty there may have been as to the relationship of the young woman to the poet, but among the European intelligentsia there was little doubt that she was the unfortunate victim of cruel circumstance, and that she made a pathetic contrast with the elegant Anne, who was received with honour in the best houses wherever she went. George Eliot's was not quite the last record of Marie Leigh. There was contact between Anne and Marie three years later, as is revealed in Anne's correspondence with her later publisher, John Murray, in connection with a public demand for a memorial to Byron in Westminster Abbey. Marie and her half-brother (Jean-Marie Taillefer) had seen their opportunity when the proposal was published in the French press.

On 5 July 1875, Anne wrote to Murray saying she was glad she had not joined in the correspondence in *The Times* since, 'I have heard from Miss Leigh that her brother wanted to write... but put off doing so because I did not send my letter.' It seems Anne had persuaded her cousin to remain silent if she did too. 'I am now writing a private letter to Mr Disraeli,' Anne told Murray, 'for surely a word from him would influence the committee.' There is no further record of contact between the cousins. Marie's exact fate has never been determined.[31]

Perhaps her grandmother's attitude decided Anne against helping her cousin as she could so easily have done. Perhaps she thought that to do so would simply make a rod for her own back. A comparable case which had come to light in January 1871, when she and Wilfrid were at Crabbet, throws a powerful light on Anne's attitudes. Ralph arrived on the scene with a letter from a family retainer, the widow Mrs Dowden, claiming that Anne had promised to support her during her life. Anne replied: 'My Grandmother earnestly advised me before her death never to promise an annuity.' GM approved of giving, she said, at 'one's own option and time'. Again, quoting GM: 'Mind you always keep the power in your own hands.' Lady Byron seemed even after death to walk beside Anne, moralising or raising an admonitory finger, and imparting every now and again magisterial severity to an otherwise gentle and generous nature. Indeed, the destructive enmity that infused the very fibre of the family found another lease of life in Ralph's marriage. Just as Anne gave birth to her only surviving child, her brother confided in her that his wife Fanny had been unfaithful before and after the birth of their daughter Mary. He divorced her just before she gave birth to a second child, a son. He announced that the child was not his. With a parting shot that would have done justice to any of the Byrons, Fanny replied, 'Nor was Mary'. Ralph never acknowledged the girl, though she inherited his title to become Lady Wentworth and was known affectionately to Anne as 'Molly'.[32]

Just at that moment of high drama, Anne and Wilfrid began the construction of a new world for themselves and their daughter at Crabbet Park, and to plan a journey to the east that would change the course of their lives.

## Chapter Six
# Drinkers of the Wind

According to a saying which comes down to us from Ali it is from the Prophet that the following tradition comes. When God thought Him to create the horse He said to the South Wind: 'Of thy substance will I make me a new being for the glory of my chosen ones, the shame of my enemies, and a robe for them that serve me.' And the wind said: 'Be that being made.' And God took, as it were, a handful of wind and said to it: 'I create thee, O Arabian. To thy forelock I bind victory in battle – on thy back I set a rich spoil, and a treasure on thy loins...' [1]

The travels of Burton and Palgrave in Arabia had fascinated Wilfrid ever since he met the former in Buenos Aires, and read the latter's description of his 1862 mission to the capital of the Al Saud dynasty at Riyadh in central Arabia. For Anne and Wilfrid alike, Arabia was the land of the purest and most entrancing of all horse breeds, the original home of the Godolphins, Darleys, Darcys and other blue-blooded strains that had been bred in Europe and

America for some three centuries. Wentworths and Milbankes had been connected with the provenance of such pure breeds for most of that time, and in moments of domestic unity Anne and Wilfrid saw a role for themselves as latter-day preservers of the Arab equine heritage. A journey to Turkey in the spring of 1873 was to prove the beginning of an adventure which would capture their hearts and minds.[2]

As they crossed the Alps, Wilfrid began a chapter of his *Alms to Oblivion* which he entitled 'First Eastern Travels', and he wrote – as did many another Englishman of his century – of the romance of the east, of pleasures which 'were not those of the flesh and almost as little of the intellect'; of 'rough lying on the ground by night, endurance of sun, wind and rain by day'; of abstinence and that absence of 'passionate longings bred of idleness'. Here was an unfamiliar side to Wilfrid and Anne entered happily on a new honeymoon.

They had left their daughter behind in England in the care of a nurse and Anne was missing the child already, but nothing could detract from the magic of Stamboul and Smyrna and the eastern sights and smells that would lead them on to desert lands, where few westerners had gone before. Wilfrid wrote a sonnet and they slept in a white tent with a brown lining and a striped blanket over the entrance. They bought a small grey horse, Turkeycock, not of pure Arabian blood but the first of eastern breed to find a place in the stables of Crabbet.

'I have been almost too happy,' wrote Anne, on returning to England, 'I suppose in our being alone.' Blunt saw in the Turkish peasantry a happiness denied to their counterparts in England, freer despite the absence of civil rights, and without the petty regulations of civilised Britain, a people free to wander as they pleased, to work or not to work at will. Blunt's brittle political conscience became more articulate as he travelled eastward, as did the incipient rebelliousness, the instinct to oppose everything his own country did and stood for in the world.

It did not take long for the effect to wear off once he was back in 'civilised' Europe. He devoted himself increasingly to Madeline Wyndham and Minnie Pollen. Anne tried ineffectually to find compensation in Judith. A bad cough prevented her from holding her child, 'my own little thing'. And then maternal doubt: 'it is of no use to try and alter my nature. I cannot manage very young children. I don't know how.' Her own mother's inadequacies began to show themselves.[3]

Minnie came home from a trip to Germany determined to throw off all restraint in her relationship with Blunt and to pray for his true adherence to the Catholic faith. In return, Blunt lent his other home, Newbuildings, to the Pollen family on condition that Minnie mothered Judith – and Ralph's daughter Mary – when he and Anne were abroad. For the next 15 years the two families lived almost as one, and Blunt firmly believed that neither partner suspected the true relations existing between himself and Minnie.

A journey to Algiers in the following year, 1874, kept up the eastern connection. In January they were crossing the desert by mule when Anne had another miscarriage. 'I was ill – could not go on and so we have lost both the chance for the future and the journey now. I did not think I was doing a folly – but it seems to me I should have known I was trying the impossible.'[4] It was another premature male child. Wilfrid erected a heap of stones over the spot where the foetus was buried. With courage and wilfulness all too reminiscent of her mother, Anne insisted on continuing a journey which became for her husband 'the bleakest week of all my wandering life.'

In mid-February the dismal scene was relieved by a strange figure, alone except for a single guide, which came into view one day as they approached the wells of Mahdi.

It was brother Ralph, munching a large sausage and carrying his violin (he had been taking lessons with Anne's old teacher Tansa and played the instrument excruciatingly).[5] Wilfrid's misery was compounded by his brother-in-law's determination to play scales at nightfall. Anne painted the Sahara and Wilfrid wrote a sonnet. When they arrived home in April, it was to discover that Minnie had miscarried at five months – a boy, and very likely Wilfrid's. Minnie went off to London to recuperate and her husband John became Blunt's bosom companion.

Minnie's daughter Anne – known as Pansy – was now in her teens and needed 'bringing out' of her shyness. The doting mother left her in Blunt's care and told her daughter that he would be attentive. And she told him, 'she is in love with you already.' After a few days of Blunt's petting, the girl burst into tears at being made a fool of. Pansy was sent to her aunt, Lucy Laprimaudaye, who had taken the veil and was at Roehampton. Pansy followed her aunt into the nunnery.[6]

Anne, blindly following in her Tyrant's wake, wrote that she missed him 'every moment of the day'. But Ella Baird came to dash her hopes once more. She stayed at Crabbet and after Anne had gone to bed crept down to the library where Blunt was reading. He wanted her to sleep with him but she refused, though they agreed to spend the winter together in Paris, or perhaps Italy.

Blunt found himself surrounded by the fruits of his amorous labours. Anne was confined to bed again. This time the cause was thought not to be pregnancy but its opposite. The family physician Dr Lewis told her that she would never have another child. Something required treatment; perhaps it was incurable. A second opinion was needed and Dr Cumberbatch, who had delivered Judith, decided that the womb was inflamed and that she was pregnant. The effect of the pronouncement was for Anne to jump out of the bed she had occupied on and off for several months. She looked forward to the birth of the child that was there after all.

Two days before Christmas 1874 there was yet another miscarriage.[7] Blunt noted that there was little chance now of another child, and he still had no son. He turned for the first time to his daughter for consolation. Judith reached up to kiss him and he melted. Anne asked Dr Cumberbatch if the trouble with her 'machinery' might prove fatal. With remarkable insensitivity the doctor replied that cancers began in much that way.

Soon after they were on the move again, to Paris and the south of France. Wilfrid's cup overflowed. His female admirers queued up for his favours: Skittles (only occasionally now), Minnie and Madeline and Juliet waiting at Monaco, 'but only for friendship not for love'.

On 20 March 1875, he and Anne moved on to Arles. Before the train left he was on tenterhooks waiting for a note from Juliet. A man rushed forward as the train was due to depart but the note was from Madeline. Blunt felt abandoned and burst out crying. He thought of suicide but his saintly wife comforted him, made him eat and restored his sanity. Anne, too, cried that night, though she was not one for tears. He pleaded with Anne not to abandon him, as Juliet had done, and they cried together. As if that was not enough, he took Anne by carriage across the Carmargue to the village of Saintes-Maries, where he promised the saints £100 each if they would restore Juliet to him. Fortunately he did not have to redeem the pledge. So painful to Anne was the recollection of these events that she tore the offending pages from her diary, except for one fragment which followed the day marked 19 March when they were at Nice:

> I am like one who has suddenly lost everything – or rather it is worse than that, I have discovered that I never had anything to lose – I who thought myself rich! Henceforth I will care for stones and sands – birds and beasts, the stars – anything in the

universe but no human being except with a sorrowful pity –
Why did I ever dream... But there are some sufferings I cannot
bear to see and not help, only I cannot help.[8]

Back in England, there were visits to Edward Burne-
Jones's studio, negotiations with Anne's prospective
publisher John Murray and dinner with Murray and
George Eliot and her 'husband' George Lewes. The Eliot
encounter, much looked forward to, did not it seems give
rise to any embarrassing mention of the Marie Leigh matter
which had caused the famous writer so much distress three
years before. Blunt's chief concern following the dinner was
Lewes' view of his sonnets.

A more serious matter all the same, was the news that
Byron's letters to Lady Melbourne had come into the
possession of Lady Dorchester, daughter of the poet's friend
John Cam Hobhouse. Blunt was given the letters to read
and he declared that if they were published they would
'convulse the universe'. The letters showed, he said, that
Augusta was 'a good woman' who loved her brother, and
'whom he loved and honoured all the more for it.'

But letters from Juliet and Minnie to Blunt, the first
proposing a new relationship without passion and hovering
between love and friendship, were more to Blunt's liking
than the raking over of old ashes, however warmly they had
once burnt. On reflection, he found Byron's views on love
and women very like his own.

While Wilfrid contemplated his affinity with Anne's
grandfather, Lovelace dropped another bombshell. He
confided to Anne that Lady Byron had told him three
different stories of the separation, and that none of them
involved incest. And he added that he, Lovelace, had
discovered that Byron was married at the time of his
betrothal to Annabella, that the marriage was contracted
bigamously and, therefore, Anne's mother was illegitimate.
Lovelace, now almost totally alienated from his first family
and much closer to the children of his second marriage, also

revealed to Anne the horrific events of Ada's last days in which she confessed to her infidelities and her betting activities which included forgery. Though she and Ralph had known all along of the deathbed confessions, Anne was dumbfounded by the revelations concerning her grandmother. She asked Ralph to ask their father for chapter and verse. Lovelace gave Ralph a less than warm reception, and on 21 May 1875, Anne wrote to her father with unconcealed anger:

> Dear Papa, Ralph was here this morning & told me that his visit to you last night was ill received. I am greatly pained at this in every way, & especially as it was in consequence of what you had authorised me to tell him, that the visit was made. You will remember that two or three days ago... you agreed to see him without raising disagreeable matters... I hope my dear father, you will think it due to me to explain this matter, in which I find myself involved... Your affectionate daughter, A.I.N. Blunt.[9]

There is no recorded explanation of this allegation which cannot have been supported by the facts, for no examination of Byron's life has ever produced a scrap of evidence that he was married when he wedded Annabella Milbanke, that 'very superior woman a little encumbered with Virtue.' Blunt propounded the theory that it was Byron's sparing of Lady Frances Webster which hardened his heart and showed itself immediately after in the seduction of his sister.[10]

Blunt's own case now showed distinct parallels with his poet hero's.[11] Juliet's virtual rejection had soured him. No more loose affairs, for the moment at least, no more 'aesthetic' talk, or tiresome literary conversations such as he found at George Eliot's soirées. He turned to Anne and showed her his farewell sonnets to Juliet, finding refuge in her 'dutiful nature, her clear sweet voice and pure features, above all in her integrity.'

A further chapter in Blunt's prodigious record of sexual

pursuit formed the backdrop to yet another domestic drama. In 1875, Anne's cousin Robert Curzon, who had succeeded to the title of Zouche and the magnificent Elizabethan estate of Parham, married Dorothea Fraser, the daughter of Lord Saltoun. Lady Burrell, a relative of the Curzons, invited Blunt to a celebration party at the Berkeley Square house that had staged his own wedding breakfast. The dark-haired, vivacious Dorothea, 'Doll' to her family and friends, took an instant fancy to the romantic Blunt. She was just 18. To do him credit, Blunt warned Lord Zouche to call off the marriage. The wedding took place however on 17 July, and within a month Doll was in the arms of her new lover. He called her 'Swingkettle'.

Anne lamented her most recent miscarriage just as her husband began to celebrate the latest conquest: 'Oh why am I not someone else, why am I in the way of happiness... Life in spite of everything is too sweet to me, but I think I ought to give it up. Oh if God would hear me... it is too horrible.'[12]

Her husband was now involved in a new and most remarkable bedroom farce. His cousin, the young Lord Mayo, whose father had been murdered while serving as Viceroy of India, was also among Doll's legion of lovers. So was a friend from South American days, Alec Fraser. Doll told Blunt that both were in love with her but that she would prefer to elope with him. The husband Lord Zouche was aware of a procession to her bedroom in the night watches, and he directed his anger at Mayo. Fighting broke out among the men and Blunt felled Mayo, having agreed with Doll that they should love each other for ten years, 'a fixed limit on human happiness being best', they conceded.

In the middle of this bizarre drama, which transferred from Parham to the Burrells' place in London, Minnie Pollen arrived to demonstrate by her appearance that her last meeting with Blunt had borne fruit. A journey to Abyssinia with the Zouches had been proposed by Wilfrid before everything foundered on the rock of Doll's catholic taste in men. In the end, advised by Minnie to make himself scarce in order to avoid public scandal, he took Anne on a journey to Egypt by P&O, departing on 23 December 1875, with Alec Fraser as companion.[13] When they reached Cairo, Blunt learnt that Lord Lytton had passed through just before them on his way to take up the viceroyalty of India. He sent a telegram offering his services to his old friend, a move encouraged by Anne who thought it would be 'something to interest Wilfrid' and perhaps would cut out other 'interests'. When they returned from a tour of the Nile Delta, Anne having sketched the Khufu pyramid on the way, it was to find a rejection from Robert Lytton awaiting them: 'We have chosen different paths in life, you pleasure, I duty.' In the same mail was a summons for Wilfrid to appear in the divorce case brought by Lord Zouche against his wife, citing Blunt among others.[14]

They returned home in March by way of Sinai and Jerusalem, Anne threatened by yet another miscarriage. 'If only I can get safely to Jerusalem,' she wrote.[15] In the south of the Sinai peninsula there was a dangerous altercation with tribesmen. They were followed by a party of Bedouin and inadvisedly flashed their pistols in the starlit night. They survived, but only to experience thirst and real fear for the first time in their lives, which increased their mounting desire to travel in the desert and to learn Arabic. Anne stayed at Jaffa to regain her strength while Wilfrid went on to Jerusalem. There he found a letter from Minnie announcing the birth of a child, 'her child and mine'. It was a boy, and was named Benjamin.

Anne felt off-colour on the voyage home to England in April, and at Chichester a doctor told her that there was no child but 'something or other'. Dr Cumberbatch renewed her hope, but by June she was resigned to a familiar fate, 'no present prospects'. On Minnie's advice, she decided to have an operation.[16] She surely knew of Minnie's child by Wilfrid, but she ignored the subject in conversation and even in the secret precincts of her diary. Greater loyalty was called for as the Zouche divorce case proceeded. In the middle of the court hearing Doll fled with young Mayo and thus gave the kiss of death to any defence she might have presented. But Lord Zouche decided to proceed against three admitted adulterers, Mayo, Fraser and Blunt.[17] He demanded £7,000 in damages. During the hearings and the inescapable public debate which accompanied them, Anne stood by her husband without a moment's hesitation and without a single question. She entered only one caveat, that she would not on any condition set foot in 'that abomination, the divorce court'. The Prince of Wales let it be known that it would be a disgrace if her name was introduced.

Anne was undoubtedly outraged by Wilfrid's conduct but she couldn't bring herself to criticise him, even in private. A sense of duty mixed potently in Anne's make-up with that quiescence of spirit which Lady Byron had so painstakingly inculcated. Important pages were torn from Anne's diary at this period, and we are dependent on her daughter Judith's evidence many years later, though even that was taken from an expurgated version of the diary.[18] Judith maintained that Minnie Pollen had commandeered her mother's diary and made the cuts after Anne consulted her about Wilfrid's 'concubines'. Judith also insisted that her mother was 'unconscious that Minnie herself was one of them.'

The daughter's account speaks of her mother's 'piteous cry' when Wilfrid told her that he was duty bound to elope with Doll. Anne is said to have asked: 'What is to become of me and our child?'

In the end, in December 1876, an action before a special jury in Westminster court was settled by a divorce decree in favour of Zouche with costs against Mayo. Next day a telegram was delivered to Wilfrid. He pocketed it and said nothing. Anne, determined not to ask 'needless questions', waited all evening but he kept quiet. Despite the continuing evidence of subterfuge she was 'delighted beyond words' that Wilfrid had been let off the hook. Many old friends and close relations had heard and seen enough, however. The Wyndham cousins, though their own record did not bear too close a scrutiny, cut him. So did the Bourkes (Lord Mayo's family), the Burrells, and many of their neighbours around Crabbet Park.

It was Skittles who eventually came to Blunt's rescue, saving him from what would have been almost total social ostracism.[19] He frequently visited the woman who had taught him his way in the bedroom; he had written to her when abroad, cementing the Prince of Wales's friendship in the process. Catherine was now middle-aged and respectable enough to command the ear of Gladstone, entertain the exiled Napoleon III, and hunt with the Quorn. She had whispered to Bertie something of Blunt's dilemma in the divorce case, and the Prince was said to have intervened quite improperly to persuade counsel to remove his name from the list of co-respondents.[20]

The troubles he had so manifestly brought on himself turned Blunt back to the Church. Coincidentally, Anne too began to undergo a spiritual awakening. Religion of the institutional kind had so far played little part in her life, though she was imbued with her grandmother's detestation of orthodoxy. A sudden conversion to the Catholic faith was to follow two years hence. She had, of course, toyed with the thought of conversion at the time of her marriage, as part of her dowry of loyalty, but Blunt's own doubts would have made such a gesture pointless. The devout, ever fallible Minnie Pollen seems to have had some influence on her thinking. And there had been another strong Catholic influence in her friendship with Florence Nightingale, who was close to conversion in the heyday of the Oxford Movement and the young Manning who, as rector of Lavington, had been instrumental in Wilfrid's mother being received into the Catholic Church.[21]

Wilfrid's hedonistic search for love and renewal was never far from the surface, but in the first months of 1877 he decided to embark on a life of healthy endeavour, free from the deadly influence of women and sex. It began with a riding holiday based in Gibraltar.[22] As a result, three Barbary horses were imported from Algiers and introduced into the Crabbet stud. For Anne, it was a joyful interlude with a reformed husband and her beloved horses; riding, jumping, hunting, steeplechasing. Anne stuck the cards of the meets she attended in her diary.

The year was propitious for another reason. In his new-found resolution to steer as clear of sin as his nature allowed, Blunt turned with positive intent to the desert; to Arabia proper. Although Crabbet had become a paradise for the couple, they had also formed a joint ambition to explore Arabia. In June 1877 Anne wrote in her diary, 'I can't think of leaving it again.' She referred to Crabbet Park and she included in her diary a photograph of the house staff – 15 excluding grounds and stables.[23] Yet ever since the visit to Turkey four years earlier and the brief journey in the Sahara, she had looked with growing enthusiasm towards Asia Minor and the Arabian deserts.

For Blunt, however, it was a case of first things first. There was one more irresistible encounter before finally facing the harsh discipline of desert exploration. They were visited by a lady he had met and flirted with in Gibraltar, Mrs Thurlow. She was young and pretty and they were soon in each other's arms. In November 1877, Anne left Crabbet without a backward look in the company of her sated husband, bound for inner Arabia. She was in her 41st year.[24]

Less than a year before they departed, the Russo-Turkish war had led to Mr Gladstone's famous 'bag and baggage' pronouncement, but whatever liberal Englishmen may have thought of them, the Turks were still masters of Syria and Mesopotamia,[25] territories that had formed part of the

Ottoman Empire for four centuries, and they also had largely uncontested claims to much of North Africa and the Arabian peninsula.

Indifferent to the political conflicts of the day and to warnings of plague and disorder from Sir Henry Layard, the Blunts left on 20 November, travelling by way of Rhodes to Alexandretta and thence by mule to Aleppo in northern Syria.

Anne's notebooks soon became filled with sketches luxuriant with Turneresque washes which gave emphasis to sand and mountains and sky, while the men and horses – most of all the horses – stood out in confident line. She began to compile in words and drawings a graphic record of places which were still largely unknown in the west, and of people whose ways she quickly came to admire. The notion of a book, jointly composed, had begun to form. People and places began to fill her notebooks – Abu Khar, Rakka, Middin, Crusader ruins, the baths of Zenobia, Ana, Hit, Ctesiphon. On 8 February 1878 she noted: 'Wilfrid has spent some time this morning in writing a sonnet which might be a preface (I think) to the book.' She set down some of his verses in their raw state:

> *A child of Shem,*
> *the first born of man's race*
> *But still forever children,*
> *at the door*
> *of Eden found unconscious of disgrace*
> *And loitering still*
> *where all are gone before*
> *Too proud to dig,*
> *too careless to be poor*
> *Taking the gifts God gives you*
> *favourless*
> *Not rendering thanks*
> *nor asking ought in store*

*Nor arguing ought*
*tho' he withhold his face. Etc*

The verses were signed, 'WSB, Ramadi, Feb 8, 1878'.
They needed polishing, and Anne appended a postscript to
her diary entry: 'A few alterations made by me but I am not
allowed to copy them here.'

They had stayed at the home of the British consul in
Aleppo, James Henry Skene, who claimed kinship with
Anne through an ancient Scots connection, and he told
them about Arab horses and the etiquette of the desert. He
mapped out a route which would take them, with notes of
introduction, to the sheikhs of the eastern section of the
great Anaiza tribal federation. Before leaving they bought
an Arab stallion named Kars, for £69. The horse had been
badly treated and was named after the battle in which he
had been hit by a cannon ball and left for dead. To Anne,
he was the most beautiful of all the horses she had
ever known, the foundation stone of the Arabian stud
at Crabbet.

Baghdad was a disappointment. They were shown the
Pasha's stables by the British resident, Colonel Nixon, but
since women took no part in the social or business life of
the community, only Wilfrid was invited to call on the
Turkish Pasha, Akif. Anne thought none of the horses
worthy of interest except perhaps 'an old white mare',
which she was told was partly of 'Najd blood'. The horses
of Najd, in the heart of Arabia, were the goal of their
journey, but they had to make their way carefully,
familiarising themselves with the ways of the desert and its
wandering people as they went.

They left Baghdad on 24 February, making their way
along the right bank of the Tigris to Deir and Kalat Shargat,
the site of the ancient Assyrian capital of Assur. They were
accompanied by two servants, Hajji Muhammad, who had
been with them since Alexandretta, and Hanna, a Christian

from Aleppo; and they slept in a tent made for them by an old Jewish craftsman in Baghdad.

Pencil and colour sketches marked the route: Samarra, Al Hadda, and then, by mid-March, Deir. They had intended to join up with Jedan bin Mehed, a sheikh of the Fidan Anaiza, who was currently pursuing an allied and much more powerful tribe (also part of the Anaiza confederation), the Ruwalla. Instead, they had stumbled on the encampment of Sheikh Faris, who disputed with his half-brother the leadership of the eastern Shammar tribe.[26] Far from joining the powerful Anaiza, therefore, they had found their intended hosts' deadly rivals in the desert. Anne sketched the imposing Faris, and Blunt and his unexpected Arab host swore eternal brotherhood after a display of shooting skills in which Blunt, by his own account, outgunned the lord of the desert 'by a wide margin'. They had made *dakhala* (refuge), and no Shammar should henceforth harm a hair of their heads.

The Blunts' plans now centred on the book they were determined to write. 'It will be leaving the thing but half done if we cannot see the Anaiza, and in that case the book cannot be written now and I foresee if not written now it will never be written.' Wilfrid went back to Deir to seek the whereabouts of the sheikh, leaving Anne by the Khabur river, with Hanna as her only guard. When he returned Wilfrid brought news that the *kaimakam* (local governor) of Deir had ordered that they proceed direct to Tadmor, ancient Palmyra, and then on to Damascus. They must not meet with the Anaiza sheikhs.

They expected to be arrested as spies, but Blunt bribed their escort, Muhammad bin Aruk, to take them slightly off course in the hope of meeting Jedan. By 25 March they were given to understand that Jedan was only a day's journey away on the Tadmor road, his tents pitched under a white slope of the Amur mountains. They reached Tadmor on the 29th.[27] Money was running low. Their last horse purchase had left them with just £25. At breakfast next day Anne sat on the roof of their guide's house, drawing the 'singular mix of ancient and modern' which was Palmyra. She noticed that one of their mares, Hagar, oozed blood from a foot after Wilfrid had taken it to the blacksmith.

By mid-March the Blunts were at camp when news came of Skene. Travelling musicians announced that 'a great man' had been seen with a body of soldiers, 'a stout man with white beard or whiskers'. Anne confided to her journal 'this would do for Mr Skene. I hope it is so.' She already had plans for the Consul in her equine scheme. For the moment, 'Owls are crying and I must sleep.' On 2 April they heard that Skene was nearby, having left Aleppo on 24 March after being delayed by the late arrival of his relief, Mr Henderson. Wilfrid and Anne rode off to meet the consul on their best mares. Anne's mount behaved in a 'charming' manner, 'pulling only just enough to make it a pleasure to let her go with her smooth, long striding gallop.' The horses were exhausted by the heat however, and after a 15-mile journey the riders dismounted and walked the last two miles.

Skene had brought with him two mares – Sherifa, a magnificent creature they had seen at Aleppo, and one bought for £500. Sherifa, 'noble lady' was faultless, Anne considered, except for her colour, white, which her new owner thought a pity.

In the specialist equine terms which Anne was already using to construct a genealogy of the 'pure-bred 'Arab', the mare Sherifa was a 'Hamdan Siri', sent by Ibn Saud of Riyadh to the Turkish governor of Mecca in about 1870. The date suggests that the Ibn Saud in question must have been Abdullah bin Faisal, who remained in Riyadh during the interim regime which followed the death of his father Faisal bin Turki (Faisal the Great) at the hand of the conqueror from the northern town of Hail, Muhammad bin Rashid.

The latter prince was now the ruler of all central Arabia.

Sherifa was said to be in foal to a chestnut sire of her own breed. 'She has the finest head I ever saw and I am delighted with her.' Anne added: 'I think Sherifa will be pleasant to ride. She has a good walk and trot but will not try to gallop well, this I fancy because she is tired. She has been four or five years in town and in a stable and seldom exercised and is not yet in good condition for going.'

They finally met Sheikh Jedan on 4 April. His Fidan tents were set up with those of the S'baa, a competing tribe belonging to the same Anaiza brotherhood. The desert prince was not as impressive, not as *asil,* or well-born, as they had been led to believe, and was lukewarm in his reception of Skene, with whom he had sworn affinity. The English sense of aristocratic worth has its mirror image in the desert, and Anne felt perfectly at home in deciding that Jedan, though dignified, was not a true thoroughbred, 'in fact of no family – a parvenu.' Over the ritual offering of coffee, dates and *lebban,* the sheikh began asking about Sherifa. Anne thought his tone offensive.

Anne was convinced Jedan was trying to effect a swap with his own mare, 'not a horse I should care for.' They rode off with the Fidan, the sheikh mounted his white mare and put on a riding performance for the guests as they made their way towards the Ruwalla, one of the greatest tribes of the desert, presided over by the Shalaan family of Damascus. A hawk was let loose on a *hubara,* or lesser bustard. The prey showed courage as it outflew the hawk, the falconer having to call in his bird. A saluki coursed and killed a fox, which was presented to Wilfrid for his wife. A gazelle fawn was caught and brought to Anne tethered like a horse. It was about ten days old, and was being suckled by a goat which was away at the time so the infant gazelle curled up in Anne's lap and went to sleep.

In the stony Hauran desert about three days' ride from Damascus they met a sub-tribe of the S'baa led by Farhan bin Hadab, a young and handsome sheikh who spoke bitterly of the Ruwalla and its leaders. In Farhan's tent conversation turned inevitably to horses, and Anne asked if there was any tradition among the S'baa of mixing English blood with Arab. It was said in Aleppo that English blood had been introduced there 40 or 50 years earlier. When they understood the question, the assembly erupted with cries of *kidb*, *kidb* (a lie! a lie!). 'Our horses are still the same in blood and form as those our forefathers had before our tribes left Najd and as those of our tribes remaining in Najd still possess,' said one of them. The tribes abused their horses, but they were proud of their purity of blood. They called their brave lean steeds 'drinkers of the wind' and Anne had come to know the joy of their sturdy character and vigorous stride. Nevertheless, she noted in her Aleppo journal that there was evidence of English blood having been imported.

They departed to the call of the cuckoo on the morning of 12 April towards the encampment of the Ruwalla in the Hauran desert. Sotam bin Shalaan sent scouts to bring the visitors to him, and they arrived at his camp after two days' travel. The scene was staggering. A sea of black tents stretched out before them, some 20,000 in all, with 150,000 camels, the hallmark of stature among the great princely tribes of Arabia.

Two days before, the Ruwalla had raided the Wuld Ali tribe and captured a thousand camels. Fires of victory burned in celebration of the successful *ghazzu* as the English party approached. Sotam turned out to be an old, tired man who had lost control of his great tribe. The horses too were a disappointment. Anne made a drawing of Turkiyyah, Sotam's beautiful wife, who was angry on account of her husband's recent acquisition of 'one, or perhaps two, other wives'. By the 15th they were making their way from the desert to the sown.

'I am lying under the trees in one of the gardens of

Damascus, looking up at the pink and blue sunset sky and listening to the beebirds flying high in the air and keeping up a ceaseless twittering,'[28] Anne wrote two days later. At last they could go to the Ottoman Bank to see about money, sadly depleted by their horse purchases. More importantly, they were invited to the home of the heroic figure Abdel Kader, the Algerian exile who was one of the world's leading experts on the horses of the desert lands, and whose nobility during the massacres of Maronites by Druzes and Muslims in the 1860s had brought international honour to his name. They were introduced by the Beiruti banker Mr Sioufi who, as a boy of 12, had been saved from death by Abdel Kader. They found the great man full of dignity, kindly and without pretension. The conversation quickly turned to horses.

Were the breeds of Arabia – Keheilan, Seglawi, Abeyan, Hamdani, Habdan – known in Algeria? No, in north Africa horses were named from the tribes who bred them. What of the antiquity of the Arabian breeds?[29] He answered that Ishmael, the son of Abraham, had tamed the wild horse, and the breed that came down from Ishmael was called *benet al ahwaj* (daughters of the humpbacked) on account of one horse that had a lump on its back. Solomon, he continued, had obtained his five remarkable mares through the Ishmael strain, one of which he gave to the tribe of Uzda, and from her, the Amir believed, all Arab breeds derived.

The Amir's words were to find their way into the voluminous notes on central Arabia and the Arab horse, qualified by subsequent discovery, that Anne was to work on for the rest of her life and eventually leave unpublished at her death. She would write in an essay entitled 'The First Voice' of Islamic traditions, 'stripped of their semi-religious imagination', of the 'pre-Islamic tradition of a wild horse in Arabia of great antiquity, the capture of which is placed as far back as Ishmael, about 1800 to 2000 B.C., or earlier';

of the 'desert horse which stumbleth not' mentioned in the Book of Job, and of the Islamic tradition of Solomon's Arabian horses and his 'reputed pride in them'. In the same breath she wrote of the 'eccentric folk of Nejd' and their one great consistency, 'their race pride, their own and that of their horse, which are so blended as to be inseparable.' In a memorable passage she added:

> Truly is that horse prized by them above all else in the world, believed in by them as being theirs in origin, and that from all time in an immeasurable past. You hear the very same words used now in prose as those uttered so many centuries ago in verse, by uncounted Nomad poets, before the rise of Islam... You hear the very same remark made now: "Children of mine may hunger and thirst, but never my mare", in the very same tone of mind in which the pre-Islamic warrior made it.

She was presented with Abdel Kader's book on horses, 'an encouragement to me to learn Arabic'. She and Wilfrid had already read extracts in Daumas's *Les Chevaux du Sahara*. They bade farewell to the distinguished Algerian, who was living out his last days in Damascene exile. His eldest son Muhammad, made an inscription in her diary, giving her a first informal lesson in Arabic as he did so. Since Muhammad spoke French but no English, the lesson became an exercise in anglicised Franco-Arabic: 'Lady Anne Blunt min Muhammad fils de l'Emir, ibn el Emir Abd el Kader el Husseni, seize Rabih le second, sittasher Rabih el thani, 1295 alf wa maiatein wa khamset wa tessoun de Damas, min ash-Sham.' (The Lady Anne Blunt from Muhammad, son of the Amir Abdal Kader al Hussaini, 2 May 1295 AH (AD 1878) at Damascus.)

## Chapter Seven
# Pilgrimage to Nejd

Nejd – 'pretty nearly co-extensive with our term Central Arabia. I hold, then, to the correctness of our title, though in this matter as in the rest, craving indulgence of the learned.' W. S. Blunt, Crabbet Park, 1 August, 1880, from Preface to *A Pilgrimage to Nejd.*

On her birthday in September 1878 Anne remarked, 'my 41st birthday is one of the pleasantest I have spent... but... happiness is of a sort which comes from a greater repose of mind, from a confidence in the rule of a Supreme Power, greater than... I have hitherto felt.'[1] She had been gripped by an all-embracing transcendental force, though diaries and letters had so far given no hint of its approach.

She had not expected to reach so ripe an age, still less to find at last her heart's desire. While she was recovering from confinement at the time of her 37th birthday she remembered the cause of her mother's agonising death and rejoiced at passing her age. She recalled that in a moment of delirium Ada had told her, 'You will not pass 40'.

In May 1878, when they arrived back in England, she felt an optimism that she had not known since girlhood when she rode and strolled in the fields of Sussex and Somerset. Wilfrid too had found a new lease of life in his discovery of the Bedouin, the desert-born 'sons of Shem'.

Before leaving Damascus, the Blunts had met another remarkable Englishwoman devoted to the desert people, Jane Digby, the former Lady Ellenborough, who was married to Sheikh Medjul of the Misrab tribe. The imperious 'Lady Jane', generally known to the Arabs as Deegbee al Misrab, was 70 at the time of their visit. She showed lingering traces of very great beauty, and 'even with the most unfavourable style of dress', the appearance of a 'person of distinction', though Anne was sorry to find that she had adopted the Arab fashion of blacking the rim of the eyes and darkening the eyebrows.[2]

Mrs Digby at first refused the Blunts' request to call, sending back the message, *Ma fi makan.* 'Not at home.' They later discovered that she had heard that Mr Skene was with them and would not have him in the house. She never went into the street except in black lace and veil. Anne found her quiet, dignified and unassuming, and admired her drawing, especially her sketches of the ruins of Palmyra, and not in the least resembling some famous sketches of her by Richard Burton's wife Isabel.

They arrived home to await the appearance of their Arab steeds, which had been shipped from Beirut, and to find that Blunt's theological tract *Proteus to Amadeus* was on the verge of publication. His publisher had changed the final offensive word in the question 'Has God a smell?' to 'scent'.

Arguments about God and Christianity[3] appeared to Wilfrid in a new light after his first brief tour among the Bedouin of Syria, with their 'bird-like minds', their 'nonchalance' and untroubled consciences. Both Anne and Wilfrid were struck by their 'lack of spiritual fantasies, a freedom from all bondage religious or political, above all their practical unbelief in any but the corporal life...'

Wilfrid persuaded Anne to write up her diary of their recent travels, much more detailed and complete than his own, and to publish it. In six months she produced the first part of a two-volume work of surprising authority on a part of the world they had as yet explored only cursorily. On 28 August she wrote to John Murray suggesting several possible titles for the book and in October delivered the second volume.[4] In November she was writing to her publisher from the Hotel d'Orient in Paris asking for proofs to be sent to her brother Lord Wentworth, and suggesting that a lady she had met in France should be entrusted with a French translation.

*Bedouin Tribes of the Euphrates* bore her name as author; underneath were the words, 'edited with a Preface and some account of the Arabs and their Horses by W.S.B.'. Subsequent scholarship would show that Wilfrid's contribution amounted in the main to interference of a kind that was not always helpful or disinterested. As the present-day writer and equestrian authority James Fleming has said: 'Blunt's alterations to the Journals are far in excess of the wildest hopes of the most zealous editor. In the first place he allowed himself licence to rearrange the material in a general way and to transpose events in both time and place so as, one must assume, to lend Lady Anne's account a more rounded and pleasing appearance. Passages were then added or subtracted according to his own recollections. By and large, the descriptions of individuals were lengthily embroidered and those relating to horses omitted or emasculated.'[5]

Many of the original references were changed, giving rise to inaccuracies and even to mistaken identity in the case of important sheikhs and princes of the region.[6]

Certainly Anne was the better scholar, fitted by temperament and an orderly mind to systematic study.

Blunt flitted from subject to subject as the mood took him, unable to stay long enough with any one topic to hear the other person's point of view, much less to comprehend it. Anne was in many ways too much his opposite. In writing as in drawing and music, she tended to pedantry, but in her command of languages, her assessments of Arab notables and the oral history of the tribes, and her marshalling of facts and sources of information on horse genealogy and breeding, she was vastly his superior and was greatly assisted by single-mindedness and the absence of preconceptions. She set to work on her Arabic as soon as she arrived home from Syria and within a year, while she worked on her first book, she had mastered it. Wilfrid boasted of his knowledge of Arabia and the Arab language but never truly knew the one or spoke the other. His descriptions of desert life often contained inspired grains of poetic truth, but they were more often as emotive and biased as his politics.

The first practical steps in Anne's new world of thoroughbred classification and breeding were taken soon after the return to England in May 1878, in a mood of marital harmony that was to prove sadly transient.

In April, while still in Syria, Anne had listed the purchases made through Skene, according to the names they had given the horses. Among the first, apart from Sherifa and Kars, were Lady Hester (a tribute to her distinguished aunt), Basilisk, Tamarisk and Damask Rose. Between them they would produce offspring giving new strength to specialist breeding in many parts of the world.

The horses arrived on 3 July. Anne's first act was to snip off a lock of Sherifa's hair and seal it in an envelope. 'We went out the first thing this morning to see the mares and horses. They all have colds from their journey.' They took Kars for a gallop; 'all agreed that he is magnificent, just enough of action, and a good stride with his legs well under him.' He was the biggest of the bunch, 15 hands, most

Arabs being 14 hands or less. 'In short he leaves nothing to be desired as to shape, action, colour, temper.'

The Arab horse, Anne thought, had deteriorated in the north, away from the royal stables of the Al Saud and the Al Rashid. The answer must lie in the lack of stud horses and 'in-and-in-breeding'. They set about the creation of the Crabbet Arabian Stud which would remedy the defects and deficiencies for the benefit of all the world.[7] Although their daughter was to say years later that the stud was originally the idea of Mr James Weatherby and Wilfrid, it is clear from Anne's notes that it was Skene who first suggested it to them in Aleppo. He was to have been an original partner in the enterprise but was unable to raise the money needed for partnership. Anne talked Ralph into participation and he invested an initial £750 for the purchase by Skene of more horses. Anne noted, 'We (or rather I) paid £573, so that I must send £157 [to Skene] to be equal with Ralph.' The arithmetic was not quite correct, but near enough. If the enthusiasm was shared, the money spent to date was all hers. Ralph subsequently invested several thousand pounds.

The personal income which Anne had made available to Wilfrid, and which was afterwards supplemented by inheritance through family deaths, was fast disappearing. His habits were costly and his attitude to money dismissive. 'I do not quite understand how Wilfrid manages his money matters,' she wrote.[8] The money for Crabbet, she noted, referring presumably to new stud buildings, was hers and Ralph's.

The disapproval that Blunt's involvement in the Parham affair brought in its train had affected them both and showed in their social calendar. There were few invitations from friends in high places, which Blunt, in particular, found so essential. He received an invitation from Lord Salisbury however, at which he expounded his views on near eastern politics. Anne went to see the ageing Edward John Trelawny, her grandfather's friend, who told her that

Lord Byron would have liked to have been a man of action, but had always felt that his lameness militated against his desire. At such moments, he said, Byron would rise from his chair and suddenly, feeling his infirmity, would throw himself back with passionate violence.

By November the book was complete. The Crabbet stud was developing well, though with some inevitable teething troubles, and Blunt was restless. Anne would have liked to stay with her daughter and her horses for a little longer, but her husband could not be denied, and she in any case had built up high hopes of a journey to the heart of Arabia. There they would be able to see and study the true Arab thoroughbred horse in its birthplace, research the history of Najd, as central Arabia was then called, and study the language and its poets among people who had retained the 'speech of the angels' unsullied by urban degeneracy. Even if it meant leaving home and daughter behind, it was for Anne as much as for Wilfrid an inspiring prospect. When it came to leaving Crabbet though, regret overcame her. 'Rain. Miseries, oh miseries!' she wrote on 15 November 1878. 'But for Wilfrid's sake we must go and immediately. Goodbye my happy house – God grant not for ever.'⁹

The last days before setting out from England had been spent in assembling the family portraits painted during the blissful months at Crabbet by Mr Molony, an old friend of Wilfrid's who lived in Spain and was most reluctant to charge for his work. He had painted oils of Wilfrid and Anne, as well as Ralph and his new fiancée (his divorced wife Fanny, had died earlier in the year and he was currently wooing Mary Stuart Wortley) and Dr Meynell, to whom Wilfrid had turned for guidance on the question of evolution some 20 years before. Anne liked her own portrait best: 'it should make a favourable impression on my descendants. W[ilfrid] likes it so much he has asked Mrs Pollen to have it sent to the Academy exhibition next spring.' Minnie had moved into Crabbet to look after things in their absence.

They called on Bitters Currie in Paris before finally departing for Beirut, where they arrived on 4 December. Alarming news awaited them of their friend Skene, to whom they had sent over £1,000 for the purchase of horses.[10] He was now a private businessman in Aleppo, maintaining tribal contacts at Deir and other places. Henderson had telegraphed to say that Skene might try to get out of the country and should be stopped and arrested. Skene was alleged to have debts of £2,000 or more and an order for the seizure of his property had been issued.

At Damascus they found Edward Malet, who was on leave from the Constantinople embassy and was about to take over Britain's diplomatic post in Cairo. They left him with the task of finding Skene and rescuing their investment, and moved on towards Najd, the heartland of Arabia.

Only eight Europeans had made recorded journeys to central Arabia since Roman times. The last of them, their countryman Charles Doughty, had completed his solemn journey only two years before. Another, Charles Huber, made the first of four remarkable journeys that were to lead to ultimate disaster in the same year as the Blunts. But he took a different path. Al Jauf, the northernmost town of any size, was the Blunts' first destination. There was frost on the ground and nights were bitterly cold, but for Anne the theme of life from here on was quickly established:

> The charm of the East is the absence of intellectual life there, the freedom one's mind gets from anxiety in looking forward or pain in looking back. Nobody here thinks of the past or the future, only of the present; and till the day one's death comes, I suppose the present will always be endurable.[11]

By Friday 20 December they were deep in the desert and sleep was fitful. The night echoed with the barking of dogs and it was bitterly cold, 'melancholy as the nights are when the moon only rises late & is then mixed up in a haggard light with the dawn.' They were accompanied by six servants and guides, eight camels and three mares. Hanna, their cook from the year before, was with them. So was Muhammad bin Aruk of Tadmor, who sought reunion with relatives in the desert and a truly *asil* or noble wife. There were also Awad, a black *agheyl* (guide), and Abdal Tahman, a young white guide. One of their servants, Abdullah, had 'played them false'. The offender was a mere boy. He cried to be released and they let him go, but he rejoined them after a few days, loath to leave his friends. They made their way by the old Roman road, through the stony Hauran desert of Syria, towards Wadi Sirhan, the bleak path to Arabia proper.

Their next camping ground was covered with immense flocks of sand grouse. Wilfrid, by now in the habit of shooting at everything that moved even though the proposed illustrated book of birds had fallen by the wayside, bagged eight birds with a single shot. Frost still covered the ground but they reckoned four days would take them to Esrak and Kaf. Between lay the Harra, black stones as far as the eye could see, with here and there a tell, or mound. On the 22nd they were joined by two sheikhs of the Bani Sakhr tribe, Khreysheh and Sutam ibn Fendi of the Faiz family, who said they would accompany the travellers to Al Jauf.

Christmas Day found them in Wadi Rajjil. Blunt and the Arabs chased gazelle for Christmas dinner but neither mares nor greyhounds could catch the prey. Then they spotted a lone camel, young and unprotected, traditionally the property of first-comers. Anne felt remorse as the creature was despatched, but enjoyed the meal. On 27 December they reached Kaf, where the Italian Guarmani had ended his quest for Arabian horses on behalf of Napoleon III and King Victor Emmanuel in 1874. On the 29th they passed into the territory of Ibn Rashid, the ruler of inner Arabia whose capital, Hail, lay about 500 miles before them in Jabal Shammar.

A sandstorm blew up, Anne was thrown from her camel, and she struggled with a painful knee and injured pride. Some of Muhammad bin Aruk's relatives were at Kaf. Others were in Jauf beyond the Wadi Sirhan, which they entered with a new guide, a Sherarati.

They were now in one of the most dangerous regions of Arabia, the forbidding rocky corridor leading from Syria to Arabia proper; a region inhabited by the most aggressive and ill-disciplined tribes and a place where many a traveller had met his end. No European woman had ever been known to pass that way.

Looking back after many troubled years to their five-day journey in that steep and treacherous region infested with robbers and wild animals, Wilfrid was to say of Anne: 'There was never anybody so courageous as she was. The only thing she was afraid of was the sea.'

The Sherarat tribe was famed in the desert for its music, and Hamdan the Sherarati guide sang as they marched through the long valley.[12] The song was about a girl and a boy, and Anne annotated the music in her pocket diary. The greyhounds ran a hare to earth. Anne was told to stand by with a shotgun lest the quarry should slip through their hands while the men dug furiously. They killed it with a hatchet. With poetic justice a hawk descended from the sky and snatched the still-warm creature, leaving a fragment for Muhammad who chased madly after the bird in a hopeless attempt to retrieve their supper. In her excitement, Anne dated her diary incorrectly, '1 January 1878.' She meant 1879, an uncharacteristic error.

The knee was still painful and she became convinced that she would never again walk properly. She drew the blue hills ahead of them with a red mound in the foreground, and was distracted by the sound of galloping horses. Wilfrid, feeling unwell with a recurrence of his chest trouble, shouted to her, 'Get on your mare. This is a ghazzu.' The desert raid was beginning.

I saw a troop of horsemen charging down at full gallop with their lances, not two hundred yards off. Wilfrid was up as he spoke, and so should I have been, but for my sprained knee... I fell back. There was not time to think and I had hardly struggled to my feet, when the enemy was upon us, and I was knocked down by a spear. Then they turned on Wilfrid who had waited for me, some of them jumping down on foot so as to get hold of his mare's halter. He had my gun with him... but unloaded; his own gun and his sword being on his *delul*. He fortunately had on very thick clothes... so the lances did him no harm. At last his assailants managed to get his gun from him and broke it over his head, hitting him three times and smashing the stock. Resistance seemed to me useless, and I shouted to the nearest horseman 'ana dahilak' (I am under your protection), the usual form of surrender.

The Bedouin raiders were Ruwalla. Muhammad shouted to them that his companions were 'Franjis', friends of Bin Shaalan. The raiders, mostly young men, reluctantly handed back the stolen mares and the 'beautiful gun'. They could not afford to risk the wrath of their lord. Presently they gathered in a circle on the sand, eating dates and passing round a pipe. 'In spite of their rough behaviour, we could see that they were gentlemen,' Anne declared. As for the spear, they had seen only a person wearing a cloak, and did not for a moment suppose that it was a woman. For Bedouin to have killed a woman in combat would have been an almost unimaginable act of cowardice.

The 190 miles from Kaf to Al Jauf was covered in eight days.[13] From Damascus they had travelled about 400 miles. They had read Palgrave's account of his visit in 1862. Al Jauf was a small walled town with outlying houses and palm gardens, but neither Palgrave's nor their own geography was assured. The difficulty lay to some extent in the constant change of ownership of this vulnerable northern settlement with its pleasant climate and attractive fruit gardens, on the edge of the great Nafud desert. Al Jauf actually signified a region. When they and other travellers said that they were at Al Jauf they usually meant Dumat al-Jandal, where there were three mud-brick and stone castles used by several dynasties of the Shaalan and Rashid. Several miles to the east of Dumat is Jauf al-A'mru, named after the A'mru tribe who once inhabited the region, and beyond that Sakaka (the Blunts called it Meskakeh). Muhammad's kinsmen, the Ibn Aruk, lived in one of the outlying settlements of Dumat, and the Blunts were warmly welcomed by the head of the house, Hussein. Abdullah ibn Aruk expressed a desire to join them.

That evening they were invited to the governor's fortress, Kasr Mitaab Rashid which had been built by the Rashid since Palgrave's day. In fact, they were received by the deputy governor, Duwass, who entertained them with offerings of 'wild cow', which Anne said was the best beef she had ever tasted. It was the flesh of the oryx, the creature that travellers over the centuries had seen side on and taken to be the fabulous unicorn.

As soon as it was discovered that they wished to go on to the Rashid capital of Hail they were told they must speak to the governor Johar, and they went to Sakaka in search of him. There they stayed with Nasser, head of another family of Muhammad's cousins, where they enjoyed three days' rest and found an opportunity to negotiate a suitable wife for their young guide – a pretty 15-year-old girl belonging to the host family.

Back at Dumat they inspected the tumbledown fortress of Marid, the best-known landmark of the region, facing a glistening dry lake with sand cliffs beyond, dividing this urban settlement with its hints of Roman and Nabataean occupation from the Nafud desert. Kasr Marid, with suq and mosque built into its shaggy fabric, had been the residence of earlier Rashid and Shaalan rulers, and would become so again.

On 6 January 1879 they returned with a Shammar

*khayal* or bodyguard to Kasr Mitaab ibn Rashid, the guard riding alongside Anne mounted on a yearling colt which she much admired. They entered the castle by a concealed door in a corner tower. Fear of tribal attack or insurrection was ever present. At that moment, Ibn Rashid held hostage the son of the noblest family of Al Jauf, just in case of trouble.

At the entrance were two small cannon, nicknamed Nasser and Mansur, and probably of British origin, perhaps gifts from India to one of the princes of northern Najd.[14]

The anxiously-awaited conference with Johar the Rashidi took place in a house below the *kasr*. They sat and listened to the governor, flanked by forbidding-looking black slaves, as he derided some of the tribes, especially the locals, the Jufiyah, who he said ate the locust, 'a disgusting habit'. The guests' mares were greatly admired, and the Blunts were surprised by their host's insistence that Ibn Rashid hadn't a single mare to compare with theirs. They would have to wait to find out the truth of the matter. Their visit to Hail would not be long delayed as the governor promised them a guide across the great Nafud sands, after accepting a handsome gift of a black and gold *abba* or outer coat.

Conversation in the hospitable *diwans* of Al Jauf gave the Blunts a clear and not altogether reassuring picture of the Rashid ruler they hoped to meet at Hail. The Amir Muhammad bin Abdullah, known far and wide as Muhammad Kabir (the Great), had entered Hail on Christmas Day 1869, murdered the reigning prince Bandar bin Talal along with all his supporters, and made himself the ruler of all central Arabia. On 10 January, Anne's diary noted: 'Nothing more is needed but a gold piece, just one *dahab* for a sort of silence money.' It was an obscure remark, perhaps referring to some confidence received or given. Wilfrid kissed the Aruk family all round and Anne went to the harem to say her farewells. On the 12th they stepped into the red sands of the Nafud.

We have been all day in the Nafud, which is interesting beyond our hopes, and charming into the bargain. It is, moreover, quite unlike the description I remember to have read about it by Mr Palgrave, which affects one as a nightmare of impossible horror... The thing that strikes one first about the Nafud is its colour. It is not white like the sand dunes we passed yesterday, nor yellow as the sand in parts of the Egyptian desert, but a really bright red, almost crimson in the morning when it is wet with the dew.

Her recollection of Palgrave's words was not quite accurate. He did describe the desert's colour and its changes in the seasons, particularly when the north wind, the *shimal*, blows and even the hardiest explorer is tested to the limits of endurance.

Huge hollows, some a quarter of mile across, began to bar their way; the travellers compared them to giant horseshoes. Two days from Sakaka they found water at the wells of Shakik, 225 feet deep and lined with cut stone, worn with the marks made by ropes over the centuries. Ruwalla tribesmen were there and one man recognized them from the previous year, 500 miles away in the north. Wilfrid lectured the Arabs on the dangers ahead, as though he knew more about them than the Bedouin. As they made their way to the wells of Jubba, they expressed their satisfaction with the guide Radi, supplied by Jofar; 'a curious little old man, as dry and black and withered as the dead stumps of the *yerta* bushes one sees here...' Radi rode a *dhalul*, a she-camel, who looked like a bag of bones; he spent hour after hour in silence, pointing now and then with his shrivelled hand towards the road they were to take.

When he did speak, the guide told them of travellers who had perished on the same journey. There was confirmation in the hollows; camel and human bones signifying the penalty of running out of water in a region where, in summer, temperatures rise to 55°C in the shade. Dried shreds of skin were still visible on some of the bones.

To while away the evening hours, Radi told them the tale of a Turkish garrison left to guard Hail in the days of the first Ibn Rashid, Abdullah bin Ali, who ruled at Hail between 1834 and 1847. Ubaid, the brother of Abdullah, whom Palgrave met and described, resolved to destroy the Turks. When about 500 of the garrison decided they could stand their remote duty no longer and set out for home, Ubaid instructed their guides to abandon them in the desert. Every one perished of thirst, though some of the horses found their way to the waters of Jubba.

On 16 January they saw the reassuring peaks of Alam, the twin hills that mark the way to Jubba. They had taken a tortuous route and began to distrust their guide. On the sixth day out, the men had to walk to spare their camels.

Abdullah ibn Aruk was an inspiration to everyone with his good humour and willingness to be the first to face any hazard, but after only a few days some camels showed distinct signs of distress and there was little if any pasture. On the 19th Anne wrote: 'a terrible day for camels and men'. Two of the baggage animals were too thirsty to eat, and could not stand under their loads; a third was too exhausted to keep up. Occasionally Wilfrid gave a lift to Hanna their aged cook, on his *dhalul*.

They arrived at Jubba just in time to avert disaster. Anne wrote that they had added a new chapter to old Radi's tales of horror. Perhaps she paused to reflect that Palgrave, who had travelled when the temperature was nearly twice the benign level it reached in January, was not exaggerating.

At the wells of Jubba in Jabal Shammar they were treated as interlopers, 'Nasranis', who had no business there. They were in the midst of a vast, endless ocean of sand and they believed themselves the first avowed Christians ever to enter this mountainous region, cut off by nature from the rest of Arabia. Soon, however, they heard talk of another Nasrani who had passed that way a few months before: Khalil, as the Arabs called Charles Doughty. And Palgrave had come close enough, likening the Nafud to that circle of hell conceived as a plain of burning sand in Dante's *Inferno*.

Anne, at least, could take comfort from the knowledge that if a handful of men had been there before her, she was the first Christian woman ever to make a recorded visit to that remote region. They had crossed their Rubicon and there was nothing to be done but to proceed on their way. As they went, Radi filled in the gaps in their knowledge of the Ibn Rashid.

He told them of Muhammad's bloodstained rise to power, of his murder of his four nephews and almost all his cousins, and how the people of the desert attributed his childless state to God's anger at his crimes. 'All this was anything but agreeable intelligence to us as we travelled on to Hail. We felt as if we were going towards a wild beast's den.' They heard too about the powerful military brain of the family Ubaid, who in his lifetime gave away all his property and on his death, nine years before the Blunts' journey, had bequeathed his sword, his mare and his youngest wife to his nephew Muhammad. 'These he left... with the request that his sword should remain undrawn, his mare unridden, and his wife unmarried for ever afterwards.' Muhammad had respected his uncle's first two wishes, but had taken the wife into his own harem.

High spirits returned. Before leaving Jubba, Anne had drawn Abdullah ibn Aruk standing on his head. 'There is something in the air of Najd which would exhilarate even a condemned man, and we were far from being condemned.' They discussed with Muhammad bin Aruk their mode of introduction at Hail, but thought his suggestion of Wilfrid being a merchant on his way to Basra far-fetched.

'We intend to tell Ibn Rashid that we are persons of distinction in search of other persons of distinction.' Her words were reminiscent of the Queen of Sheba's on her visit to Solomon, and Radi approved. They reached the mountains of Shammar on 23 January.

The view in front of us was beautiful beyond description, a perfectly even plain sloping gradually upwards, out of which these rocks and tells cropped up like islands, and beyond it the violet-coloured mountains... The outline of Jabal Shammar is strangely fantastic, running up into spires and domes and pinnacles, with here and there a loop-hole through which you can see the sky, or a wonderful boulder perched like a rocking-stone...

And then:

It is like a dream to be sitting here, writing a journal on a rock in Jabal Shammar. When I remember how, years ago, I read that romantic account by Mr Palgrave, which nobody believed, of an ideal state in the heart of Arabia... and how impossibly remote and unreal it all appeared; and how, later during our travels, we heard of Najd and Hail and this very Jabal Shammar, spoken of with a kind of awe by all men who knew the name... I feel that we have achieved something which it is not given to everyone to do. Wilfrid declares that we shall die happy now, even if we have our heads cut off at Hail.[15]

Their reception was encouraging. They were met in the square outside the ruler's castle by 20 handsomely dressed guards, and a venerable old man in their midst whom the visitors thought was Ibn Rashid himself. It was only the chamberlain.

Salaams exchanged, they were shown to the great pillared *kahawa*, the entertainment hall, where Palgrave, Guarmani and Doughty had been received before them.

Then the Amir Muhammad appeared, splendidly attired. The guests all stood, the great man pronounced his salaams, there was a chorus of 'Wa aleikom as-salaam,' and Muhammad held out his hand to each guest in turn.

'It was plain that we now had nothing to fear.'

Muhammad bin Rashid was by now master of Arabia as far as Asir, Aleppo, Damascus and Basra. His rule was ruthless, though he was not a keen soldier, leaving such matters to Ubaid in the latter's lifetime. But Ubaid was a devotee of the Wahhabi version of the faith adopted by the Al Saud. The other side of the family were opposed to that strict doctrine, and when Ubaid died (at Riyadh in 1869, in the care of Abdullah bin Faisal), the rupture with the other royal house of Arabia was complete. However, by 1874 Muhammad had subdued the Ibn Saud of Riyadh.

Anne described their host as having a thin sallow face, careworn and wrinkled. He reminded her of Richard III, with a 'barbaric' love of finery. He was dressed in silk and gold, 'with an *agal* [head band] half gold and wears gold and a jewelled sword – a handsome weapon.'[16] They were taken to a gallery of the great *kasr* for a meal of dates floating on molten butter with crisp bread. Then through a garden with cheetahs, antelope and gazelle to a yard teeming with mares, ready at a moment's notice to go to war. Bin Rashid asked them if they were interested in horses.

They had been worried that they might not be permitted to see the famous horses of Hail. Yet there they were, within a few hours of their arrival, in the legendary stables of the Ibn Rashid. First impressions disappointed. A grey mare was brought to them. Anne found her extremely plain with a drooping hindquarter. Then she looked again at the Amir's chestnut mare, which she had found 'inferior' at first sight. 'I ought not to call her head plain, and she is a fine mare altogether and very strong.'

The pick of all the mares they saw belonged to Hamud the son of Ubaid, one of the few surviving princes of the blood. 'If I could have my choice I would take Hamud's mare. Next the brown, third the chestnut.' But the mares of Arabia's royal stud were not for sale.

They were shown the Persian caravan, its pilgrims waiting outside the city walls to resume the journey from Mecca back to Iraq and Persia along the Darb Zubaidah, the pilgrim road said to have been built for the wife of

Harun Rashid. They sat with Bin Rashid at his *majlis*, the daily council of the desert, as he conversed with the people and dispensed a justice not always understood by westerners but somehow appropriate to the Arab who has the precepts of Islam for guidance.

They were positively dazzled by the next spectacle. Anne estimated that 800 soldiers, beautifully attired, lined the square. Muhammad bin Aruk, so well behaved till now, began to show off disgracefully. The Blunts were a little ashamed of the presents they had brought, having no idea of the magnificence or power of the ruler, and they had deputed Bin Aruk to make the presentations. The scarlet cloth cloak they had brought from Damascus which the Blunts had thought the height of splendour paled against the gorgeous robes of Hail. After making the presentation, Bin Aruk suddenly became garrulous and let it be known that he was the important man of the visiting party, boring his hosts with the story of his family's migration from Najd in the distant past.

The visitors were shown more horses, dismissed by Bin Rashid with a wave of the hand as 'the horses of my slaves'. There were about 40 mares, eight stallions, and 30 or 40 foals. 'I was almost too excited to look,' said Anne. They were not allowed to linger but she was satisfied that they had seen what they had come to see. She was convinced that in spite of the Amir's disclaimer, these were Bin Rashid's famous mares.[17]

Several more days were devoted to courtesy calls and to conversations with Hamud, the Amir's only surviving kinsman at Hail. They found him the more sympathetic of the two princes, a judgement that Doughty also made. Anne found his manners as good as any that could be found anywhere in the world, and he was besides intelligent and well-informed. Hamud was poisoned in 1909, by which time the Amir Muhammad had been dead for 12 years, poisoned it was said at the instigation of foreign powers.

When Anne left Hail, but not until then, she wrote the notes which would enable her to compose her account of the Amir's homicidal regime, of the murder of almost all his nephews and their families, of the mutilation and slaughter of his cousins, 'beautiful to look at', as they took coffee in his castle. Such ghastly crimes, some Arabs believed, accounted for the fact that, though he had many wives, Muhammad was never blessed with a son or even a daughter.

For Anne, the other highlight of the visit was her call at the women's quarters in the castle. The women had all put on their gayest clothes and jewellery for the occasion. Anne was escorted by a slave to the reception room where she was received by Amusheh, the principal lady of the harem. All the women rose to their feet when she entered.

> Amusheh could easily be singled out from among the crowd, even before she advanced to do the honours... But she, the daughter of Ubaid and sister of Hamud, has every right to outshine friends, relatives and fellow-wives. Her face... is sufficiently good-looking, with a well-cut nose and mouth, and something singularly sparkling and brilliant. Hedusheh and Lulya, the next two wives... had gold brocade as rich as hers, and lips and cheeks smeared as red as hers with carmine, and eyes with borders kohled as black as hers, but lacked her charm.[18]

Amusheh wore crimson and gold clothes, her sparkling necklace of gold chains studded with turquoises and pearls. Her hair hung down in plaits, plastered smooth with 'reddish stuff', and on top of her head was a gold and turquoise ornament like a small plate. Each woman wore a nose ring in the left nostril, which was taken out to dangle on its chain while the wearer ate and drank. Anne found it hard to understand how these women could be content with lives of idleness. She asked one of the princesses, Zehowa, 'Then you never ride as we do?'

'No, we have no mares to ride.'

'What a pity! And don't you ever go to the countryside outside Hail?'

'Oh no, of course not.'

'But to pass the time, what do you do?'

'We do nothing.'

'When I am at home,' Anne told them, 'I always walk round the first thing in the morning to look at my horses.' The ladies were clearly baffled.

After four days, the Amir's cordiality cooled. He was offended by young Bin Aruk's vain talk. Wilfrid found himself involved in a dangerous dispute with the Amir, and Anne tried to cool the temperature.

'Hail was a lion's den, though fortunately we were friends with the lion. We began to make our plans for moving on.'

*Part Three*

———

# Disillusion
# &
# Exile

———

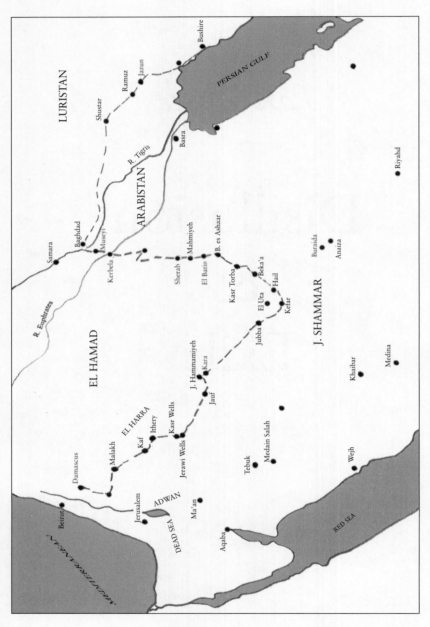

*Map of the Blunts' journey in Arabia in 1879*

*Chapter Eight*

# Fantasia of the Mares

They left Hail with the Persian pilgrims on 1 February 1879, making their way along the Darb Zubaidah, the pilgrim road which leads to Najaf on the river Euphrates. This Shia stronghold was the city of Ali, son-in-law of the Prophet, and thus known by the alternative name of Meshed Ali. After the hazards of their journey thus far, it was an easy road, well trodden by the faithful of the centuries, and more or less free of marauders.[1]

Their last day had been spent riding with the Amir and the Rashid sheikhs. Shammar horsemen in the scruffy regalia of the desert fighter – bandoliers across the chest, rifles at the ready, red patterned *keffiyeh* (desert headdress) held in place by goat's hair *agal*, or rope, clattered up and down the cobbled street as the princely party saddled up. Bin Rashid stayed at Anne's side on his grey mare, while Hamud on his splendid bay kept a respectful distance. When she came to write about it Anne recalled the experience as, 'Fantasia of the Mares'.[2]

They attached themselves to the leader of the Persian caravan, Ali Kuli Khan, who rode a Najdi mare 'like a good little boy in an old-fashioned frock gathered at the waist.'[3] Ali Kuli Khan's family were the titular heads of the Bakhtiar tribe which has often played a decisive part in Iranian politics. That fact alone was enough to attract Wilfrid to the prince of the pilgrim caravan, the amir-al-hajj. There was the added attraction of a fine Arabian stud in the Bakhtiari highlands of southern Persia. Anne was less enthusiastic about the hordes of pilgrims with their ragged dress and heaps of rubbish. There were 4,000 camels and even more people, winding their way towards Najaf in a procession three miles long.

They found more relatives of the Ibn Aruk on the last stage of the journey. A hyena was shot and consumed, and the leader of the caravan was reported missing. Ali Kuli Khan had wandered off on business of his own and was caught in a fierce north wind and an accompanying sandstorm.

Wilfrid worked on his travel notes for an article in the Royal Geographical Society journal and Anne made a record at the back of her diary of the touching story of Ali, towards whose city they were heading. Ali had engaged in a bitter struggle with his Muslim brothers for the leadership of Islam following the death of Muhammad, a conflict that was to lead to much suffering through the ensuing strife between Shia and Sunni Muslims.[4]

On 27 February the caravan sighted the gleaming gold dome of the mosque of Meshed Ali rising magnificently above the town, a line of cliffs on the far side of the lake framing the splendid picture. On 6 March they reached Baghdad, having completed the 600 miles from Hail in little more than a month. Telegrams were sent from the British residency to Minnie Pollen at Newbuildings, Jane Digby in Damascus and the Lyttons in Calcutta. They had decided to go on to India and Minnie, who had ten children of her own, was asked to look after Judith for a further six months. The idea of going on was probably Wilfrid's, for Anne commented with resignation that 'his thirst for exploration had not yet been slaked.'

Ali Kuli Khan had turned up again and they would visit him on the way to India. Anne telegraphed Lady Lytton, 'En route from Central Arabia to Persia. Shall we pay you a visit in April or May?' While in Baghdad, where they were known to be on the lookout for horses, they were shown several 'Seglawi Jed'. Anne observed: 'Now as all the Seglawi Jedran in the world are but few, and as the owners of those few are well known among both Anaiza and Shammar Bedouin, you may imagine the improbability of there being a single drop of that blood in the horses offered for sale at Baghdad – their history unknown.'

They were shown a Jabal Shammar mare whose owner could not remember its pedigree, but Anne thought it the finest they had seen in Baghdad. Another, a black mare with a blaze though of unknown breed, 'must be *asil*'. Blunt bought a grey off the resident, Colonel Nixon, but Anne refused the generous offer of Mrs Nixon's black mare: 'Of course I could not take the gift, though it was extremely agreeable to have it offered to me by a person for whom I have real regard and affection.'[5]

While they were in Baghdad, Ali Kuli Khan went on pilgrimage to Kerbala, the other holy city of the Shia on the Euphrates, the city of Ali's son Husain. The Blunts dispatched a messenger there to ask him to write to his father, the Bakhtiari chief, to say they were on their way to Persia. They had received an answer from Lady Lytton on 10 March, a cordial invitation to visit the viceregal lodge at any time in May. They were off within a fortnight of experiencing the rare luxury of a made-up bed in Baghdad. After paying off the retainers of the Hail journey, they took on a new retinue of servants and left by river boat on 18 March with two armed guards, Ali and Hajji Muhammad, the cook Ramazan, and Muhammad their guide. Next day they were at Kut al Amara on the Tigris.

Blunt, inveterate hunter and cavalier shot that he was, regarded anything that moved on four legs or flew in the air as fair game, and he threw out his chest at the appeal of some *fellahin* along the marshy stretch of the Tigris between Iraq and Iran, to help them rid the countryside of the wild boar. On 22 March he slew five boars and a sow.[6] Later the same day he set out on his mare Ariel with Anne and a large party of attendants, singling out a large, rust-red creature for pursuit. Blunt, the bullfighter-turned boar hunter, shot and wounded the animal. As the men with him dashed to the scene in triumph, the 'hideous beast' – the words, surprisingly, were Anne's – jumped to its feet and charged. Wilfrid shouted to Anne, 'Could you not turn him, and prevent his crossing the river?' Anne was taken by surprise and the boar turned on her instead, coming at her with a savage grunt and a toss of its head. The crazed creature jumped into the river and tried to escape by swimming. Wilfrid shot at it in the water and wounded it yet again. Blood was streaming from its mouth and from several other wounds. The hunters were sure that it would die but they hadn't bargained for the creature's courage. One of their men had chased it through the river and marsh in a *kellak* (the Iraqi rivercraft kept afloat by inflated goat skins). A sheikh with them fired and missed. Then Wilfrid tried. The boar made a sudden charge out of the water. Anne described what followed:

> He charged exactly like a bull and to my horror seemed to lift the mare by a sort of double toss of his head. I shouted, for I was close behind, to Wilfrid "Your mare, your mare is hurt" but he did not believe it was more than a slight scratch... and he made her again face the beast while he fired again. I could not see what effect either shot produced at the moment (but the boar died in a few minutes) for I was too much alarmed about the mare, and screamed as loud as I

could "Your mare is streaming with blood" – indeed it was a horrid sight – the blood pouring down like a fountain and spreading all over the ground in pools.

The lower of two gashes had cut an artery. They tore off their Arab headdresses to use as tourniquets above the wound. The ground was too hard for them to dig sand, a styptic of the desert, and so they used dry dung to fill the wound and stem the flow.

Blunt's moment of glory had been tarnished. Had they not hunted the boar, they would have been quietly on their way, since their camels and baggage had arrived as they set off. In the event, they were delayed and distressed. Two days later Anne wrote: 'I can talk of it now calmly, as we hope the mare will recover, but yesterday we were in despair and both miserable and I got a feverish attack of violent headache all the evening and most of the night... we were encamped by half past four and the mare laying down on her side and afterwards sitting to feed.' An old man arrived with *alum* to arrest the bleeding, and afterwards the wound was dressed with ointment.

Already the journey was ill-starred.[7] On their way into Persia, rain and hailstones bucketed down and they ran into the Bani Lam, a tribe whose rough habits Sir Henry Layard and other travellers in the same region had noted. They were forced none the less to ask the disagreeable sheikh for guides. These were not respectable Bedouin; in fact they reminded Anne of gangs on Epsom Downs. The sheikh, Ghafil, had a squint and his deputy Sadun only one eye. The night after their meeting, Hajji Muhammad, a Sunni, heard the 'accursed' Shia plotting to rob and murder the unbelievers. Later, Anne was awakened by the sheikh opening her tent flap. A brief challenge of 'Who's there?' had the desired effect and Ghafil retired. Anne and Wilfrid kept their revolvers at the ready just in case. The cook and a groom deserted them and a camel was killed. Before long, however, the Bani Lam began to treat the Blunts as possible allies in the event of another tribe attacking them and called Blunt 'Bey', a term of respect. Crossing rivers and streams on rafts with the 'forty thieves' the party made its way into Luristan to meet the powerful deputy Karim Khan, though Husain Kuli Khan, father of Ali the pilgrim caravan leader and owner of a noted stud, was their chief objective.

At Shustar they found pleasant quarters wherein to wait for Karim Khan. 'Here, at Shustar, all our troubles were, we thought, to end. So little can one foresee what is to come.'

In the night Wilfrid was seized with violent pains, sickness and diarrhoea. Only the camels seemed happy with their lot; in the Shahzade's palace where they were staying, marrows covered the grounds and the animals found them a rare treat. Wilfrid was weak next day but just able to speak to the deputy and the doctor for a few minutes. The eagerly-awaited meeting with the Bakhtiari chief Husain Kuli Khan was disappointing. He was on his way to Teheran and was unable to show them his stables.

Woe piled on woe. On 13 April Wilfrid suffered another violent bout of sickness and Anne thought that he might die. Though she made no reference to it at the time, she was later to recall 'a very strange and important experience' at the moment that Wilfrid was lifted on to his camel to resume the journey. In her own simple words, she 'had a vision'; a vision that was to prove one of the most momentous events of her life and to lead her within a year to convert to Roman Catholicism.[8]

There can be little doubt that their desert travels had had a profound effect on Anne. There was certainly a deeply religious strand in her make-up, a sense of wonderment and gratitude that had been enhanced by the suffering of recent years, but she seldom gave expression to it even in the privacy of her journals. What was within her waiting to come into the open must have been nurtured by the thought of a renewal of her married life, perhaps the thought that Wilfrid's Catholic religion, with its uncompromising values, and its clearly defined elements of faith, would contribute to that end. Whatever her motives, the ascetic life of the desert, the clear sky revealing the infinity of the universe beyond the open tent flap, must have given her many a moment to pause and consider the direction of her life.

They moved on in painfully short stages towards Sultanabad, with Wilfrid suffering sudden uncontrollable seizures. Accompanied on the last stage of that route by the great one of Sultanabad, Kaid Muhammad Jafar, they were invited to gallop the last few miles and Wilfrid's condition seemed to improve as a result. Anne's red *dhalul*, fast but temperamental, spoiled the occasion, however, by sitting down in the last river they had to cross, submerging all her personal baggage, including her clothing.

At last they turned south to the civilisation of the Gulf coast, 'lovely pasture, barley, in which the horses stand grazing knee deep, and the camels have been feeding not far off.' They admired the beautiful little mare belonging to the son of a chieftain, Muhammad Jafar, whose family came originally from Najd. A handsome chestnut mare with four white feet was said to be Kehileh Sheykbah, 'a new name to me'. They went on along the Gulf coastline to Dilam. 'Never since we left Baghdad on this unpleasant journey had we been so quiet and comfortable.'

Persia had not impressed them so far. Elaborate courtesies and hospitality were, they believed, offered simply in order to obtain money from those they flattered, unlike Arab welcomes 'in return for which payment would be an insult'. On 28 April they arrived at Bushire, where the residency held sway over the Persian Gulf, that 'British lake' as it was to be dubbed, patrolled then by a single gunboat.

It was a strange sensation but very agreeable to find oneself suddenly at rest after all our anxieties and after the many difficulties and delays which had at moments made me doubt if we ever should get down to the sea-coast and when there if we should reach Bushire. Then there was the small pleasure of washing and eating and drinking like Christians – which we never thought to do again.[9]

Wilfrid was still suffering from the Persian journey when they docked at Karachi on 7 May, but was well enough nine days later when they saw the viceregal flag fluttering over the '*Peterhof*' in the breeze of Simla, and Edith and Robert Lytton with outstretched arms on the steps to greet them. [10] Anne arrived wearing a headscarf tied under her chin with a cap perched on top, and a straight woollen skirt. Priorities being what they were at Simla, arrangements for a ball the next evening occupied hosts and guests. Anne's ballgown had been ruined by the river crossing disaster in Persia, and Edith quickly adapted a Worth dress she had just received from Paris.

They saw her book – Blunt called it 'their book' – advertised by a Calcutta bookseller. On 27 May Anne wrote to John Murray to protest that copies had not been dispatched either to the Viceroy or the consul-general in Baghdad, but that she had found a copy in a bookshop. She was vexed at the positioning of her table of Arab pedigrees, and her drawings had been mysteriously altered so that they were quite unlike the real animals. Unforgivably, they had substituted the mare Wilfrid was supposed to be riding for Beteyn's, another creature whose head, neck and legs had been 'improved'. There were the inevitable printer's blunders also.

Almost as tiresome was a ten-year-old boy kept by the Viceroy, who claimed to have the powers of a medium. Lytton told them some of the lad's curious answers to questions he had put to him about the next world. Anne found his confident assertions frivolous. But that was the only discernible cloud in an otherwise perfect Simla sky. They rode the horses to unstiffen their legs, took lessons in Hindu from a certain Moonshee Ali – 'the language seems strangely easy' – and went to parties, balls, gymkhanas, race meetings and had 'fascinating conversations' with

Lady Kerr, with whom Anne said she could go on talking forever.

Anne had toothache. She painted the horse Brownie while Wilfrid sketched Edith Lytton. The grand ball on 4 June was the highlight of the season. Supper produced by Lytton's French chef Bonsard was declared a triumph. Simla smiled on its visitors.

Edith, 'more lovely than ever' according to Anne, saved her husband a good deal of censure during his term of office. When he was appointed to the post, Disraeli is said to have walked up and down by a picture of Robert Lytton's father Bulwer, rubbing his hands and saying, 'Ah, my dear old friend, if he could know that I have made his son Viceroy of India, how pleased he would be.'[11] But had they been present during the viceroyalty, neither Bulwer Lytton nor Disraeli would have been altogether pleased. Wilfrid observed the 'fast' set of Simla with a sympathetic eye, and noted his friend Robert's flouting of the rules of even this 'immoral world' of empire. He smoked constantly, and on all occasions refused to attend church on Sundays. Often he sat through an entire social occasion with one pretty woman guest, pointedly ignoring everyone else. The Viceroy would walk on the lawn with his arm round the neck of his finance secretary Sir John Strachey, and he habitually addressed members of the Viceroy's Council as 'my dearest fellow'. He flirted with the young wife of his secretary, despite the ever-present guards who had become mandatory after the murder of his predecessor, Mayo. The same lady, Mrs Batten, focused her attention on Blunt, admitting to him that she did not love her older husband, and giving him a blow-by-blow account of her own love affairs and those of others. Blunt thought it all 'deliciously amusing' and told Mrs Batten that he found her attractive.

Blunt kept a red notebook in which he made a record of his more official confidential discussions.[12] The Viceroy told him that the first Afghan war (1839-42) had been necessary to establish a 'scientific' frontier between India and Russia and to prevent the Tsar from annexing Afghanistan, rather than for the 'extension of territory'. Later, in his *Alms to Oblivion*, Blunt wrote, 'Thus for these few weeks I may truly say that the whole machinery of the Indian government was laid bare to me with its hidden weaknesses as well as its strengths.'

He had been given a similar insight into British policy in Egypt, and to his country's attitude to the Ottoman Empire under its new Sultan, Abdul Hamid, on the way to India. Travelling to Egypt the year before, he and Anne had met Sir Garnet Wolseley in Cyprus, where he ruled as the first British governor following Disraeli's secret negotiations at the Congress of Berlin and the Russian occupation of Armenia and Adrianople. Anne thought Cyprus 'not a desirable place or worth any sacrifices'. Such meetings must have played an important part in the metamorphosis that was beginning to take place in Blunt's political thinking. Whatever reservations he already had about British imperial policy were underlined by the fate of the man he found most sympathetic in Simla, Sir Louis Cavagnari, who was sent to Afghanistan by the Viceroy soon after the Blunts left only to be assassinated by fanatical Muslims, along with the entire British agency staff in Kabul. These were salutary events, and the blame which attached to Lytton quickly encompassed Whitehall, helping to bring down the Disraeli administration and sending a reluctant Gladstone back to Downing Street.

By July it was time to relinquish the high life of Simla, though not before a somewhat premature plot was hatched with Lord Lytton and his foreign secretary, Sir Alfred Lyall, to make a return visit to Hail the following winter, taking viceregal gifts and cementing the position of Britain in central Arabia at the expense of Ottoman power. Blunt was to write later that he left India with his faith in the British empire and its ways in the east 'shaken to its foundations', despite his membership of the Carlton Club.

Despite Wilfrid's qualified dissent, the stay had been enjoyable. He had formed an attachment to Edith which he called a 'new kind of love', and from that fact he made a further deduction:

> There is no more certain rule in friendship... than that, unless one makes a little love to one's friend's wife, the love that was with him soon languishes. There is a point where it becomes a condition of its continuance, just as the continuance of one's love for a married woman depends so often on the pleasant relations one may establish with the husband. These are the secrets of the heart which are not known even to our best novelists.[13]

At the beginning of July they paid a fleeting visit to Agra. Anne described the Taj Mahal as 'a ghostly balloon on the horizon' adding that it had a 'sepulchral gleam'. Wilfrid called it a 'wedding cake'.

They moved on to Bombay where the stables, as elsewhere, were the chief attraction, though in the event they were disappointing. At the leading stud they saw only 'third or fourth rate' horses. In discussion with one of the dealers, Anne discovered that some of the best Indian horses came from the tribes.

'What tribes?'

'From the Shammar.'

'Then they are Shammar horses.'

'Yes, they are Shammar and Anaiza.'

'I fancy a great deal of this horse trade with India goes on with the Shammar of Ferhan and his sons and that with very rare exceptions the horses called Anaiza come from them – the Najd ones coming from Ibn Rashid,' Anne wrote in her diary.[14]

They sailed for home on 11 July. On Saturday 2 August they were up at five in the morning walking about the Crabbet estate, anxiously examining the horses. 'All are well,' Anne noted.

Their daughter Judith was already six years old by the time they returned, and they had seen little of her.

They called her Bibi, and in writing to each other used the initials 'BB', tokens which, on the surface at least, suggested an affectionate concern.[15] In truth, neither Anne nor Wilfrid was disposed by instinct or choice to parenthood. If Anne grew closer to her daughter, it was due as much as anything to her husband's endless appetite for self-gratification. And that need was complicated by his desire to give a boyish hardiness to the girl he had acquired, as it were, by default. However, a solution to their problems stared them in the face, and if Wilfrid pushed for it Anne did not resist.

Minnie Pollen, designed by nature for motherhood and conditioned by her religion to unhindered conception, gathered Judith to her bosom and hoped in her incurably optimistic way that the adoptive girl might grow to love one of her own sons.[16] Minnie and her large family were waiting with Judith at Crabbet, and the Blunts were delighted to see them, and to include their daughter in the exciting regime of victualling and exercising the new influx of Arabs. The arrangement worked well at first. Mornings were spent exercising the horses.

'Wilfrid, Mr Pollen and I rode at half past six. Beyteyn's mare is splendid,' wrote Anne. Next day it was to be Damask Rose, Basilisk and Hagar, full of the promise of great things in performance and breeding.

'Tomorrow we expect more visitors to the horses – so the stud is getting a reputation,' Anne wrote within a month of their homecoming. Judith had received an early baptism in riding and equine management and was destined to share her mother's obsessive delight in the Crabbet stud and all its creations.[17]

Music and drawing remained important influences in the home however, and her daughter's enthusiasm matched Anne's; as did a decided lack of true musicality. Anne had acquired more violins – by Steiner and Maggini – to add to the two 'Strads' already in her possession, and on the way home she had made a note in her diary which indicated the direction of her own musical enthusiasms. 'People in India,' she wrote, 'seem to be in the Mozart and Rossini stage of taste – a stage to be got over, as Wilfrid says of the "fox terrier" stage in dog fancying.'[18]

The progress of the Crabbet stud had become her dominant interest and for the moment this passion was shared by Wilfrid. However, old habits died hard.

Mary Batten, the wife of the Viceroy's private secretary who had impressed him at Simla, arrived at Crabbet in July 1880. He had described her as 'quite depraved, but tinged too with romance'.[19] As so often happened with Blunt's affairs, there was a circular history; Mrs Batten's sister Emma was married to Edward Bourke, Wilfrid's cousin. Lytton, who was also back in England, his reputation somewhat tarnished by the Afghan affair, had secured from her a promise not to have an affair with his friend. The promise was short-lived. Blunt found her bedroom door ajar and stayed in her bed until daybreak. It was Goodwood time, and next morning he drove a team of Arab mares from Arundel station to the racecourse. He was in high spirits.

If Minnie had provided scope for his ideal of love – a nest of shared sexual experience with the husband's acquiescence – Mary Batten and her compliant husband seemed an even more enticing prospect. There were other pleasant diversions. Madeline Wyndham's daughter Mary, hardly pubescent, blushed as he kissed her goodbye after a visit to Crabbet and was scolded by her mother who only too well understood the implication. And a more experienced lover came his way just as he was beginning to feel rejected by Minnie Pollen and Anne who, he thought, were 'ganging up'. She was Minnie Singleton, otherwise the writer Violet Fane, who was known as 'Angelina' after one of her characters.

On 8 December, Anne accompanied Wilfrid to the Royal Geographical Society at Burlington House, where the president, Lord Northbrook, had asked him to speak on the Arabian journey. 'Wilfrid spoke extremely well... The audience appeared much interested and the speech, for he spoke, only referring to notes of the order of mentioning things, was followed by a discussion of the limits of Najd.'[20]

A few days later they went together to Westbourne Place in London to meet their distinguished predecessor in the Arabian deserts, William Gifford Palgrave.[21] The traveller who had gone before them to Hail and on to Riyadh 800 miles to the south, had been born into a Jewish family, had subsequently become a Jesuit, and was currently in philosophical limbo. Anne had expected great things of the meeting. She was still haunted by the vision that had come to her on the day of her husband's sudden rising from his 'death-bed' in Persia. The episode had a biblical quality and Anne recalled a year later the exact spot on the road to Bushire where the vision had come to her. She was at the crossroads of faith, and the meeting with Palgrave had a special significance. 'I was curious to see whether his long career in the S.J. [Society of Jesus] had left a mark. Whether a man who is a traitor bears any mark or sign of his history – and yet I expected to find much to like in him.' But the man of whom she had expected so much was a disappointment. 'He is as clever as he can be and learned in Arabic and Arabian history, but trivial and flippant in his talk, most irreverent indeed, which sounded all the more shocking to anyone who knew his past life... Mr Palgrave had what seems to me to be a bad countenance. I would not trust such a man with anything great or small.'

Anne busied herself with the day-to-day care of house and stud at Crabbet, but her thoughts were elsewhere, turning increasingly to the implications of her spiritual rebirth.[22] All the same, the stud remained a high priority and she recorded every available detail of pedigree and each horse's physical characteristics, while Wilfrid showed old friends round the stables with unconcealed pride of ownership. Among the early visitors he entertained were Skittles and the admirer she was popularly supposed to have married, Alec Baillie. The explorer Robert Cunningham Graham and Joseph Edgar Boehm, sculptor of the Wellington statue at Hyde Park Corner, were also given conducted tours. Graham sought out Anne to congratulate her on her 'Euphrates Valley' book.

Visits to race meetings at Newmarket and Goodwood gave Blunt the opportunity to show off 'his' horses with a panache hitherto reserved for the display of his paramours. Now he was able to combine one with the other. A lady visitor who took his fancy at the beginning of 1880 was Miss Wodehouse. On 13 January Anne noted that 'Wilfrid again devoted himself to Miss Wodehouse and the four in hand with Darley.' Two days later she recorded that the lady had left for the railway station escorted by Wilfrid.

On 31 December 1879 she had recorded the 'last day of an eventful year – a year of hair's breadth escapes and adventures which now in our "happy home" seem almost like a dream.'

She had come to a final determination to enter the Roman Church. There were lengthy preparations for a visit to Birmingham to seek Cardinal Newman's blessing and guidance and in the meantime she went with Wilfrid to Tunbridge Wells to see the Stratford de Redcliffes.[23] After being received downstairs by Lady de Redcliffe they were called for by his lordship and found him sitting in an armchair wearing a pink dressing gown with a purple shawl over his shoulders. The one-time ambassador to the Sublime Porte (the European name for the Ottoman Government) still possessed sharp blue eyes at 93, and with his white hair and pallor had an 'ethereal look'. He had played cricket for Eton against the Harrow eleven which included Anne's grandfather in 1805. 'Lord Byron played fairly well but had someone to run for him on account of his lameness,' the old man told her. They had met subsequently in Constantinople, when he, Byron and Hobhouse rode together almost every day for three weeks. It was Byron's *Childe Harold* period; 'a young man of very engaging manners and with most beautiful eyes'. Anne wrote later that Lord Stratford had said there was something about the lower part of Byron's face which registered his feelings about people. She could not remember the word their host had used but she thought it suggested contempt. He also told Anne that he had spent a week at the home of Sir Ralph and Lady Milbanke at Seaham before her grandmother Annabella had married Byron. John Wilkes was there at the time and Lady Milbanke's favourite dog Jim had just died. Wilkes composed an epitaph:

*Alas poor Jim*
*I'm sorry for him*
*I'd sooner by half*
*It had been Sir Ralph.*

In March 1880, Anne took the final step in her conversion to the Catholic faith an act which Lady Byron would have abhorred more than any other. Wilfrid was amusing himself with Mrs Georgie Currie at Brighton, 'serious in his usual duty', Anne noted parenthetically before setting off to meet Cardinal Newman at Birmingham.

Ralph had said that he would accompany her but cried off at the last moment. He promised to follow on next day however, so that if she achieved her aim and was received into the Church he, if not her husband, would be with her at what had become a moment of supreme importance. John Pollen had also agreed to accompany her and was as good as his word.

It was an anxious moment. Pollen went to the Oratory to announce her arrival while Anne waited nervously at the Plough and Harrow public house nearby. Then they went together to the Oratory to see the ageing cardinal who had known both Byron and his virtuous 'princess', and most of Lady Byron's coterie.

'He spoke of my grandmother and of Lady Olivia Acheson and Miss Kate Bathurst. I think I was alone with him for about 20 minutes. He was very weak in consequence of his late accident... and I was distracted from the conversation to some degree by the fear of tiring him for this was the first time he had come (or been carried) down stairs.' Olivia Acheson had suffered the wrath of Anne's grandmother when she had embraced the fashionable 'Romanism' of the Oxford Movement. As for the audience with Newman:

> What he said was very much to the point. I came to the conclusion that there would be nothing in the Church that would clash with what I can see of certain truth. Nothing that filters through imperfect channels such as human expressions and words... can seem a complete expression of the Divine. But this is the nearest and best... If I asked he would receive me. He wished to do so but he is considered too weak and so it was arranged between Mr Pollen and the Cardinal and me that this should be done by Father Pope, in the shortest and simplest form. Father Thomas Pope came in the evening and I sent a telegram to W. to tell him what I intended.[24]

Ralph arrived next day and Anne made a revealing comment on the relationship with her brother that had caused so much anxiety in her adult life. 'Ralph... arrived... a piece of kindness I shall never forget. It is perhaps the only time he has ever put himself to some pains for my sake but it was an act of true affection – and being the only one deserves special mention.'[25] On 14 March she was confirmed at Westminster by Cardinal Manning in his private chapel. Wilfrid and Judith went with her on that occasion and they returned to Crabbet after breakfast.

As soon as she arrived home Anne began writing her next book, this time covering the journey to the Arabian heartland, and took up Arabic lessons in earnest under the tuition of the Christian Syrian Louis Sabunji. Between the joy of the Arabian stud, writing, perfecting her Arabic and attending to Wilfrid's needs in a year that he described as 'a carnival of folly', there were only occasional social engagements. She and Wilfrid dined with the Tennysons, and Anne was seated between her host and another poet, Robert Browning. She was virtually ignored by both men. Tennyson struck her as 'a profoundly selfish and self-satisfied person', and she did not get on well 'as to conversation' with him or Browning.[26]

But the Crabbet stud was now uppermost in her mind, and her daughter Judith, old enough to ride and to demonstrate that she had the makings of a good horsewoman, was constantly at her side.

The tradition of horse breeding within the Milbanke and Wentworth families was manifested at Crabbet by a veritable art gallery of famous horses. Many of the pictures that had adorned the Milbanke and Wentworth homes came to Anne after Lady Byron's death. Under her mother's instruction, Judith became a child authority on bloodstock, and developed an affection for the 'Arabian' which would be with her for the rest of her life. It was the visit of James Weatherby to Crabbet that set the seal on its fame and authority. Arabs had, of course, been eligible for registration for centuries, but the Arab section of the General Stud Book had fallen into disuse in the nineteenth century. Weatherby agreed to a special section with an introduction to the subject in Volume XIV, in which was set out the belief that an Arabian strain, improved and developed as a 'non-running auxiliary to the Thoroughbred', would be a valuable reserve outcross in view of its proven success in the past, of its threatened extinction in its own country and of its possible use in the future (however remote) when inbreeding of racing stock might become a serious matter. Wilfrid had already persuaded the Newmarket authorities to include an Arab race in 1883, and he wrote to the *Nineteenth Century* in 1880 advising owners of Arabs to 'go for increased size,' advice that he subsequently retracted.

All the detail of the stud was in Anne's care. She had been responsible for the selection and purchase of the original stock and supervised the breeding programme, though she usually sought her husband's opinion. Ralph had now invested £10,000 in the project; the rest of the capital was hers. But it was Wilfrid who took the honour and glory. As Anne's daughter was to write in her maturity: 'To her was due the success of the venture, and she alone studied the pedigrees, strains, and history of the horses. It is to her that we owe its survival of the many vicissitudes caused by Wilfrid Blunt's often reckless disregard of common sense in the treatment of horses.'[27]

Judith was to castigate her father on many counts, but on none did she harbour more resentment than the part he played in the Crabbet stud. Indeed, she maintained to the end of her life that his actions were responsible for its final decline. Her mother was a martyr here as elsewhere: 'She always had to contend also with the sudden whims by which he would insist on presenting some precious mare to some undeserving lady who generally rode like a sack of oats and broke its knees, or got run away with and broke her nose and abused Arabs ever afterwards with shrill vindictiveness as nasty, wild, savage creatures!'

Wilfrid acquired a pied-à-terre at this time in Buckingham Gate, and rented a temporary love nest opposite Victoria Station from the Duke of Bedford's French chef, representing himself as Walter Bingham, an Irishman residing in Streatham. He also agreed to elope with Angelina Singleton to Italy, although she was worried lest he have a 'papistical twist' and abandon her. As it happened, she abandoned him and went off with his cousin Philip Currie. Blunt is said to have kept to the end of his days a bunch of everlasting flowers she had given him.[28]

By November 1880 it was time to go east again though Anne was on tenterhooks about the latest book, which, after various attempts to arrive at a title she eventually decided to call *Pilgrimage to Nejd*. Just before they left, John Murray wrote to say that he approved of the manuscript and title.

'The last thing I saw was Judith's face looking through the lattice of the dining room window,' Anne wrote of their departure from James Street. Wilfrid wrote that they were off 'perhaps for ever', adding, 'I beg my wife to believe I love her truly, in spite of all, and my daughter with a pure and honest love.'[29] He had chatted to Gladstone before they set out, finding the 'grand old man' totally ignorant on the matter of the regeneration of the east, which Blunt thought rested largely on the restoration of the caliphate to the Arabs after four centuries vested in the Sultan of the Ottoman Empire. Gladstone seemed interested in the idea and circulated a note to the Cabinet. Excited by the interest he had aroused and citing his many 'correspondents' in the Arab world, Blunt asked Dilke at the Foreign Office to make him consul for the Hadramaut or some place on the Red Sea. He was proposing to go back to central Arabia to foster the scheme dreamt up with Lytton in Simla, a mission to Hail to bolster Britain's prestige in the eyes of Bin Rashid. A consulship would enhance his own prestige. Foreign Secretary Granville would have none of it.

Anne wrote to her publisher on 19 November from the Hotel du Nil in Cairo, asking him to send her a copy of the book as soon as it was out, care of the consul-general in Cairo or Jane Digby in Damascus.[30] There was a brief voyage along the Red Sea coast of the Hejaz in December before they returned to Cairo in January 1881.

In February they were on their way to familiar Syrian pastures in search of Mrs Digby, Abdel Kadr, Sheikh Farhan, and additions to the Crabbet stud.

They reached Damascus on 15 March 1881 where Jane Digby had received a copy of 'our new book', *Pilgrimage to Nejd*. Anne flicked through it anxiously and decided that it was, 'on the whole satisfactory'. Her diary went straight on to the topic of the moment. 'Managyeh mare – a lovely white mare I saw in the afternoon (head something like Sherifa).' On 26 March she wrote: 'He rode a Managyeh mare, his younger brother a Hamidi mohra, a strain brought from Ibn Saud 15 years ago... a two year-old I suppose.'[31] Journals and sketchbooks filled with the technical jargon and the detailed sketching of horses, as they made their way to Damascus and on to Aleppo, to the camp of the Gomussa tribe.

On 12 April, Anne listed the purchases so far. They totalled some 27 horses at a cost of about £2,000. Entire days of her diary were taken up with agonised arguments as to whether they should purchase this or that animal, comparing physical details, analysing pedigrees. It was hard work, mentally and physically, and at one despairing moment she considered giving away all the Crabbet stock and finishing with horses. A letter from Judith and another from Minnie Pollen in praise of her daughter consoled her; '...what matters else?', she asked. It is not clear whether she referred to Judith or her Arabs, or both.[32]

There were last-minute hitches with visas and travel permits and eventually they had to appeal to Mr Goschen, the ambassador at Constantinople, for help.

On 12 May they supervised the unloading of their Syrian horse purchases at Marseille. The cargo was swung down in boxes onto a floating platform. 'Jedrania was put into the empty horse box hitherto occupied by David, Rasham and Fly, and the foal, with a rope round its neck to lead it, was lifted down separately... Next Meshura, Rodania, Kebeysha and lastly Dahana were taken.' All were finally loaded on a barge along with bales of cotton. Wilfrid, never one to take a back seat on such occasions, squatted on top of the bales armed with sword and spear, looking like a caricature of Britannia.

## Chapter Nine
# Who Waits Wins

There was a familiar edge to Anne's diary entry of 8 June 1881: 'Probably I am the only person who remembers that this is the anniversary of a marriage which took place 12 years ago.'[1]

The depression was soon thrown off. There was encouraging news about her latest book: Hachette of Paris had decided to publish and in August she was able to thank Mr Murray for her first royalty cheque. 'Very satisfactory,' she wrote, while declining an invitation to dine at Albermarle Street – that distinguished publishing address to which Byron had so often repaired – because Judith was unwell.

While preparing for the next journey abroad – suggested to Wilfrid by widespread talk of revolution in Egypt – Anne busied herself with the horses. A show at Islington provided an opportunity to assess the current state of the thoroughbred market. Anne took Minnie Pollen with her to London and they picked up Wilfrid at the Travellers' Club on the way to Islington. The event only underlined her belief that the English horse scene was dominated by corrupt amateurs. 'There are at the Horse Show several real and sham Arabians and the prize has been given to Lady Wilson's grey Egyptian horse – the pair she has sent have no pretension to being thoroughbred.'[2]

Oppenheims and Rothschilds began to consult Anne about their Arabs, and substantial offers came in for the progeny of Crabbet. Wilfrid was offered 800 guineas for Pharaoh and Anne said he should take it on the Arab principle that it is unlucky to refuse a fair offer. She was tormented by the thought of being away from her beloved home and stables; 'it is more difficult to get through the pain of going away because I have got ill somehow and I am obliged to seem well.'[3] At the beginning of November she noted that she was tired and unhappy at the thought of leaving England and Crabbet. By the 30th of the month she and Wilfrid were installed in the Hotel du Nil.

Wilfrid had already attempted to influence British policy in conversations about the caliphate with Gladstone and Dilke, and the idea of a Euphrates valley rail scheme as being inimical to Arab interests. He had also suggested to his friends in government that Syria and Egypt might be encouraged to join together in opposition to the Ottoman power. Lord Salisbury, according to Blunt, was impressed with his arguments and with his 'integrity'.[4]

When the Blunts arrived in Egypt, forces as yet unknown to this radical-Conservative Englishman were being released on a tidal wave of nationalism.[5] The secret agreement of 1878 between Britain and Turkey had guaranteed the Asiatic dominions of the Ottoman Empire in return for the promise of reforms and British control of Cyprus. Within a month of that agreement being signed by Disraeli in June 1878, the Congress of Berlin had given France permission to occupy the Ottoman province of Tunis in return for French recognition of British supremacy in Cyprus. Britain also recognised the French right to protect Christians in Syria (in contravention of an earlier agreement between Britain and Russia), while France and Britain would jointly administer the finances of Egypt. Gladstone called it an 'insane covenant'. The Suez Canal was of course at the heart of the arrangements, designed to protect British commercial interests in the face of that perpetual threat to the balance of imperial power, the break-up of the Ottoman Empire. Almost 40 years had passed since the Tsar Nicholas told Lord Aberdeen that Turkey was 'a dying man', and that Russia should take Constantinople while Britain occupied Egypt and Crete. Such an eventuality was never far from the minds of the great powers.

The Caisse, the Anglo-French Public Debt Commission, had been established in Cairo in 1876, assuming responsibility for the Egyptian national debt at seven per cent interest, the estates of the Khedive being mortgaged as security. In Constantinople George Goschen, had made the arrangement with his French counterpart Joubert. Evelyn Baring was English commissioner of the Caisse and, in a cabal of old diplomatic friends who were about to become bitter enemies, Edward Malet was Britain's consul-general in Cairo. Love, politics and horses would go hand in glove for Blunt, and one way or another Anne would become embroiled.

Sir Rivers Wilson, the Treasury minister sent out to Egypt to advise the Debt Commission and who had first pointed the Blunts towards Skene and the horses of Aleppo, and whose wife had, in Anne's view, been unjustly rewarded at the Islington show, was Blunt's political guide as he stumbled into the Egyptian political arena. The country's figurehead, the Khedive Tewfiq Pasha, ruling as the viceroy of the Ottoman Sultan under the dispensation granted to Muhammad Ali and his sons in 1840, was autocratic and inept. The prime minister, Riaz Pasha, was unliked but honest, a Jew turned Muslim. A mishmash nationalist movement had grown out of opposition to the schemes of Britain and France, its members bound together by the pan-Islamic appeal of the religious leader Jamal Ad-Din al-Afghani and the moderate counsels of Muhammad Abdu and Saad Zaghul. A second strand of nationalism was the Constitutional Party represented by Sherif Pasha, a delightfully indolent French-educated Turk whose passion in life was billiards. In 1881, an officer who sympathised with the poorer classes came to the fore. He was Ahmed Arabi, son of a smallholder, graduate of Al Azhar University, and commander of the 4th Regiment. Blunt liked him.

The high politics of Egypt, set to determine the course of Britain's policy in the Middle East for decades to follow, was meat and drink not only to Wilfrid but to Anne as well. She would have liked to be an intellectual support as well as a comfort in his increasingly forceful activities. But it was not to be. As the Egyptian crisis came to the boil, Anne was ill again. 'In bed. I suppose I am worn out with tiredness – wish I could get well but have been getting less well for the last few months.' All the same, she found enough strength to visit the stables of Ali Pasha Sherif. His was the only Arabian stud left in Egypt and she had seen his horses before. 'He seems to have parted with a good many [horses] and his foals (ie. nearly yearlings), this year are in bad condition. He said to me "J'ai vendue plusieurs et j'ai donne qelques uns."'[6] However many the Pasha may have sold or given away, only one really took Anne's fancy, a white mare called Nura that took her breath away. But she was not impressed by the offspring. 'If we could ever get the bay it would be the glory of the stud. She is exactly the colour of Kars (though less black points).'

By 14 December she was feeling better and went with Wilfrid to meet Ahmed Arabi.[7] She did not at first share her husband's favourable impression. 'We found there a crowd of officers who all left when we entered leaving Arabi Bey alone with us. He is tall and fat, with nothing to attract in his personal appearance, not a single good feature in his face, but a look of extreme earnestness that makes ugliness seem of no consequence.' Arabi impressed his guests with the sincerity of his wish to achieve good government in his country, while stating that the Anglo-French control of Egyptian finance must remain. Subsequent double-dealing involving the British and French governments and the Khedive seemed to decide Anne in favour of Arabi and the Egyptian nationalist cause, and she began to record minutely the movements of politicians and diplomats on all sides and once more to hope that she might take an active part at her husband's side.

Priorities remained much as before, however. The Blunts were in and out of the desert beyond the eastern bank of the Nile, returning to Cairo every now and again to look for horses and keep up with political events. The journals became a pot-pourri of equine information and diplomatic conjecture. Before leaving Paris for Cairo, Blunt had been told by his cousin Philip Currie, 'Perhaps you might find in Arabi just the man you have been looking for'. By the new year Arabi was the hero of the populace, and the Englishman and his interpreter Louis Sabunji,[8] Anne's Arabic teacher, had to push through a crowd of supplicants to reach him. Arabi had heard that Blunt was married to Byron's granddaughter and paid homage to the legendary 'freedom fighter'. Blunt had now become the unofficial mediator between the British and Egyptian sides, though he saw little good in one and plenty in the other. Anne, hurrying between morning mass, visits to stables and one meeting after another, kept notes and drafted letters to the press. On 1 January *The Times* published the nationalist programme, composed by Blunt in the name of Ahmed Arabi.[9] Malet had warned Blunt against publishing, but Gregory, a retired governor of Ceylon, had encouraged him to ignore the consul-general's advice. When Malet was shown the article he questioned Blunt's judgement and good faith. Blunt was furious that the article, published in the form of a letter, had been attributed to Arabi, who had been made Secretary for War by the Egyptian government. Clearly there had been a misunderstanding. The Anglo-French note, ostensibly supporting the Khedive in the face of nationalist insurrection, followed on the 6th. On that day Anne and Wilfrid were in the desert camping near Halwan, where there were horse races. The bungling of the article by *The Times* rankled more than ever when *Al Ahram*, the Cairo newspaper, published a disclaimer by Arabi himself, which Anne neatly copied into her diary. Blunt's credibility was at stake and Anne noted 'Wilfrid must see Arabi tomorrow.'[10]

At 5 p.m. on the 7th she was with Lady Gregory at the Hotel du Nil. Wilfrid arrived, his face showing that 'it was all right' – that Arabi had not betrayed his party nor abandoned his principles – 'he sticks to the programme.' Arabi wanted Wilfrid to telegraph *The Times*, confirming the authenticity of the letter. In Arabi's presence, Blunt there and then composed a long telegram to the newspaper. It read: 'Arabi Bey confirms to me correctness and genuine character of programme I sent you. The official contradiction as far as authorised by him applies only to report of his having signed and sent it himself to Times. He is staunch to his opinions. Please publish this with full guarantee and explanation of circs, in my name. Blunt.'

There followed telegrams to French, British and Egyptian journals, with copies of the despatch he had sent to *The Times*. It had its own distinguished correspondent on the spot, but its editor must have wondered sometimes if Blunt had replaced him. Each telegram ended with Arabi's favourite dictum: 'Who waits wins.'

When Blunt met Arabi on 9 January the Egyptian, according to Anne, 'was in a great rage with England and its government and Minister [Malet].' He accused Malet of neglecting to show him vital telegrams and documents, although Malet had promised to keep him fully informed. But even Blunt could not bring himself at this stage to accept allegations of the consul-general's guilt. He had breakfasted with Malet the day before and been shown all official telegrams for the past three months, 'and,' wrote Anne, 'says he has throughout been perfectly straight and fair.'[11] Anne and Wilfrid both blamed the French and Whitehall for the Anglo-French note. Loyally following her husband's line, Anne wrote indignantly: 'The fact is the note was drawn up by Gambetta himself (and no doubt Dilke consenting) and the Ministry in England busily acts at his bidding in order to gain something with reference to the commercial treaty now being argued about.'

Blunt was asked by Malet to go back to Arabi with an official explanation of Britain's interpretation of the note – 'that the English government would not permit any interference of the Sultan [of Turkey] with Egypt and would not allow the Khedive to go back from his promises or molest the parliament.' Anne, as angry now as Wilfrid with the British administration and its ambivalence, wrote: 'It is certainly not the meaning the words of the note seem to point to, and the explanation was neither believed nor accepted – Wilfrid returned saying "they are irreconcilable". No wonder.'

For the first time in her life Anne had come to grips with the realities of everyday diplomacy and political horse-trading. Almost to her own surprise she found that she had a ready understanding of the complexities and the implicit immorality. Still, the more open life of country and desert beckoned her. On 10 January she wrote:

> when we can leave Cairo we don't alas, know – I long to go away to the desert and live with our camels – But we cannot leave this turmoil and confusion – and Wilfrid even thinks that when the immediate crisis for which we must stay is

past it may be necessary to go to England when he could bring more pressure to bear on the Government than from a distance out here. I shall regret it if we must go so soon into the cold – But [it] must be risked if it is right and just and we cannot go back from what we have promised.'[12]

Tennis, riding, occasional visits to the desert filled in the time as January's air of crisis grew into open talk of rebellion.

At the end of January Sir Auckland Colvin, who had succeeded Baring in 1880 as Britain's Comptroller of Egyptian finances, told Blunt that annexation by England was the probable result of all that was happening. Blunt passed the warning on to the nationalists.[13]

Anne meanwhile wrote her weekly letter to MMP (Minnie Pollen) asking for news of Judith,[14] and Wilfrid dashed off another letter to *The Times*, before packing their baggage camels and going off for three days in the desert. They had been looking for an apartment and had found something opposite Shepheard's, but they were somewhat put off by the rent demanded, £20 a month. They camped in the luxuriously fruited garden of a large estate known as Sheykh Obeyd, and after some consideration decided to buy it.

At the end of the month they were back in Cairo entertaining familiar members of the British and French colonies when rumour came of war preparations. 'They could give no fresh news except rumour of the fleet being sent from Malta to Alexandria, which I hope to Heaven is not true – while we sat talking a group of camels appeared on the horizon.' On 3 February Anne noted that Wilfrid had had a letter that day from Prime Minister Gladstone, regretting that he could not in the present climate, give any reassuring reply to Blunt's appeal some weeks earlier, reminding him of some of his, the PM's, essays on Ottoman matters. Gladstone added that Wilfrid should read his article of 1877 in the *Nineteenth Century*, 'since which he has seen no reason to change his views about Egypt.'[15]

February 6 was a day to disarm the fearful. It was Judith's ninth birthday, and the day on which a letter from Foreign Secretary Lord Granville to Lord Dufferin, Britain's diplomatic trouble-shooter in Cairo, was published, indicating that Britain was 'not bound' to make an armed intervention 'to avert anarchy in Egypt'.

Wilfrid then went down with mild food poisoning, and he began to speak affectionately of home and BB. They gave up the idea of a farewell dinner party for Egyptian friends. 'It might occasion official jealousies.' On 20 February, Mr Barnard, correspondent of the *New York Herald*, called. Even he, said Anne ruefully, did not understand the true state of affairs. On the 27th they went with Lady Gregory to say their farewells to Arabi. This time Blunt quoted his wife's grandfather, reciting his warning to the Greeks: 'Trust not for freedom to the Franks.'

They arrived at Victoria Station in London on Sunday 5 March, where John Pollen and Cowie met them. They had arranged to spend the night at Pembridge Villas, the London home of the Pollens, where Minnie and Judith waited anxiously at the front door. Their daughter had grown tall and wore a becoming pink frock. 'Here turns over a new leaf of life,' Anne wrote.[16]

Anne had taken the Egyptian cause to heart. 'Everybody says, "Oh, if what you say is correct of course we sympathise with the Egyptian nation" – the thing is to make them believe it to be true.'[17]

Wilfrid moved to the James Street house, just off Oxford Street in London's West End, where he felt he could pursue the cause of Egyptian nationalism without domestic interruption. His devoted wife sent on his 'things', and remained within call at the Pollens' home, Pembridge Villas, so that she could copy his letters and entertain the mighty on his behalf.[18] On 9 March 1882 he went to Westminster and Whitehall to lobby old friends. At the Foreign Office he found Dilke, the parliamentary under-secretary, 'hostile', as was Foreign Secretary Granville. If the Egyptian nationalists would not give up their claims on the domestic budget, their case was hopeless said the Foreign Secretary, and they would have to be put down, if necessary by force. Blunt decided that he would have to go directly to Gladstone to prevent this outrage. He was not encouraged by an encounter with Sir Henry Rawlinson, President of the Royal Asiatic Society and, though a prominent Conservative, the man to whom all parties looked as the expert on the Asiatic world (which tended to include Africa in the political mind). Rawlinson had an uncomplicated view of the matter. Despotic rule was endemic among the eastern races and the Egyptians like all the others would 'always be slaves'. In fact, Blunt found himself almost alone in his advocacy of the Egyptian cause.

Morley, the editor of the *Pall Mall Gazette*, to whom Blunt had looked confidently, followed the Colvin-Malet line, while Moberly Bell, *The Times's* man on the spot, was 'blinding everyone', though John Walter the newspaper's proprietor promised to send a special correspondent to Egypt. An interview with Lord Rothschild, privy to the attitude of bond-holders in the Suez Canal, fell through at the last moment. General Sir Garnet Wolseley questioned him closely about the desert region between the Nile Delta and the canal. Blunt wrote in his diary that if there was armed intervention, 'troops will be landed from that side', and he warned his friend Arabi accordingly.

The meeting with Gladstone proved the final nail in the coffin of conciliation. The consummate politician easily convinced Blunt that he was on Arabi's side, that he always had and always would be on the side of small nations. At the end of what seemed a promising interview, in the course of which the PM sent his foreign secretary from the room so as to give Blunt an absolutely private hearing, the impressionable visitor asked if Gladstone would send Arabi a message of goodwill. The PM replied, 'I think not. But you are at liberty to state your own impression of my sentiments.' But he was not at all sure that the Grand Old Man could be relied upon.[19]

The Egyptian question was bedevilled by the concurrent Irish troubles, and Wilfrid began to give his mind to another anti-imperialist cause. Like so many informed radicals of the time, he took a naive view. Gladstone, who had to deal with the realities of each problem as it arose, could bemuse idealists like Blunt who never understood that imperialism in the nineteenth century was not about 'good and bad' or political perfidy, but about trade and commerce and administration; above all about filling the empty spaces and commercial vacuums of the world.

While Wilfrid attended with mounting exasperation to affairs of state, Anne returned to Crabbet and the horses. Blunt's artist friends Bird and Molony were busy adding to the Crabbet art gallery (along with Anne who had painted a full-size portrait of Wilfrid in Arab garb, seated on the rearing Pharaoh). Bird was painting an Assyrian warhorse after consulting with Henry Layard at the British Museum. 'The picture represents a sort of plumbox wild horse with a flaming eye and in the distance Sardanapalus or Sennacherib driving in a chariot and a burning town... This, Mr Bird says, is the war horse out of Job.' Bird had only eight days to finish his work; 'it is only rubbed in, but I paint very quick,' he told Anne. It was for the Royal Academy exhibition. 'Such is art,' she observed.[20]

On 1 April, Queen of Sheba produced a foal by Pharaoh, a bay with three white feet and blaze. Anne and Judith were celebrating the event when Wilfrid arrived home, having decided to rest from politics with a little fishing. A magnificent trout weighing nearly four pounds was hooked and sent as a present to Cardinal Manning.

But Blunt was no longer content to placate religious or secular authorities with gifts of fish or appeals to old friendships. Back in March, after seeing Lord Granville, he had dined with a Foreign Office clerk named Cockerell, who sided with Blunt and was indignant about his colleagues' view that he was simply a meddler in Egyptian matters.[21] A few days later Anne went with Wilfrid to be entertained by Lord Northbrook, First Lord of the Admiralty and one of the founding fathers of the intelligence service. Northbrook, like Granville, was suspicious of Blunt's links with Arabi's nationalists.

In late April a shoal of letters arrived from Egyptian leaders, including Arabi and Abdu. They were worried about reports, premature as it happened, that the Bedouin of the Egyptian desert were in revolt. Anne was not confident enough of her Arabic to translate the letters with assurance and so they went to Mecklenbergh Square, the London home of Edward Palmer, Lord Almoner's Professor of Arabic at Cambridge and an old hand at desert exploration.[22] The Professor translated as Anne wrote down the words. She knew enough to realise that he had left out important passages in one of Arabi's letters and that it was a somewhat inadequate translation. All the same, Blunt sent it to *The Times*, along with a letter of his own.

News came as these letters were published of Arabi calling up Egyptian reservists to guard ports in the face of naval manoeuvres.[23] On 16 May, Anne copied into her diary telegrams sent by Blunt in English and French to several Egyptian leaders.

To Arabi: 'Lord Granville states in Parliament that Sultan Pasha and deputies have joined Khedive against you. If untrue let Sultan Pasha telegraph me contradiction. United you have nothing to fear. Could you not form ministry with Sultan Pasha as Prime Minister, but stand firm.'

To Sultan Pasha: 'I trust that all who love Egypt will stand together. Do not quarrel with Arabi. The danger is too great.'

Of more immediate concern to Anne was news from Crabbet. 'Burning Bush's foal died last night.'

A telegram arrived the same night from Sultan Pasha,

President of the Egyptian Chamber of Notables, assuring
Wilfrid that all was tranquil in Cairo. A copy was dashed
off to Gladstone. On the 25th the Anglo-French
administration issued an ultimatum to the nationalists:
Arabi was to go into voluntary exile, law and order was to
be restored under the authority of the Khedive Tewfiq. On
the 28th Blunt went to sleep after penning the words 'Vicisti
O Colvine!' in his diary.[24] Next day's newspapers reported
that things had changed again. The populace had
demanded Arabi's recall and the Khedive had given in.

The delirious moment was spoilt for Anne by a quite
unconnected event. The magnificent Pharaoh was shown
that day at Horsham, and according to Anne's piquant note
was passed over for 'a mongrel'.[25] She suspected bias
or worse. In the heat of the moment Wilfrid dashed to
London and told Anne to pack her bags. They were
returning to Egypt. But events began to overtake even the
expeditious Blunt. On 1 June Gladstone accused Arabi in
Parliament of 'throwing off the mask' of conciliation.
Blunt's name came up. Was he to lead an 'insurrection'
against his own country? Dilke assured the House that
there was no truth in the allegation. Blunt had, in fact, sent
Sabunji as his emissary. Sabunji arrived on the 7th, the day
the Sultan's personal representative, Dervish Pasha, turned
up from Constantinople. Not long after, riots broke out in
Alexandria and some 60 people were killed and many
injured. Blunt believed Arabi's enemies had fomented the
riots. 'What purpose could they serve him?' he asked.[26]

As the so-called massacres took place, Anne was
receiving the Khedive's cousins Osman and Kamil at
Crabbet. They were accompanied by Arif Bey and Dr
Lampiere; the former a Kurd claiming descent through the
Prophet's tribe, the Quraysh, the latter dubbed by Anne 'an
adventurer'. The princes admired the stud and played tennis
while Anne translated a telegram from Cairo outlining the
latest developments.

The Cabinet had agreed by now that Malet and Colvin should have absolute discretion to call in the Royal Navy if circumstances demanded it. Colvin had been waiting for just such an excuse as the Alexandria riots. In mid-June the dispatch of a Turkish force to Egypt was threatened and a European congress took place at Constantinople. As if to underline the seriousness of the moment, Anne moved in with Wilfrid at the James Street house and they were visited by Lady Malet, mother of Edward the consul-general. She walked up and down muttering under her breath, 'Traitors!' She believed that they more than anyone were responsible for her son's predicament.

A few days later Malet came home with a stomach complaint, believing he had been poisoned. At much the same time, Arabi was offered a bribe of £4,000 by Rothschild to step down and leave Egypt. Lord Houghton, in the course of a heated debate in the correspondence columns of *The Times*, suggested that both Blunt and Arabi should be shot.

Anne kept her head if no one else did. On 1 July she recorded that Captain Laprimaudaye was at Crabbet and that together they had arranged a programme for Mr Edmund Tattersall. 'The great man arrived at 1 and brought with him four friends from Australia, some of whom he thought might be buyers, all were he assured us very rich.' Meanwhile, a secret service mission designed to open the way to a landing at Suez and occupation of the canal had begun to unfold. Edward Palmer, whom Anne and Wilfrid had come to know well, though they found him a trifle eccentric, was approaching by land from Gaza, making his way across the top corner of Sinai, – a land he knew intimately, – towards Suez. On the 6th, Lieutenant Gill of the Royal Engineers and Lieutenant Charrington of the Royal Navy arrived at Suez.[27] Their mission was to bribe tribal leaders into neutrality or active support, and to cut the Ismailiya telegraph which connected Egypt with the

Turkish authorities. On 11 July, Admiral Sir Beauchamp Seymour's ships opened fire on Alexandria. On the 13th, marines landed. Anne copied in her diary a letter from a businessman with substantial interests in Egypt, E. St. J. Fairman, addressed to 'a Member of the House of Lords'.

> The clique responsible for the actual Egyptian crisis is composed of Henry Oppenheim, Nubar Pacha, Sir C. Rivers Wilson, and Riaz Pacha; and Sir E.B. Malet is much to blame for his personal friendship towards them... I am convinced that a strict inquiry will explain the past and guide the future.[28]

British intervention was 'cruel' and 'unChristian'. There were dire threats of retaliatory action 'from Morocco to Penang'. The letter ended, 'I have had 25 years' experience abroad, and of a very general character, and I believe that more than one nation would rejoice at England's discomfiture and isolation.'

On that note, Anne ended her diary of the Egyptian adventure. With a realism denied to her husband, she knew that there was nothing more that she or any outsider could do. Not until mid-August did British troops under Wolseley mass for an attack on Ismailiya. In the meantime, Palmer, Gill and Charrington had gone ahead of the troops to carry out their covert mission. Tribes they mistakenly believed to be loyal to Britain took them on a fool's errand, and after a brave fight by the young Gill, a veteran of some notable Indian army campaigns, they were pushed bound and gagged over a precipice and then, according to subsequent reports, their bodies mutilated. The inquiry which elicited those few facts was conducted by Colonel Charles Warren, amateur archaeologist of Jerusalem and later Commissioner of London's Metropolitan Police.

Arabi proved, in the end, an inept commander. He began to prepare the defence of Suez too late and a one-sided battle was lost at Tel-el-Kebir on 13 September. That defeat resulted in his capture and proved the end of the dreams of Arab nationalists for generations to follow.

Blunt financed the defence of Arabi in his protracted trial, retaining A. M. Broadley QC to lead, and Blunt's old acquaintance of South American days, Sir Richard Burton, now consul at Trieste was called to Sinai to help track down the killers of the three British intelligence men. The culprits were never caught, however. Arabi and his co-defendants were found guilty and condemned to death, but their sentences commuted to exile. Blunt never forgave Gladstone; 'I believe him capable of any treachery and any crime.'

Anne made no comment on the conclusion of an affair in which she had supported her husband with characteristic loyalty. Her patient endeavour was to discover a characteristic reward. Lady Gregory, a quiet Irish woman who looked like Queen Victoria, came to share Blunt's indignation at Britain's conduct in Egypt. As he said later, identity of interest drew them closer together, and at the climax of the tragedy they found themselves 'by a spontaneous impulse' in each other's arms.[29] She copied out for him the long, angry and moving poem he wrote to assuage his indignation, *Wind and Whirlwind*, predicting the downfall of the British empire. Lord Randolph Churchill, a fellow Conservative and opponent of Gladstone's policy, joined with Blunt to condemn the hangings and floggings which followed the defeat of the nationalists.[30]

General Gordon was one of many sympathetic visitors who called on Anne and Wilfrid at the time of the Egyptian crisis.[31] During his visit, he talked about the impossibility of reform in India, due to the entrenched interests of Britain and the power of the civil service. Gordon had accepted the post of secretary to the new Viceroy, Lord Ripon, in June 1880 but resigned on reaching India. Anne regarded the 'unmilitary' Gordon, with his grey eyes and grey hair, not

as the slightly odd creature of official and public view but
as having 'perfect common sense'. India was the ideal place
for Blunt to pursue the cause of the 'common man', and
Gordon rekindled his frustrated enthusiasm in the
aftermath of the Egyptian debacle.

Meanwhile the affair with Lady Gregory came close to
'true love', and she wrote a sequence of amorous sonnets
which were subsequently published in his *Proteus*. But anti-
imperialism was now the all-embracing passion, and both
daughter Judith, with whom he felt he had begun to achieve
a modest rapport, and Lady Gregory, must be sacrificed to
the call of destiny. He became increasingly morose and
embittered as if he had suffered a personal defeat; which, in
a sense, he had. There were frequent violent outbursts, and
if they were mostly directed at the Prime Minister it was his
his wife and daughter who took the brunt.

By July 1883 preparations were in hand for the return to
India. Anne and Wilfrid had lunch with the Singletons in
London and Oscar Wilde joined them, described by Anne
as 'well curled and with a green tie and handkerchief in a
carefully buttoned coat and with a huge bunch of pink lilies
in his hand.'[32] But an amusing luncheon with Wilde did
nothing to lessen the impact of a realisation that came to
Anne at this time – that her life was in ruins. On 10 August
she composed a 'mutual pact', a statement to her husband
that was the culmination of years of insult and simmering
anger. After the long fight with officialdom in Egypt, her
unquestioning loyalty to Wilfrid had been rewarded by his
avowal of love for Lady Gregory. It was the final straw.

This paper is written to state a fact and explain its cause –
as neither the one nor the other seem to be understood. The
fact is that all keen interest I have in life is gone past recall
– the cause the shock of discovering that I have spent many
years under a false impression... This is no question of 'Me
and Thee' of 'Thee and Me', nor do I now complain that I

once was rich – and now am poor. It is too late. I accept
harsh truth, preferring it to a false dream... I have lived long
years hoarding an unreal treasure and thinking 'while life
lasts this will be there'... I believed in what was not, nor ever
had been. And the knowledge of the truth came suddenly,
like a bitter wind destroying all that had taken years to grow
up, and killing all hope. Time is needed to recover – and
someday perhaps – Alas! Time is short and that 'Some Day'
may but be the Nothing of the phantom caravan... Have I
not written this plain? Perhaps I have failed. Like the dumb
creatures that have no voice to speak their suffering I have
no words on my tongue. Then those who are poets... despise
us and think in their hearts that we have nothing to say, no
sense of grief – no souls. How often have I tried to write
this?... Shall I try once more?... All night long my ship
signalled. No answer came... I strain my eyes for a sight of
land. I care for nothing but to keep the straight path.[33]

She spoke of an earthquake that had reduced her home
to ruin, of 'unceasing pain', and compared herself to the
foolish traveller who could not see the desolate waste
beyond the mirage of a caravan. She was not withdrawing
from her part of a solemn contract. What work was still to
be done she would share willingly, 'even gladly'. She wrote
with uncharacteristic feeling of herself 'alone in an open
boat, learning to cope with long waves' – waves that had
once seemed friendly. 'Now from the sea level they seem
like mountains.' At long last she had had enough. She
signed her initials, A.I.N.B. in Arabic letters, as if to stress
the one thing they had shared innocently, unsullied by his
infidelity and disloyalty.

She simply handed him the two pages of lined foolscap
on which she had written so movingly. She did not return
to the subject. Nor for many years, did her husband seek an
explanation or offer an apology, perhaps not until Anne's
death. The date of his 'confession', inserted into her diary
for 1883 and his for 1886, is uncertain.

In the long history of my vagrant heart I have said little of
what was my conjugal life at home. This, in spite of my
many lapses, had in reality been quite a happy one. Though
I have loved other women, I have not for that reason been
less kind to my wife, nor has she had cause to reproach me
with the neglect of those duties for which matrimony... was
primarily ordained. No one in truth had ever a stronger
desire for 'the procreation of children'... and yet we had no
heir.

Even here there seems to have been a need for self-
justification, as if Anne was in some way responsible for the
lack of a son. And he sought to justify her exclusion from
the marital bed:

Now, however, the day of such hopes was fairly at an end. I
was forty-two, Anne forty-five; and with the vanishing of
what we have so long desired in common, a certain
estrangement had begun between us, for which I do not in
my conscience think I was seriously to blame.
Nevertheless... the gradual separation... was in secret
making her unhappy.

And finally:

My infidelities she had condoned as due to my poet's nature,
but my inconstancy, for so she deemed it, filled her with
despair... If I did not continue thus to love her, it was proof
that I had never loved her truly.

The 'confession' is unconvincing both as explanation and
apology. It is unlikely that Anne ever openly condoned his
amorous encounters, though she certainly turned a blind
eye to them, preferring to believe that his true affection and
loyalty lay with her. She had more than once in her diaries,
though never to friend or relative, described his sex life as
'despicable'. Once, bringing to the fore that sense of social
priority so carefully inculcated in her by Lady Byron and
her own parents, she remarked that his antics took even her
'well-bred breath away'.

Anne gave her letter to Wilfrid three days after he had slept with Lady Gregory at Crabbet. In the summer of 1883 there were frequent suggestions in her journals of deep unease. 'I am tired... Would that my thoughts could stop – it is unbearable.' Echoing thoughts leapt acrobatically over three generations of her family:

> Conversation about the hearts of poets – who have no hearts by the way, as it all dissolves in vain words. A wound years ago remains a wound forever to me – poor worm of the earth, as long as I live. But those who talk pass unscathed – I don't know which is more despicable – why should any creature have power to wound another?[34]

The stud and her Arabic studies came partly to the rescue and she entertained visitors and attended to her husband's needs as if nothing was amiss. The self-discipline and self-abnegation of childhood served her both badly and well. 'Count & Countess Bobinsky... to see the horses... Their enthusiasm knew no bounds'. Count Josef Potocki, the Polish aristocrat who had bought Pharaoh for £800, came to see his progeny. He was satisfied with Pharaoh and wanted to see if he could purchase his offspring.[35]

Ireland had begun to take the place of Egypt in Wilfrid's mind, and he thought of looking for a suitable parliamentary seat – as a home ruler. Anne was sympathetic but sceptical. 'His whole life of political action has been transparently straight and I doubt the possibility of getting into Parliament without sacrificing that.'

They left for India at the end of August 1883, stopping off at Paris to meet Egyptian nationalists in exile there. They heard talk of rebellion in the Sudan, now controlled from Cairo by the British-run Egyptian army, and of a fanatical leader called the Mahdi.[36]

In Egypt they found a new man in charge, Evelyn Baring; Lord Cromer to be, or 'the Lord' to all who knew him. Anne continued to make notes, carrying scraps of paper in her pockets so that she could scribble at a moment's notice.

Blunt had lunch with Baring at the residency, its garden running down to the Nile. Blunt proposed bringing back the nationalists, including Arabi. 'Out of the question', replied the consul-general. It was, said Blunt, a hopeless cause.

During their last, eventful stay in Cairo they had purchased Sheykh Obeyd, the 37-acre estate they had become so enamoured of near Heliopolis. They had paid £1,500 for it, and for a brief moment the enmity of a few weeks past was forgotten. They called the new home their 'apricot paradise'; Anne could not have known that Wilfrid saw it as a paradise of prospective amorous adventure. Ransacked by the authorities after the 1882 visit, when rifles and a small brass cannon were found and removed, Sheykh Obeyd would remain a memory for the time being as Baring banned Blunt from Egypt for three years after this visit.

On 5 October 1883 they boarded the British India ship *Goorkha* at Suez, and a large community of Anglo-Indian planters came aboard. Anne was struck by their constant shouts of 'Boy! Boy!' whenever they required attention. On the first day out in the Red Sea, Anne sat beside Wilfrid in the early morning breeze sipping tea. Later she went to luncheon wearing a fetching hat. She was subsequently handed a note by a servant which caused her great amusement: 'Madam you are requested not to appear at your meals in your hat and ladies are not allowed on deck before 8 o'clock. A compliance with the above rules is desired.'[37]

Wilfrid was suddenly taken ill on the voyage. Anne reported 'A terrible day and night, more fever and more weakness supported by hope of arrival this evening.' Alas they got into port at Colombo just after sunset, too late to land. By the time they disembarked next day, Wilfrid was seemingly at death's door with malaria; he was revived by his reception, however.

Arabi and his fellow Egyptian nationalists had been exiled to the Sri Lanken capital, and Blunt's reputation had gone before him to the Muslim communities of the subcontinent. He was greeted with joyful familiarity. 'Blunti! Blunti!' Responding to the welcome, he told the crowd that showered him with petals, 'The Muslims have no better friend than I.' He had taken to reading the Koran and had given up wine drinking. Had he not been so ill, he said later, he would have adopted the religion of Islam and 'attained perhaps to the honour of Muhammadan saintship, so great was the devotion of all the community to me.' He was nursed back to sufficient health by Anne's maid Cowie and was able to attend a dinner given in his honour by 450 Muslim grandees. At a farewell breakfast on 10 November, Arabi Pasha toasted Queen Victoria for giving him 'such a pleasant exile.'[38]

They arrived at Calcutta on the 12th. The long train journey to Madras and Hyderabad took a renewed toll on Wilfrid's health, but Anne was in good spirits. By December 1 they were at the stables of Salar Jung, 'like a lofty covered bazaar – horse boxes in a row on either side.' The horses were mostly Australian, and her host remarked that he knew she did not care for Australian horses. There was compensation in a white horse, however, said to be 18 years old but not showing age – 'very like Sherifa and about as fine an Arab horse, taking him all round, as I have ever seen.' He carried himself, she said, with all the fire of youth. Nobody knew the horse's history but Wilfrid thought it must have come from Ibn Saud's stables. Another strong white horse reminded them of Basilisk. The director of Salar Jung's stud told them that the horse resembling Sherifa was indeed from the Ibn Saud stables.[39]

'Did I not say so?' exclaimed Wilfrid.

Salar Jung, son of an ex-prime minister of Hyderabad, was liberal in outlook and seemed to Wilfrid to have the qualities needed to forward the emancipation of the Indian people.

Blunt would put the case for his advancement in the political establishment to Lord Ripon when he returned to Calcutta. For the moment, they moved on to Bombay and more horses.

Back in Calcutta, the Viceroy listened attentively to Blunt's plans for Salar Jung. Minnie Pollen's son Walter was one of Ripon's ADCs, and the Viceroy himself was a Catholic convert. The atmosphere of the meeting could not have been more friendly. The Nizam of Hyderabad was sympathetic to Blunt's schemes, which included a Muslim university to take the place of Cairo's Al Azhar as the centre of Islamic secular learning.

After two months of haggling, during which Blunt was involved in a fracas with the chief medical officer for the Punjab, Brigadier-Surgeon Kerr, over the doctor's blackguardly treatment of Indians, Salar Jung was elected prime minister of his state and the university scheme was approved.

The Nizam invited the Blunts to return the following winter to complete the work Wilfrid had begun so auspiciously. But for Anne, who had been photographed with the Nizam and his prime minister, with the Viceroy in the centre of the picture and the bearded Blunt just behind him, the trip had begun to sour.

> Wilfrid begins to again look much worn and tired and yet he is too independent of any sympathy from me to care about having it, so that I shall no longer venture to make even the smallest advance. I have once or twice wished I could have or hear a look of kindness or a word of the same sort bestowed on me or even in my direction but if I seem to wish such a thing my seeming is as a foreign tongue – it is as hindustani to the Anglo-Indian and I have always repented thus letting out my inferiority of race to one who soars sublime...'[40]

They left Bombay for home on the first day of March 1884, aboard the SS China. The Nizam and his young prime minister soon fell into the indolent ways of Indian politicians, and the reforming Viceroy himself gave up the struggle for change at the end of the year, making way for Lord Dufferin, who favoured the old ways. 'Nothing will be done without a revolution,' said Blunt. The horses they had purchased arrived home via Naples on 28 March, though one of the creatures, named Reformer, died on the voyage.

Anne calculated they had been a total of six months and seventeen days in India. They lunched with the Pollens and Judith and then travelled by train to Three Bridges, the nearest station to Crabbet. The next day, Wilfrid returned to the Pollens in London, and Anne's silent anger turned to irony.

> I believe that Wilfrid dined at Pembridge but my information is not exact or detailed enough to make it safe to more than conjecture what dinners he ate or what friends visited, the only light on his moves that shone on me being through the friends – I hope that he will not afterwards ask me for an account in my journal of important interviews with Weatherby or Knowles or anybody else.[41]

On 26 May she wrote:

> He went to the room downstairs to sleep last night. I am hardly more cut off from him at this antipodes of the house than in his own usual room. The last few months I have ventured to go in and ask how he was in the morning before going to fetch the milk... I wrote and read something to Judith. Then in the afternoon visitors. Wilfrid returned at 8.30. He spoke a few words.

Two months later, Anne's sense of loneliness and isolation seemed to have become unbearable, and she wrote:

> This afternoon Wilfrid took Judith out in the carriage to fish in the forest pond... she is continually asking "Mother, why don't you come? Will you please come this time?" I shall some day be obliged to tell her that her father does not like me to come and only puts up with my presence when it is unavoidable.

Her romantic cousin Edward Noel died soon after their return. He left a note for his widow asking her to support his mistress. Anne called him a 'brute'.[42]

## Chapter Ten

# Political Storms

'He was completely at the mercy of Oriental deceit and Irish blarney and believed every woeful tale of oppression by the British Government, however fantastic. A born agitator, he became an ideal 'bomb thrower' for every schemer who dared not throw his own explosives, and his house soon became famous as a hot-bed of conspiracy for the scum of every nation.' So wrote his daughter Judith, Lady Wentworth, in *The Authentic Arabian Horse*, published in 1945.[1]

Remarkably, Anne was to stand by her husband for another 20 years or more, holding his hand – figuratively at least – as he plunged headlong into the political arena and embraced one revolutionary cause after another, while she tried hard to maintain an atmosphere of normality at home.

Judith, now 11 years old, was an accomplished rider of the Arab steeds divided between the stables of Crabbet and Newbuildings. Anne was delighted that she possessed natural horsemanship, but it was obvious that there was little joy for her daughter in family life. Judith looked on helplessly as her mother's humiliation and her father's arrogance grew, forced to keep her anger from boiling over until her own adulthood. Not until her old age, uninhibited by loyalty to relatives or others who may have had a stake in the Blunt reputation, did she fire off some of the fiercest salvos that can ever have enlivened a daughter's account of her father. She called her mother's continued devotion 'a record of heroic self sacrifice', but she had to confess there was a quality of 'abjectness' in it.

She wrote of her mother's unbounded kindness of heart, but obsessed that she was no match for the intrigues by which 'her natural gentleness was exploited'. Again, 'her instinctive patriotism was no match for the all-dominating creed of subservience to a superior personality in which even the very sense of self-preservation was lost.' It should be said on Blunt's behalf that he never regarded self-preservation as a particularly high priority in political life. Other values came to haunt him, though.[2]

In 1882, at the height of the Egyptian crisis, Mrs Georgie Sumner reminded him of one of his indiscretions back in the early 1870s, when he had left her pregnant with what turned out to be the long-desired male child. By 1884, he had paid two years' boarding school fees for the boy, who had been named Berkeley. Blunt was of course using Anne's depleted resources. He had not been allowed to see the child, however, and declined to make further advances unless allowed to do so. Georgie, who like Anne had become deeply religious, refused and the payments ceased.[3]

Judith had become another bone of contention. Blunt treated his daughter as if she were the son he had been denied in marriage, taking her on long arduous hunting and fishing expeditions, forcing her to jump fences that were too high for so young a rider and laughing uproariously when she fell and hurt herself. Judith, tall and athletic, responded as she was expected to, with phlegm, never admitting to hurt or shedding tears.[4] There was the odd social call to keep Blunt busy during the fallow months between their return from the east and the next trip. In August 1883 he went to stay at Naworth Castle at the invitation of Rosalind Howard. They went on to join William Morris and Janey, the notable beauty he had married in 1859, who had been immortalised by Rossetti. Blunt was to comment that she was 'a loveable and noble woman, but he [Morris] knew he had never touched her heart.' Blunt set out to put that matter to rights at the first meeting. He noted afterwards that though Janey was 'still a beautiful woman', she was 'already on the decline'.[5]

Through the spring and summer of 1884, Anne waited for word of their next journey. Eventually he spoke, telling her they would go to Constantinople on 15 September, return for the autumn and go away again for Christmas. 'I really think Wilfrid would get on more to his satisfaction without me if it is too much trouble to say even one word. Like the Armenian Hajji in the desert "Je ne demande pas un diner complet."' She was constrained to ask herself what would have become of her had she not been of independent means. Trying to discuss these personal matters was, she wrote, like 'writing on the waters'.[6]

Paris provided a resting place to catch up on the missing days of her diary. Judith had looked pale and sad at their latest parting. 'This time she feels our going more than ever before.'

Wilfrid went ahead of her to Paris, and she had said goodbye to Judith and Minnie Pollen at James Street. There was no sign of Wilfrid at the Gare du Nord. She found him instead on the stairs of the Hotel St Romain. They took the Orient Express to Vienna and were advised to seek out the 'wonderful Arab horses' of a Polish nobleman, General Langiewitz, when they reached Constantinople. They took a circuitous route, however, so as to visit the stables of the Potockis at Lancut in what was then Russian Poland.

September 22nd (and by the way my birthday) in the train approaching Cracow... At one o'clock stopped at Lancut and were met by Count Joseph Potocki and his brother-in-law and two carriages and in the hurry of getting out and pleasure of meeting, Wilfrid left his little red pillow in the train. Countess Alfred Potocki – whom I had not seen before – was a Princess Sanguscko and through her comes the Sanguscko stud. Her father Prince Sanguscko was for many years at forced labour in Siberia... He died three years ago – there seems to be no improvement in the state of Russia under the present Emperor... How shall I describe Lancut – it would take pages and pictures – there is so much. A château with a high roof and many windows – you drive under an archway – on the left is the entrance. Before entering the door you look round and see on each side very handsome old guns – belonging to former Potockis... Up the stairs and through a long gallery with full-length portraits of Potockis – the one that struck me most was that of the Potocki killed at the siege of Vienna by the Turks...There is only one arab horse here, a little bay we saw in the stable... The stud itself is in Russia about ten hours railway from here...[7]

Anne was surprised to find that the director, Brzizicki, who had been in his post for 18 years, was 'rather an incubus not up to the mark' who neither remembered about pedigrees nor always obeyed orders. She was startled too by the household servants who accompanied the Potockis between their widely separated estates, most of whom were specially-bred and trained dwarfs. Her journal was written up as they travelled, with detailed essays on the Sanguscko stud at Antonin, the pedigree of every mare and foal carefully noted along with its markings. She was particularly interested in the 'four-in-hand' horses and concluded that there was hardly an animal without a flaw: 'The result however is very interesting in spite of the cross blood we here see the distinct Arab type, and the mares are a splendid collection and appear to be remarkably sound.'

They went on to Turkey via Odessa. Wilfrid, enlivened by the journey, planned to go on to Sebastopol 'and I know not what'. At Constantinople they waited patiently for a promised audience with the Sultan Abdul Hamid, 'Abdul the Damned', but the royal command never came. The Sultan gave orders instead that they should be given red-carpet treatment at the Topkapi.

To Anne's delight they found the stud of General Langiewitz at Scutari and were gratified that he had heard of them and their establishment. Wilfrid had been silent for much of the journey, but on the way to Therapia his usual taciturnity in Anne's presence deserted him and they began to talk of Christianity and Islam, of God and 'absolute truth'. Anne wrote:

> My question I cannot remember but only that his answer to it, putting everything of the sort aside as neither possible nor quite needful, made me feel as Paul in his dream, when he dreamt that he saw all the nations of the universe assembled and our Lord appearing to them only to say 'there was no God' – on which the whole universe was filled with wailing and anguish. Unfortunately the moment of anguish soon passed for me – at least for the time – after the first great disillusion – and I tried to be satisfied with what my chosen guide (for I believed in his guidance) led me to: nothing at all in fact.

They returned home in time for Christmas; in time for Anne to make amends for a neglected diary. November 15:

> These words written with purple pencil so long ago... it is now December 6th and from that day to this I have not put down a single word about how the time has been spent. There is something discouraging when you come home and find... But I had determined to complain no more.

Wilfrid took Judith riding and kept her out after dark in the rain, though she had just recovered from a cold. Anne's fears were dismissed. 'Nonsense! It did the girl good to get wet.'

Bullying was accompanied by a new gambit. 'I have now got to the age when I like to be amused without giving myself much trouble, and there are several women who amuse me, I don't care which of them it is, but I must have someone. There is Lady Gregory, Mrs Batten, Mrs Thurlow, Mrs Singleton, etc., I don't mind which of them.'

From a position of wretched pusillanimity Anne wrote: 'I don't agree to Lady G. having all the rose leaves while the thorns are kept for me.'

Before leaving for Constantinople, Blunt had thrown his opportunist's hat into the political ring, seeking a seat in Parliament as the member for any likely grouping of the disaffected. 'Home Rule for Everyone' was, as Judith would observe in years to come, 'his general policy'.[8] An invitation to a party given by Gladstone in June convinced him that he had re-established some rapport with the prime minister. Anne declared that the GOM's handshake 'seemed to pass me on or hand me on, as it were'.[9] A month earlier, Gordon had been under siege at Khartoum and Blunt had offered himself as a mediator with the Mahdi. Gladstone had replied briefly, 'No.' Blunt responded with a description of the prime minister as 'a pedant, a babbler, an impotent old fool'.[10] In response to his efforts to enter politics in an active role, H. M. Hyndman invited him to join the Social Democratic Federation, a tempting transition but one that would have guaranteed the political wilderness.[11] All the same, he was flattered. Lyulph Stanley – Lord Stanley of Alderley – atheist and anarchist, formed an alliance with Blunt on a number of anti-imperialist issues, and since both believed in free trade, free love and free almost anything, they had a good deal to agree about.[12] In the end however, Blunt embraced Lord Randolph Churchill's 'Tory democrats'. When he asked Lord Randolph what a Tory democrat was, the reply did not exactly surprise him. 'To tell the truth I don't know myself what Tory democracy is.' Still, Parnell had promised him a solid Irish vote if he stood as a 'Nationalist' and home ruler on the Churchill ticket. Randolph suggested that he should find a vaguer description for home rule as, 'we haven't educated the party up to it yet.'

Skittles returned to the scene to ensure that Blunt's views were put discreetly to Gladstone and the Prince of Wales[13] but in 1885 Gladstone's administration fell and Salisbury's official Tories came to power, depending for their majority on the Irish vote. The change looked propitious for Wilfrid. His friends were now in the highest places and he went off to meet some of them at the Salisbury Club, located in the imposing house of Anne's birth. For her the irony was complete.

> I should have liked to go... for the reason, perhaps foolish, that I am curious to see the inside of 10 St James's Square, the Salisbury Club, where it took place... I was born in that house and all my earliest recollections are there. None of them very delightful except that of my aunt Hester [Stanhope] coming and telling stories of her travels to us, the children. And of the room she slept in; her coming being a joy. Then I recollect being naughty when a music master... came, and having crawled under the piano on all fours saying I was 'the Queen's horse' – I remember where the piano stood, and how the chairs had brown holland covers on. Also the nursery memories of our three beds in a row, and our all three jumping up as soon as the nurses were gone... and our having steeplechases over the ditches between the beds... With all this I can't remember even thinking what was right or wrong in itself, it was whether we should be punished or not for this or that with no sense at all of guilt on my part. Then Ralph being ill and the object of much care and my wishing to be ill too in order to be thought of and Byron having a mutton chop for breakfast and my hungry glances at this and my joy when now and then he did not cut it and I was allowed to have it – a constant hunger was one of my recollections...[14]

Perhaps memories of the nursery had become confused, or telescoped with stories told her by her mother for, as has already been noted, Aunt Hester died within two years of Anne's birth. She had certainly been a welcome visitor to Ada's several childhood homes in the early years of the 19th century, and Anne's recollections of austerity also ring true.

Horses and domestic animals still offered escape from marital grievances, but even they sometimes brought sadness and invidious choices. Once the maid Cowie found Judith at the stables waiting patiently for her parents to return from a trip. 'I see you are still alone,' said Cowie. 'Of course, horses before children,' Judith replied. On another occasion Anne wrote in her diary: 'My little dog Chloe died the night before last... I cannot understand why, as she seemed [to be] recovering. Poor Chloe! I have never seen such soul in a dog – she understood too well – too well to live, perhaps.' Again: 'This is the last canter Webb will ride here – for he goes to Australia with Kars and Hadban, and these weeks are overshadowed by the regret of parting with Kars.'[15]

For Wilfrid, the summer months were overshadowed by political misfortune. He hoped that the Tories in the London borough of Southwark would adopt him as their candidate for the approaching general election but Anne's cousin 'Master Button' Bourke pulled the rug from under him by putting forward his brother Mayo, leaving the unhappy Blunt to try Camberwell. A meeting in that constituency ended in fisticuffs after Wilfrid addressed it on 'Tory socialism'. The politics of the madhouse took over with a vengeance when on another occasion, after a harangue calling for the virtual dismemberment of the British empire, the crowd sang 'Rule, Britannia!' in honour of Blunt, Randolph Churchill and Tory democracy. He was adopted, and the scent of this initial victory was heady. 'I have a conviction that I shall carry all before me, or why should this opportunity have been placed before me?'[16]

By September, canvassing was in progress. Anne went almost daily to Camberwell but her husband spoke hardly a word to her in the two months they were together. After the event she wrote: 'November 9th, a Monday, is the last day of which I have any record – it was the last on which I had time for anything but the ceaseless grind of Camberwell, up to November 27th, the polling day.'

The carefully nursed constituency was hit with a characteristic broadside by Blunt in the second week of November. He announced his total support for Irish home rule and for Parnell. Salisbury was dumbfounded. The party had gone along with Blunt's unpopular views on Egypt, India and Burma. Tory democracy was one thing, open support of an anti-British revolutionary cause another. Even his sponsor and friend Randolph Churchill was no longer able to regard Blunt as a political ally. Party and electorate began to desert a candidate who, except for that one indiscretion, would almost certainly have been elected.

On polling day Anne drove around the constituency with her husband in an open carriage, looking every inch the devoted and elegant wife of a major political figure. Blunt always overestimated his chances, but the defeat was a narrow one. The electorate was divided almost down the middle. He lost by 162 votes. Even at this bitter moment, when Anne might have gained quiet satisfaction from his having been put in his place for once, she showed her loyalty, attributing defeat to party mismanagement and treachery. Wilfrid thought the anti-Catholic vote decisive. 'I take defeat as final,' he wrote. Churchill told him that if he wanted home rule he would have to go to Gladstone for it. 'We cannot touch it.'

On 23 March 1886, Blunt suddenly announced that he was leaving for Ireland, 'alone, alone. I never thought it would come to this.' He was feeling very sorry for himself, and conscious of approaching old age. He was 45. Anne had refused to go with him, and even the devoted Minnie failed to turn up to see him off. Paranoia began to set in. 'In public life I have striven to do justly and the world is full of my enemies. In the world of my own life I have striven to be loved, and none loves me – not one.'[17]

His daughter looked back on this period of her family life to quote an anonymous observer of her father's conduct: 'He has a way of kicking you downstairs, and then carrying on as if his life wasn't safe.'[18]

Ireland was in a familiar state of turmoil. Blunt found the land war at its ferocious height and the Catholic clergy rampant for home rule. The Archbishop of Dublin, Dr Walsh, was unable to contain himself as he predicted the doom of landlordism. The battle of Aughrim against William of Orange was conjured by the Bishop of Clonfert. 'They call it the last battle but the battle is still going on,' said Blunt. 'They adore Davitt here, as Arabi used to be adored in Egypt.' Davitt was founder of the radical Land League. Most of the nationalist MPs were at Westminster, where Gladstone's ill-fated home rule bill was being debated. Press publicity greeted every statement Blunt uttered.[19]

When he arrived home in April even his mistresses had turned against him. First Egypt, now Ireland. What next? Lady Gregory was up in arms and Skittles reported that the Prince of Wales was 'very angry'. Cousin Button said that everyone was angry about his comments on Lord Kingston's evictions. Blunt thought their anger meant that he had 'hit them hard' and was pleased with his efforts. He was not so pleased to receive a cheque from a 'benefactor of the Sussex peasants'. It was for three guineas and was signed by George Meredith. Blunt's friend Wilde once said of Meredith, 'As a writer he mastered everything but language' but on this occasion he had made his point well. Blunt instructed his land agent to lower one or two rents on the estate. 'It will not do to neglect the mote in my own eye while plucking the beam out of Lord Kingston's.'

A huge blow to his new political cause came in June, despite Gladstone's famous speech in which he pleaded so prophetically with the House to 'think not for the moment, but for the years that are to come.' By a slender majority the vote was lost, chiefly because of Liberal waverers. For the moment, Anne allowed things to simmer and got on with the care of Judith, the horses and Crabbet. Blunt found comfort in another Irish tour and with the ever-accommodating Skittles.

Ireland was to be the focus of his attention from now on, but in the meantime he had need of spiritual refreshment. Perhaps Ireland had given him renewed faith. He resolved to take himself 'to that third and concluding phase of all rational existence, the life contemplative.'

The family went to Rome for Christmas, and on 2 January 1887, Anne joyfully received communion at the side of the husband, who was not quite sure whether to embrace Islam or Catholicism, or neither.[20]

Having obtained special permission from Evelyn Baring, they went on to Egypt, but Blunt's exclusion was not to be regarded as forgotten. Prime Minister Salisbury had serious reservations about the desirability of letting the firebrand loose again in the country, though he relented as Baring had no objection. The first three months of 1887 – at Sheykh Obeyd, camping in the desert, attending race meetings and meeting old friends – helped to restore a rapport of sorts. Anne was her old self for the moment and so Egypt was restored to her favour.[21]

'The air full of sounds – camels grumbling, sheep bleating people shouting, girls trilling, guns firing.' The pilgrim caravan was assembling for its long journey to the holy cities of the Hejaz. They even corresponded with Mr Dickson, the consul in Jerusalem, about a grey horse belonging to one Ibn al-Derri. Dickson was authorised to pay up to £150 for the celebrated grey plus two other colts or mares, if their messenger Zaid could find suitable beasts.

On 6 February Anne thought of Judith, whose birthday had come round again, her 14th. In contemplation she played her violin under an orange tree; 'it was delightful – a perfect afternoon.' They had seen the squat-faced Henry Stanley in Cairo, and Blunt hoped the journalist-explorer might leave his bones halfway between there and Zanzibar; Europe's only contribution to Africa so far, Blunt said, being 'fire-arms, drink and syphilis'.

Sheykh Obeyd, its gardens restored to their full glory, was left in the care of a Muslim friend. They departed for home on 20 March, feeling to the last moment that they were being followed by spies.

The British government was making another desperate bid to solve the Irish question, putting forward a 'coercion' bill designed to force the country into cooperation; if that failed, the Salisbury administration recognised that home rule would be the only answer. On Easter Monday 1887, Blunt took part in a massive Hyde Park demonstration against the bill. Blunt rode one of his Arabian steeds onto the platform at another meeting, where he took the chair and T. P. O'Connor spoke. A rival socialist platform was graced by Michael Davitt and May Morris, daughter of Janey and William. Blunt had become an accomplished speaker, master of all the platform tricks, and even the women's suffrage movement made use of his splendid voice, though in their case he maintained an attitude of friendly neutrality. The Oxford Union followed as a matter of course.

In July, Cardinal Manning persuaded Blunt to return to Ireland to explain the agrarian question to the papal envoy who was on his way to Dublin. He dallied at home for a brief flirtation with Dora Swinburne, the 21-year-old daughter of Sir John Swinburne, and to form a new club, the Crabbet, devoted to 'convivial association', and intended to 'discourage serious views of life by holding up a constant standard of its amusements.' He then set off on his third visit to Ireland. On the 19th he met Monsignor Persico, the Pope's representative, at the palace of the Archbishop of Dublin. The papal envoy, a diplomat of the old school, posed the large question facing all reformers who turn to revolutionary means. 'How should people behave when the law is bad, until it was repealed?' Blunt avoided the question and concentrated on the justice of the peasants' fight, adding as an afterthought, 'There is no means of forcing attention except by breaking the law.'[22]

Back at Crabbet at the end of July, Blunt pledged his support for a campaign to bring Irish tenants into open hostility with their landlords. John Dillon, William O'Brien and Tim Harrington were the three leaders of the campaign. Blunt had offered the sickly Dillon a holiday at Sheykh Obeyd, and promised the Irishman his support for the programme based on the proposition that tenants should offer their landlords a fair rent. If the offer was refused, the money would be paid into a national fund. The Conservatives' defeat of Gladstone's Liberals the year before had brought a new Irish secretary, Arthur Balfour, to Whitehall and he was in uncompromising mood.

Blunt's time of trouble over Ireland did not soften his attitude at home. In the first week of August, Anne had written to Ralph and his wife Mary (he had by then been married to his second wife for seven years) to discuss her plans for the working men's club she had decided to finance as a memorial to her grandmother. On 12 August she was compelled to write to Ralph to ask urgently for the return of the letter 'as Wilfrid demands sight of it'.

At about this time Anne, Wilfrid and Judith went together to Clouds, the family home of the Wyndhams and, for the moment, of Madeline's daughter Mary, Lady Elcho, who had been one of Anne's bridesmaids. Blunt decided she was the most beautiful woman in the world.[23] The Marchioness of Queensberry, another cousin for whom he had entertained a childhood fancy, was also there, with her son 'Bosie', Lord Alfred Douglas. George Wyndham was private secretary to Balfour at the Irish Office. At Clouds Blunt met Balfour, who was devoted to Mary, along with the novelist Henry James. When they had finished discussing the Irish question, with James 'trying hard to keep up with the talk but always a little behind hand', Blunt decided that Tory policy was based entirely on aggressive racialism, a pseudo-scientific belief in the survival of the fittest deriving from an unwarranted deduction from Darwinism. Balfour he thought 'cynical'. He feared for his friend Dillon.

Blunt was entertaining Rosalind Howard at Naworth when news came of a police clampdown in County Cork in which two people had been shot and killed. He rushed off to Ireland to the scene of the action and spent two days with Dillon and Davitt at Mitchelstown where the shootings had occurred. 'I have so often resolved to wait for the first blood and now it has been shed,' he wrote. And again: 'I cursed my country with its red coats and black coats and its absurd truculent ministers of an infamous law.'[24]

He returned to Dublin on 14 October and telegraphed Anne to join him. On the 15th he went to Limerick with O'Brien without waiting for Anne. Meetings were held in Limerick to throw the police off the scent, and then Blunt and his Irish confederates, together with the English MP Rowlands and two journalists, went to Woodford in Galway.[25] As they approached the town, the surrounding countryside burst into flame from gorse fires and turf flares. The telegraph wires had been cut. The government proclamation banning meetings in their area was publicly burnt by O'Brien. Blunt and Rowlands made impassioned speeches.

By now Anne and Cowie had joined Wilfrid, and with characteristic thoroughness she made notes of preliminary court proceedings which began next day at Wexford, in furtherance of Balfour's 'no mercy' policy concerning evictions. Edward Carson appeared for the Crown, Tim Healy MP for the defence. No sooner had the magistrate's hearing been adjourned than news came of more evictions in the Woodford area.[26]

Blunt took Anne with him this time as he sped off to organise an anti-eviction meeting. On the night of the 21st a telegram arrived from O'Brien telling them that the government had specifically banned Blunt from speaking. Wilfrid and Anne slept at the home of a nationalist militant named Roche. The host's children, used as military-style scouts, reported a large police presence and a company of Scots Guards. A proclamation accusing Blunt of intended intimidation and breach of the peace, signed by the Lord Lieutenant and Arthur Balfour, was posted on the town bridge. Blunt tore it down and then drafted his own proclamation for the benefit of the police and the officer commanding the Scots Guards. 'I do not recognise the right of the Lord Lieutenant causelessly to interfere with a meeting convened by orderly Englishmen.' He added that his purpose was to encourage the victims of Lord Clanricarde's rapacity 'to a steadfast patience and endurance of their wrongs.'

As soon as Blunt took his place on the platform at the anti-eviction meeting, Major Byrne the magistrate appeared and asked him, 'Are you the Mr Blunt whose name is on the handbills?' When Blunt admitted his identity, the magistrate told him it was his duty to prevent the meeting. Blunt replied that it was his duty to hold it. As Blunt began his address the police stormed the platform. Anne and Mrs Rowlands pushed from the platform, together with the men. Anne clambered back up with Wilfrid who began his speech again with the words, 'Men of Galway!' Another charge followed. Blunt fought with the police and they all toppled over the edge. Several policemen pulled at Wilfrid's overcoat and Anne noted that the garment was 'astonishingly strong'. The magistrate grabbed Anne by the throat and nearly asphyxiated her as he tried to separate her from her husband.

'Thanks be to God, I was able to hold firm,' she wrote afterwards. A policeman twisted Blunt's arm until he yelled something about torture having been abolished. He lay down passively. 'Let him go or you will kill him,' Anne screamed, believing him to be unconscious. Blunt added fuel to the fire by shouting to the police, 'Are you all such damned cowards that none of you will arrest me?' The police sergeant was equal to the challenge.

'It's all right now,' Blunt told Anne as he was marched off with Roche. The case came up on 24 October before two magistrates, one a 'bookie' soon to be arrested himself, the other a grocer. Carson appeared again for the Crown. Blunt was sentenced to two months' imprisonment and immediately lodged an appeal, having been refused permission to cross-summons Byrne and Balfour. He was released on bail and returned with Anne to London. He had been blooded at the sharp end of political struggle.

Looking back on the incident, Blunt regarded it as one that 'deserves to be remembered in Irish history'. He was gracious enough to say also that it was most rare at that time for a woman to take part in 'political scrambles'. He showed off in a letter to Judith but did not mention her mother's role, though she was nearly throttled and was hit on the wrist by a stone.

When Wilfrid decided to stand for Deptford as 'Anti-Coercion Conservative' candidate, Anne declared that 'political mania' had gripped him.[27] All the same she was soon playing her dutiful part, canvassing the riverside electorate. Neither local Conservatives nor the electors in general seemed happy with the firebrand foisted on them. Blunt was heartened by letters of support from Minnie Pollen and Skittles however, and most especially by a note from Janey Morris in which she told him that she had dined the night before with the Burne-Joneses, who were loud in his praise. As a nominal and somewhat fickle Conservative, Blunt must have been heartened, and wryly amused too, by Sir William Harcourt's remark that his popularity with the Liberals was second only to Gladstone's.

The sentence for the Woodford misdemeanour was confirmed by a higher court in January 1888. Anne sat in court taking notes and illuminating her record with drawings of the defendants and the prosecuting counsel – Carson. The prosecution reminded the court that Woodford was a place of crime and murder and that the agent of Blunt's opponent Lord Clanricarde, had been shot the previous year. The defence barrister MacDermot ridiculed police evidence in the magistrates' court that as Blunt fell to the ground a constable heard his wife whisper the word 'conspiracy'.[28]

The verdict, all the same, went to the other side, and the judge had no hesitation in awarding the culprit two months' hard labour. 'With deepest pain I must confirm the sentence of the court below.' The judge also wondered about Blunt's 'good feeling as to the risks to life and limb – of the danger to the lady.' Anne accompanied him to Galway gaol. Balfour had threatened to kill off the nationalist leaders in prison, and though the remark was not to be taken too literally, Anne wrote that her husband was on his way to 'prepare for death – for two months anyway, and maybe for altogether.' They spoke Arabic to each other on the way to the prison in the manner of two people who shared a secret, and crowds gathered to cheer them, to bless Wilfrid, and to execrate Balfour. As their omnibus drew up at the gates, mounted police with drawn swords brought up the rear. They were allowed to say their goodbyes inside the prison. That night in her hotel Anne dreamt of the events that had led to Wilfrid's imprisonment and of the police onslaught, waking her maid Cowie who slept next door. The Irish troubles had highlighted another side of the ladylike Anne's character, an aspect that had shown itself clearly in childhood – a delight in action spiced with a little danger.

Blunt resolved to take out a civil action against the magistrate Byrne in the Dublin courts, and looked forward to his next political contest, the Deptford by-election, and to another confrontation with Irish justice.[29] A distinguished team of barristers, including H. H. Asquith, had told him that he had a good case against Byrne and Balfour. Anne returned to Ireland for the appeal hearing, which opened on 11 February, and they were photographed together, she in jacket and bonnet, he in prison jacket (his overcoat had been taken away by the authorities in a celebrated act of vindictiveness). Wilfrid described the photograph of Anne as the 'best likeness ever taken of her'. His action was rejected by the court on a deciding vote and he returned to prison to finish his sentence. The contest at Deptford, where news of the rejection of his suit was well known, was left to Anne and the Pollens, who worked like demons on Wilfrid's behalf and found the poor of Deptford 'wonderfully nice'. 'The Anti-Coercion' candidate, opposed by an official Unionist and deserted by his friends, even by Cardinal Manning, was defeated eventually by 275 votes in a poll of over 8,000. *The Times* commented, without mentioning Blunt's name, that Englishmen were repelled by 'martyrdom'.[30]

Blunt was released on 6 March, 'in a spirit of revolt against all society'. Anne took him for drives around Dublin in the few days following. The marriage might have been saved in Ireland, a country Blunt had come to admire as devotedly as he had previously admired Egypt and which Anne found congenial. They even looked for an estate where they might found a new Crabbet stud. But it came to nothing and disillusion soon set in for them both.

In retrospect, Blunt regarded his term of imprisonment as penance rather than punishment, as a kind of spiritual retreat, 'a softening influence on my life'. Oscar Wilde thought it made him a better writer, converting 'a clever rhymer into an earnest and deep-thinking poet'.[31] Gladstone had written to him kindly during his captivity and saw the possibility of using Blunt's popularity among radicals in his next Liberal campaign.

He went back to Ireland, accompanied again by Anne, in early June. It was to be the last visit.[32] On 26 June, back at Crabbet, he was in a gloomy frame of mind and wrote his political epitaph: 'Here ends the History of my political life'. Although this period was to prove the start of a renewed interest in the pursuit of the opposite sex, Wilfrid, at the age of 48, was also worried about grey hairs appearing in his beard.

Anne's journals had become spasmodic, often with several blank months. The gaps in the record of her life were the result of the growing estrangement from Wilfrid, who had been the focus of her attention for so long, but they were not indicative of a defeated spirit. Church and faith sustained her, and her Arabic studies had reached the point where she could claim genuine scholarship in language and Islamic history. There was an increasing flow of distinguished Arab visitors to Crabbet, to see the now-famous horses and to discuss with her the poetry, religion and history of Islam. Her records of the pedigrees of her own Arabs and of the breed in general had become voluminous, and would prove in the course of time to be her chief claim to fame, though at this point her studies in equine history were for Judith's benefit, designed to provide her daughter with a complete record of the stud she would inherit.

Another event of the year 1887 helps to explain Anne's long silences. While she was embroiled in Ireland, her brother Ralph had printed privately and circulated within the family a document called 'Lady Byron and the Leighs'.[33] It told, from their grandmother's correspondence with

Augusta, the one-sided story of the separation and illuminated Lady Byron's relationship with Augusta and her children, particularly Medora and Marie. It was an incomplete story however, since Lord Lovelace still had in his keeping some important correspondence. As long as the document remained within the family, Anne was not too concerned, though she may well have suffered qualms of conscience over Medora's daughter Marie. Blunt asked Ralph, should he ever decide to make the disclosures public – as he did when he eventually took possession of Lovelace's papers – not to be too hard on Lord Byron.

Not until the autumn of 1888 is there a revival of Anne's painstaking daily recollection of events. Wilfrid's waning political fortunes had been counterbalanced by another passion, this time for Blanche Hozier, mother of four children including Clementine, who was destined to marry Winston Churchill.[34]

Anne penned a final note on the Irish question, commenting that the Primroses had 'ripened into Oranges'. Home rulers were 'falling like ninepins'.[35]

## Chapter Eleven

# Love is Two-edged

Blunt was not slow to follow up a pressing invitation from Rosalind to Castle Howard. Blanche Hozier would be there and Rosalind promised frivolity 'in abundance'.[1] Lady Blanche had married the divorced Henry Hozier, to the surprise of society, in place of the 'other woman' cited in the courts. That marriage had witnessed four children, two girls (Kitty and Clementine) fathered by a cavalier Austro-Hungarian, and twin boys whose paternity Hozier denied.[2]

Such a femme fatale was just what Wilfrid needed in the depressing aftermath of Ireland and Deptford, and by July 1888 Blanche and he had moved off to her little cottage in Forfarshire.

By September Blanche was committing her passion to paper. 'I want you – so much, so much, your pleasant talk – your kindness – your dear and beautiful face to look at.' He had written her a torrent of love letters, but he was becoming anxious lest there should be another scandal and he asked her to send back his letters and to use 'restrained language' when she wrote to him. A domestic drama proved a timely diversion.[3]

Judith was complaining of the attentions of the Pollens' 22-year-old son Arthur. He and Judith had been brought up in close proximity at Newbuildings, Crabbet and Pembroke Villas and they had written innocent, affectionate letters to each other over the years. Now at 15, the tall attractive Judith held a more powerful attraction for Arthur, and he kissed her, held her hand and professed his love. Judith had come to dislike Minnie and now spoke of her son Arthur as 'vulgar'. The young man's actions could hardly be described as offensive, but Anne, only too well aware of a family history of youthful grand passions, was worried. At first Blunt treated the matter quite sensibly as one of calf love. In any event, several of the Pollen boys were interested in Judith. But he used the incident for his own tortuous ends.

He had tired of Minnie Pollen but wanted to finish the relationship on grounds other than sexual disenchantment. He already had marriage plans for Judith, which he had confided to Minnie rather than Anne, involving a squire he had met at Kidderminster during a political campaign, 'an arrangement which appealed to my imagination as consonant with Arabian ideas where a return to some faraway strain of kindred blood is so much in fashion.' But there was a more material reason for Blunt's taking up his wife's call to raise the matter with Minnie. He wanted the Pollens out of Newbuildings.

The Pollens had fallen on hard times. Impoverished and unable to afford sufficient fuel to heat their grace-and-favour home in winter, they were eventually evicted not on the excuse that their son had become a menace to Judith, but because, Blunt insisted, he wanted to sell or let Newbuildings. All the same, there was for Anne at least the worry of the boys and Judith. Anne recorded 'floods of Billingsgate' from Minnie. Arthur Pollen spoke with calculated irony of 'the great eviction'. Perhaps not all bad landlords were to be found in Ireland.[4]

Blunt ranted and raved, more perhaps from conscience than anger, and Anne gave vent to her feelings in the language that had come to represent her route of escape. In Arabic scrawl she wrote, 'I must listen to my own child, when distressed.'[5]

Years later, in an essay entitled *Myself and Others*, Judith (quoted by Blunt's biographer Lady Longford), presented her revealing version of the story:

> A terrific parental explosion followed the discovery of the rival lovers, in which high words of blame revealed the possibility that one young Apollo was my half brother – an extraordinary resemblance to my Father's outstanding good looks seemed to confirm this. In a storm of vituperation the families parted and I was summarily removed to Egypt...[6]

Judith claimed that four of the seven Pollen boys had fallen in love with her at different times. At least the cause of her mother's concern was made apparent.

A month after the storm Blunt left for Greece and Egypt with Anne and Judith in train, and with the delights of Blanche very much on his mind. They were at Marseille on 16 November 1888, and arrived in Greece to celebrate Byron's birthday on the 28th.[7] Blunt read *Childe Harold* to Judith, and the daughter of the Greek patriot Tricoupi, who had orated at the poet's funeral, showed Anne a miniature of her grandfather given to Tricoupi by the Duke of Sussex. Ada had asked to see it before she died, but the message could not be conveyed to Greece in time. They met some Noels at Achmetaga, and Anne painted the hill opposite Kandili mountain where her illustrious ancestor had roamed, 'all shining in the sun', before the family left Piraeus on the Khedival steamer for Alexandria and what turned out to be a terrifying voyage. A massive wave carried away one of the lifeboats, and the ladies were disturbed by a 'monster' who carried onions, wore a fez and fought with a Greek. He was in fact Sarah Bernhardt's theatrical agent.

They were in Cairo on 1 January 1889, and before Judith could draw breath she was taken by her mother to Ali Pasha Sherif's stables. Wilfrid had gone on to Sheykh Obeyd.[8]

Anne and Judith's delight in being able to visit Cairo's finest stud and ride together was tempered by the apparent decline of Ali Pasha's fortunes. 'I am afraid Ali Pasha's stud will soon be a thing of the past. It seems to me if he once begins to break it up and is in the hands of creditors it cannot last.'

Blunt planned extensive changes to the buildings and gardens of Sheykh Obeyd, and by 31 January the foundations of the new house had been laid and oxen were ploughing and pulling trees from the gardens ready for replanting. As the ladies arrived on the scene preparations were being made for killing a lamb to commemorate the laying of the first stone of the house. Anne averted her gaze.

Anne's diary filled with anniversaries and journeys. On 6 February the family gathered in the grounds of their Cairo home to celebrate Judith's 16th birthday. She was presented with a colt by her proud parents. Wilfrid gave her an Aleppo headstall. Anne knew that payment had been made from a cheque she had written for horse purchases, but she was happy if it pleased Wilfrid. 'This, Judith says, is the happiest birthday she ever spent, and I am sure I never spent such happy days as now.' Ali Pasha Sherif, generous even in the relative poverty of his last years, made a present of rose trees and vine cuttings for the garden.

The euphoria lasted a few more days. Local riding companions proved congenial and Judith had become attached to them and the animals, but they had to move on – 'our last day here, then goodbye to orange flowers and the three chestnuts and Zeyd and the pale cow and calf and Abu.' By late March they were in Hungary seeking more horses, this time from Prince Roman Sanguszko's stable. Restless to see Paris again, and to take up old liaisons in

England, Wilfrid then went on alone, leaving Anne and Judith with instructions to make a leisurely way home, stopping off at Venice.[9]

They eventually reached England and Crabbet on 27 April to find Blunt in a depressed mood, thinking nostalgically of Galway gaol and his brief martyrdom. He was ageing and convinced that his life was 'in decline'.[10]

Anne went to London on a shopping expedition and ran into Arthur Pollen at the Army and Navy stores. The young man accused her of maligning his family to friends. Anne, unaccustomed to public dispute, lost her composure for a moment and denied the charge angrily. Wilfrid, who certainly had taken to maligning the family that he had once regarded as his own, removed himself to London in May, and on the 28th Anne picked him up at his club to go on to dinner at the London home of Sir Charles Russell, who had been his counsel in the Irish affair, 'a remarkable and historical dinner party'. London's entire political and intellectual élite seemed to be there and Gladstone offered Anne his arm. 'I was immensely surprised but not at all sorry.' Anne told the GOM charmingly that she felt alarm 'at the prominent position and honour' that fell to her lot. She couldn't help thinking that he usually 'feared my trying to get some political remarks out of him and that he wished to avoid talking to me.' On this occasion he talked 'with great liveliness about everything under the sun', everything, it appeared, 'except politics'. Wilfrid was concerned about his host's wife, Adeline, whose love of poetry he was shortly to turn to personal advantage.[11]

Another grand old man arrived at Crabbet two days later. 'Old Mr Weatherby is over 80... came from Eastbourne... to spend the day looking at the horses.' Weatherby had talked about buying an Arab but seemed put off by the shoulders of the animals he studied. In August Blanche Hozier and her family arrived for a short stay, but as luck would have it Wilfrid was away. The daughters and Judith momentarily took over from horse genealogy and physiognomy in Anne's diary. 'Kitty is very nice, but I think the little one Clemmie still nicer and less spoilt.'

A familiar matter consumed her husband. He was looking around for a replacement for Minnie, and the William Morris household provided an immediate answer in the shape of Janey. He said that they had 'loved each other on and off' for some nine years up to this point, though there is little evidence that they had seen much of each other since their encounter in 1883, or that they had known each other before that time. Janey had already had a passionate affair with Rossetti, which Blunt thought her husband had forgiven but not forgotten.

When Blanche Hozier and her children arrived at Crabbet, Wilfrid was at Kelmscott, where William Morris was printing his *Love Lyrics and Songs of Proteus*. Unusually in his experience of women, and in stark contrast to Blanche, Janey was so silent that they could become intimate only 'through the physical senses', and Blunt wondered whether it had been so with Rossetti. She wrote to Wilfrid, 'I move about in a sort of dream as if a spell had been cast over me and the whole place. Are you sure you have brought no magic arts from Egypt and have employed them against a poor defenceless woman?'[12]

Egypt, now a regular winter haunt since the authorities had permitted his return, lost none of its magnetism for Blunt even in the face of such competition. If Wilfrid left behind at least two bleeding hearts and one furiously flickering flame (in Minnie Pollen), Anne's love for Crabbet and its horses was in truth an even harder tie to break. As they prepared in the autumn of 1889 to travel by way of Rome she wrote, 'Alas, Alas goodbye to home for I suppose 6 months, if we remain alive and all is well. Goodbye to Crabbet, and to my little Bangle and Bushra [her pet dogs]; both seemed to know and almost had tears in their dark brown eyes.'[13]

Wilfrid was still anxious about his inability to come to terms with his faith – despite having kissed the hands of Pope Leo and Cardinal Newman. In Rome he kissed St Peter's toe, but it was all make-believe. As he entered the 'naughty nineties', love of Woman had very definitely superseded love of God. 'I am convinced that a religious life is best, and equally that I am made for pleasure. Love is to me what a dram is to a drinker.'[14] As for Anne, devout in her faith and constant in her relationships, Rome held the visible manifestations of all that was now dear to her;[15] but even in the celestial palaces of her faith, horses filled most of the available space, just as they filled the last few pages of her 1889 diary. Christmas and the new year were spent uneventfully, largely on finalising the additions and alterations to their Egyptian home, but the visit had to be cut short in the spring.

Cowie, whose devotion to Anne was a real consolation in her increasingly lonely existence, had become ill on the journey across the Mediterranean, and her condition worsened in Egypt. Anne was anxious to take her home to England.[16]

> April 11th, 1890. I felt regret at leaving our garden home and I think that a fortnight longer would have been well spent there, it is too beautiful to leave with all those roses and pomegranates in flower, and we shall find it cool enough in England. Not that when once packed and having gone through the agonies of goodbyes I would have delayed. No: I said goodbye to Khatila with pieces of sugar and last caresses. Judith did the same with Mesaoud. I don't believe Wilfrid cast one glance at Merzuk, or his Hamdani... I had not said goodbye to the poor little gazelle but I hope I have spoken enough about its being taken care of to ensure this...[17]

Paris on the way home offered Wilfrid the prospect of more of his favourite sport. He found much-needed 'illicit love' with Margaret Jane Talbot, wife of Reggie Talbot the military attaché. She was the elder sister of Ralph's wife Mary, happy in her marriage. Wilfrid kissed her hand on first parting and three days later they took tea together in Bitters' apartment in the rue Mazarine and consummated the affair in two idyllic hours.[18] He returned to Paris in July in the grip of yet another raging storm of passion, and they made love again at Bitters' place; 'no more flights or hesitations... we are to enjoy our love as nature wills it to our lives' end.'

He described her as being 'of that divine chaste type we only find among our own people and the noblest of them.' Next day she was penitent, fearing that her devoted husband would ask questions and that she would not be able to lie. 'Go from me, go – go.' He went off to Switzerland to nurse his *amour propre* and Cousin Bitters, who was dying. Bitters expired on Wilfrid's 50th birthday, and left him a thousand pounds. Lytton, whose Paris circle had provided the meeting ground for Wilfrid and Margaret Talbot, had warned him that she was by disposition a flirt but that she worshipped her husband.

Wilfrid's reply might have been anticipated by Lytton. 'Danger in love always acts with me as a physical stimulus.' The fact that she loved her husband made her all the more attractive to the suitor. She promptly confessed to her husband, and Blunt decided to seek sanctuary in his family. He prided himself on an 'ideal' daughter and a marriage in which he and Anne were 'like two ships in the regular trade winds, going on together without trouble and without anxiety.' Anne's now sparse diary seemed to bear out the suggestion of a resigned acceptance of advancing age.

Her diary entry for 24 September suggests marital peace, or at any rate *modus vivendi*. Her dog Bangle strayed in September and Wilfrid gave her Bulbul, tied up with blue ribbon, in compensation. Three weeks later he was able to tell her that her favourite dog had been found. Anne was ecstatic.

In October she recorded a poem that Wilfrid had written when Judith was six years old. It began:

*Judith creature of my love*
*What is this! You love me not?*
*On the stair you stand above*
*Looking down distrustfully*
*With the corner of your eyes*
*Watching me in mild surprise*
*Me, your father, only me.*[19]

Blunt had begun to realise that his daughter doubted his earnestness and perhaps his honesty in matters affecting her and her mother, and verse which seems to fall between bathos and a foolish attempt at justification ends with an admonition, lyrical words that the daughter would one day throw in his face:

*Yet remember this one word*
*Love is two-edged like a sword*
*Mind this only, only mind.*[20]

Anne bought Wilfrid a red-lined cloak and a pillow case of the same material for his birthday. But the hoped-for reformation was far from complete. Before the 1890 winter visit to Sheykh Obeyd he announced that he looked forward to perhaps ten more years to finish his poetical work, and to 'a constant element of romance'. All the same, peace was in the air and Anne was more reluctant than ever to leave Crabbet. Now that the Pollens were in exile, she was mistress in her own house and that fact increased the melancholy of parting. But the routine was by now established. By the first week of November 1890 they were in Paris, complete with Judith. They stayed at the embassy and Wilfrid told Anne he had been so happy there that he would gladly exchange Crabbet for Paris. Anne added, 'the "personnel" included I suppose'. In Egypt they went riding together for the first time in ages, even though Wilfrid was stricken with a cold. He told her that at no other place did time pass so fast as at Sheykh Obeyd and she agreed. Judith and Wilfrid played games after dinner, usually chess, and Anne would wait patiently for her daughter to go to bed so that they could pray together.

'10 o'clock. Waiting till Judith is ready for me to come. We say our prayers together, and however long I have to wait I will not risk breaking through this custom.' The year ended on the happiest note for a decade or more:

> December 31st. The year ends happily indeed. I feel myself here 'happy as the day is long' and my last word must be one of profound gratitude to Almighty God for His great mercies and favours. How have I merited? I have certainly not merited a 1000th part of the peace and delights showered upon me here; these as to the general tenor of life and also as to the millions of details full of enjoyment – the place, the air, the sun, the trees, fruits, flowers, the horses, the donkeys, the cows and calves, the foxes in the garden and out, the news of horses and mares possibly to be bought, the good news from home. All I leave in His hands. May He be praised and glorified for ever. Amen.

The horse Mesaoud, which they had purchased for Judith the previous April, was entered for his first race at the Ghezireh course on 20 February 1891. The start was bad and though he was a long way behind for much of the distance overtook three of the nine runners. Mesaoud failed to gain a place, however, and Judith went to bed disappointed. She couldn't understand her horse not winning, 'knowing how good he is, and not being prepared for the chances and accidents of racing.'[21]

Wilfrid met Evelyn Baring on the way to the course and the two men had an amiable discussion, but the consul-general made it clear that Blunt was welcome in Egypt only so long as he obeyed the injunction to keep out of political matters.

At the end of March Anne was awakened by noises which she at first took to be the sound of galloping horsemen. She seized her gun and cloak and ran to the stairs only to find that the disturbance was being caused by the collapse of parts of the newly-built house. Crash followed crash as walls tumbled around her and ceilings caved in. The day before, she and Wilfrid had wandered through the house inspecting the rooms, 'all the windows and doors being in and floor being levelled so that we proposed occupying them next week, as soon as they were plastered.' What might have been looked on in the past as a calamity was merely a temporary setback for the contented Anne. They would have to leave their head man, Hassan, to have the house rebuilt in their absence.[22]

Just before reaching England, Anne recorded the banter of an evening of chess played by her husband and daughter aboard ship.

'Checks bobo.'

'Now my chickabiddy.'

'There goes the last of your little hopes.'

'It's a deadcock certainty for me.'

'Stale mat.'

'Oh, that's a mistake. I can't see the pieces with this rolling.'

'Don't talk stuff.'

'Check mat.'[23]

Anne's rose-tinted view of Sheykh Obeyd was echoed by Wilfrid's April diary, a 'child's life' devoted entirely to Judith and made up of 'chess, dawdling, donkey-rides, talking nonsense'. But he had not abandoned his libidinous ways.

Lady Edmund Talbot (Mary Caroline, related by marriage to Margaret Talbot) provided a halting start to the sensual 1890s. She stayed at Crabbet after a visit to the theatre to see Ibsen's *Hedda Gabler*, and Blunt went to her room at night by prearrangement. The door was bolted.

Though the pursuit continued briefly, the 'end of love' which he sought was never achieved.[24] Three other sirens quickly came to his aid. Sibell Grosvenor, Margaret Talbot's sister Caroline Grosvenor and Dora Chamberlain were on the scene and all willing to play Venus to his indefatigable Adonis.

Lady Helena Carnegie, 'inquisitive, unbelieving, sad, but with a wild love of life and love', was also willing.[25] And Margaret Talbot was still in evidence, obsessed with a sense of sin and overcome by remorse at every assignation. Paris was once more the amorist's venue, and Skittles was back in the city she had once dominated, recalling perhaps the lines of Villon about the youthful enchantress who came back in old age, 'Who now no thief in all the town would take'. Skittles sent for Wilfrid but he had other more urgent appointments. She only wanted money, anyway, and he sent it by post. Sibell Grosvenor, who said she was in love with her husband George, Blunt's cousin, kept him on a tight rein and he turned for consolation to another Grosvenor, Mrs Algernon or 'Queenie', but there too 'the love we talked of... could not be.'[26]

While Wilfrid rekindled the spluttering flame of love, Anne pursued her own dual passion – Crabbet and the horses – and wrote long erudite treatises in Arabic on the poets and horses of the heartland of Islam.[27] But she was not blind, and when Blanche Hozier came back on the scene she was incensed.

> God knows I ask not to know anything from curiosity, not even from 'taking an interest'. It is simply from the wish that things should be straightforward and the bitter memory of past experience which taught me that whenever there is a concealment there is danger of evil consequences... And when those people who are the occasions of little secrets turn out to be noxious or to have behaved noxiously, one can't but think instinct was a true guide.[28]

That was written on 2 June 1891. A month earlier she had vowed to give up the violin. 'I see it is impossible to do my duty to my family unless I do so, or play so little that it would be only a weariness not worth the trouble of it.'[29]

Crabbet was buzzing with clamourous wit and portentous political chatter. The recently formed Crabbet club, presided over by Wilfrid dressed as an Arab Sheikh, was about to meet and Anne was asked to make arrangements for the accommodation of the guests.[30] All her suggestions were dismissed and she described herself as a 'cypher'. The assembly burst into laughter and she realised she had laid herself open to ridicule, 'exactly like the Candle of Punch so the Messrs and Lords of the tournament must take their chance.'

She listed the chief guests: Mr Harry Cust, 'the great Harry'; Lord Houghton, poet and peer and 'past the extreme youth suitable for dormitories and roughing it generally'; the Hon. George Curzon, rising politician and traveller and author of a work on Persia; the Hon. Richard Grosvenor, commonly known as Dick. These people needed a room apiece. 'Oh, there is a fifth new person I forgot! Oscar Wilde. Certainly he would expect a separate room.'[31]

Finally she wrote in exasperation, 'Leave it to Head of the Family' (the satirical name by which she and Judith now regularly referred to Wilfrid). As the guests gathered she took to her newest steed, Sobha, 'much more delightful as a companion.'

After tennis and crumpets one day there was intellectual entertainment. Wilde read out the poems submitted by fellow guests on the subject he had chosen, 'In praise of myself'. Curzon paid homage to his hosts in deplorable verse:

*In tents of wandering Bedouin I have*
*harkened more than once*
*To tales of prodigies performed by the great race of*
*Blunts.*

On 8 June, as the party reached its climax, Anne in self-imposed confinement remembered her wedding day:

Twenty-two years ago I made the acquaintance of this part of Sussex. For this is the anniversary of my marriage day on which we drove down with four horses from London to the cottage. It was a drizzly morning, the anniversary I mean, and is very cold. A begging brother from Dulwich has come and takes a pound from me. I would hate to go round to beg.

While Anne lamented, the Crabbets played on. The plump Wilde with his thick brown lips and the pink and glossy Curzon fought a famous war of words under the appreciative eye of president Blunt, who looked like a displaced desert sheikh. Wilde's account to Frank Harris, described Curzon's innuendo and 'sneering side-hits at strange sins' and his, Wilde's, catalogue of Curzon's mediocrity 'toiling and moiling for a second-class degree, destined for a second-rate career.' Fellow Crabbets cheered and shouted as the contestants savaged each other. There were high jinks next morning when they all went down to the lake for a swim, schoolboys all, 'so lovable'. Afterwards, Wilfrid changed into pyjamas, appearing cross-legged on the balcony, 'looking down at the mad game of lawn tennis, for all the world like a sort of pink and green Buddha.'

The club came to an end in 1893, victim of Wilfrid's dominant obsession. In the penultimate year, the handsome if overweight political journalist Harry Cust presented a telling verse on the chosen subject, this time marriage:

*Yet even cursed Cust, who may*
*not nibble*
*Those darling dainties made for*
*married man*
*May envy still the spouse of*
*Lady Sibell*
*And bow before the lord of Lady Anne.*

Autumn became winter and while Blunt had a last fling before the annual visit to Sheykh Obeyd, Anne entertained the agent of Cecil Rhodes, prime minister of the Cape, who had instructions to purchase two colts.

Princess Wagram also came to buy horses and insisted that Wilfrid should flirt with her depressed friend Lady Wenlock, who was not satisfied with her husband, 'excellent' though he was. Unfortunately the lady was deaf and after some abortive attempts to read poetry to her even Wilfrid gave up. Sheykh Obeyd called, and there were 'plenty more fish in the sea' – or pebbles in the desert.[32]

## *Chapter Twelve*
# Emily's Story

When they stayed with the Lyttons at the Paris embassy on their way to Egypt in 1891, Wilfrid's earliest mentor in poetry and the cultivation of the senses was terminally ill. Robert, first Earl of Lytton, died a fortnight after the Blunts departed, on 24 November.

Anne regarded this last meeting as a happy one, in spite of Lytton's illness, for she had come to know Edith better and to like her. 'I feel I have got to know Edith so well now, and that all which I instinctively loved in her is there, and more than all, in her admirable character. That unswerving and absolute devotion to duty in the most heroic sense is what makes her delightful, and illuminates that most sweet face which never can become old.'

When news of Lytton's death came to them in Cairo, Anne's saintly generosity glowed:

I feel so intensely for my poor Wilfrid but it is so difficult to say anything to him. I tried to however. But he will never know, I think will never choose to know more than just the edge of my thoughts and feelings, because I need help to express them, and so far from help all I can hope for is to have a rebuff and to feel I have gone too far in assuming that my sympathy could be welcome. Yet I know how much he suffers and am grateful this time to have no rebuff.[1]

Blunt had received two promising letters that day, one from Edith Lytton and the other from Margaret Talbot. In the evening he surprised Anne by sitting with her and reading Edith's description of her husband's death. 'All was over in a moment, no struggle.'

The blow of his friend's death was lightened for Blunt by the appearance in Cairo of the young diarist Margot Tennant, who was destined to marry 'Squiffy', the future prime minister Herbert Henry Asquith.[2] Anne heralded her arrival:

> December 31st. The tea party went off very well. It was composed of Mr Webb (the lodger) and Miss Blanche Fane and Sir Charles and Lady and the Miss Tennant known to fashionable society as 'Margot', who was of course in a way the most conspicuous.... W. went to meet them and I missed seeing the arrival... It must have been a curious sight as both Miss Tennant and Miss Fane rode the donkeys astride, or as Miss Margot expressed it 'we rode like boys' – I dare say Miss Fane managed with her dress but the scantiness of skirt of Miss Margot must have looked odd...[3]

Anne approved of the guests at first meeting but on reflection found Margot wanting in manners. Strangely, Wilfrid found the lady visitor no more than 'very charming and very amusing'. He made a bigger impact on her. She thought him as 'vain as a peacock... He is very handsome and cultivated and, I am told, extremely susceptible. I saw nothing of this.' Webb amused Wilfrid but was the bane of Anne's life, so often in residence that she called him 'the lodger'.[4] There were, in fact, three Webbs in the Blunt circle. Sam Webb was a groom at Crabbet. There was Webb, just

Webb, a travelling groom who drank excessively and looked after the horses in transit between Egypt and Crabbet, often residing at Sheykh Obeyd. And there was Godfrey Webb, the lodger, otherwise Wilfrid's bachelor cousin 'Webber', House of Lords clerk, who was present at the July meeting of the Crabbet club, and was always looking for a vacant bed at Crabbet or Sheykh Obeyd. Both Anne and Judith regarded him as one of the 'pawing set', Wilfrid's back-slapping fraternity who found it hard to keep their hands off any young woman.

One morning Judith showed her mother the manuscript of a review by Wilfrid of a book of Lytton's poems. It was an affectionate obituary and a testament to Lytton in his private and public roles; a vivid picture, said Anne, 'of Lord Lytton as a friend and a poet from the best point of view, and yet true for their affection was a touching and beautiful thing'. She lamented that she had not been able to share with her husband the pleasures of a friendship which had begun when the young men took rooms at old Mr Lawrence's inn near Lisbon so many years before. 'I never could bring myself to ask questions, because, in the beginning when, believing he would like to tell of his life, I did ask a few I found there were apparently things considered out of my province.'[5]

Now Anne feared for her own daughter, brought up in an atmosphere of falsehood, Judith told her one day that she feared that she might be treated by her husband as her mother was by hers. 'These are things one cannot think of and live. They must be buried or else they would wound mortally.'[6] The daughter had more to fear than she yet knew of. On their last evening in Paris, Blunt and Lytton's daughter Emily teased each other. The plump 16-year-old was a match for him and would soon have the opportunity to observe her father's old friend at close quarters.

The annual visit to Egypt in the first months of 1892 was devoted to the purchase of more horses from the declining

Ali Pasha stud and they returned with their latest acquisitions to Crabbet in April. Webb arranged an awning around the horseboxes so that the animals would not be frightened by the sight of the sea, and Anne's opinion of him was enhanced despite a recent bout of drunkenness for which she had reprimanded him. 'Of him I cannot speak too highly.'

By the time they arrived back, the Hozier divorce action was going through the courts and Wilfrid was worried.[7] Dinner with Philip Currie (Mrs Singleton acting as his hostess), at which Oscar Wilde and T. P. O'Connor were fellow guests, restored his morale for the moment, however. Love was still alive in the shape of Caroline Grosvenor, Margot Tennant – about to admit him to the 'shrine of Venus' for the first and only time before marrying Asquith – and Janey Morris (in their favourite venue, a horse-drawn gig). In fact, Janey was fast losing her appeal. She had pleaded with Blunt to go to Kelmscott in the September of 1891 and although they did enjoy a few encounters in their mobile trysting place, she had been foolish enough to introduce him to her friend Marie Stillman, another model beauty of the Pre-Raphaelite school. Blunt averred that she was 'the most beautiful woman that ever lived or ever will live', but by summer 1892 his gaze was fixed on other prey.[8]

In June, Edith and Emily Lytton arrived at Crabbet. Judith and Emily, like their two mothers, had become close friends, though after an earlier visit with her mother and brother Emily had declared Judith to be 'rather a peculiar girl' whose only amusements were riding and driving, shooting and wrestling. On 29 June she wrote in her diary: 'Crabbet Park, Three Bridges, Sussex. I like Lady Anne, for she is so extremely kind and so dreadfully snubbed by her husband. Mr Blunt and I sharpen our wits upon each other.'[9]

Emily's confident personality shrouded a sensitive soul. She was embarrassed by her lack of skill as a rider and hated the country sports on which Blunt insisted: 'fishing and shooting harmless animals'. She rode all the same, led by Blunt, Anne bringing up the rear and fussily insisting that she should sit straight, go faster, and 'do this and that'. But a day or two later she wrote: 'I had a delicious ride yesterday alone with Lady Anne through the most lovely woods where each turn seemed to bring us to something more beautiful than before. Lady Anne is much nicer by herself than with other people and she was charming to me yesterday.'

The young visitor quickly picked up the bitter atmosphere that permeated the beautiful Sussex home of her hosts; an atmosphere in which Judith became increasingly the butt of parental disdain.

'I pity Judith very much for the position she holds between her parents,' Emily wrote on 1 July.

> Mr Blunt is always scolding Lady Anne for not letting Judith go out more and bringing her more into the world, and though Lady Anne dare not scold Judith while he is there, directly she is left alone she scolds her as a kind of revenge for the scolding she herself has received from Mr Blunt. They both simply worship Judith and yet quarrel about her.

On reflection Emily added, 'They do not actually quarrel, for they hardly ever speak to one another.' Emily resented the silent animosity and felt uncomfortable, and she offered up to her diary a piece of advice that might have served the unhappy couple well: 'Be what you ought to be in yourself and you will always find people to love and respect you.'

The following year Emily wrote endless letters of the most intimate kind to the Reverend Whitewell Elwin, her confidant and father confessor through the tortured years of young womanhood. Elwin, 76 years of age, relished his vicarious role. Emily told him, for example:

> I became very much attached to Judith Blunt, and unfortunately that attachment was extended to her father... No doubt my rather flirtatious and chaffing manner

encouraged Blunt to believe that I felt more friendly towards him than was actually the case at first. But he understood my feelings for him long before I understood them myself. He drew me out, flattered me, encouraged me in playful chaff, leading me on until I unconsciously found myself deeply in love with him. I was shocked and horrified when I discovered that his intentions towards me were strictly dishonourable, and yet it took me three years before I was able to break the spell he put on me.

On 22 September, Anne acknowledged her 55th birthday.

What a monstrous age for one so unprepared for old age as I am. I really don't know how to behave suitably. However, I had every encouragement towards happiness. First – at our early breakfast Wilfrid presented the 2 little white and gold bound volumes entitled "Blunt's Poems" to me and I have got my name written in by him in red ink. Judith gave me a china bowl – really Chinese I think – it is beautiful thin paste.[10]

Judith's horse Mesaoud had arrived from Egypt and Anne rode him for the first time in England. 'I like him, but he has two or three bad habits...'

Less than a month later, Wilfrid's volume of poems entitled *Esther* arrived from the publisher Kegan Paul; 'it was given to me for my very own,' Anne wrote ecstatically. She found the story in sonnet form with which it began both painful and pathetic. It portrayed scenes which she had only vaguely imagined in the early years of marriage, scenes 'one would rather not have before the mind, but it may be a valuable warning.' But she admired the beauty of the language and the passages which she could read without pain.

She read to Judith in verse the story of Wilfrid's meeting with Skittles when he was a young attaché in Paris, and the unfolding story of seduction and passion.[11] A week or so later, she had a note from Margot Tennant asking her to contribute 'a column or 2' to a magazine she proposed to launch with her father's money. It was to be called *Petticoat*, which Anne thought a 'foolish' title.

There was plenty to take her mind off domestic troubles. On 18 November, she had taken Judith and Cowie to Horsley Towers to stay with the Lovelaces.[12] She had hardly visited her old home since her marriage and seen even less of her father. Jane, the second wife to whom he had now been married for the best part of 30 years, was as ever most amiable. The 'Stern Earl' spoke of being at the close of a long life. Anne wondered if it had ever occurred to him 'how much happiness he could have spread and did not'. In the evening Judith played Greig, Chopin and Spanish dances. It was the last time daughter or granddaughter would see the grim, luckless William King, Earl of Lovelace, though Lady Lovelace would maintain a friendly if distant relationship with her stepdaughter.

Before leaving for Cairo at the end of 1892, Anne went to lunch with the Chancellor of the Exchequer, Sir William Harcourt, at 11 Downing Street. Cecil Rhodes sat next to her and praised the horse Azrek he had purchased from Crabbet, 'praised him to my heart's content'. They celebrated Judith's 20th birthday at Sheykh Obeyd on 6 February 1893, and Anne wrote, 'This is the most valuable day of my life, so its anniversary is the happiest.' Wilfrid had bought his daughter a new foal and they all went out to inspect it. 'It was a lovely evening, sky like a golden flaming sea with purple islands and mountains.' Her optimism was not allowed too much rein. Within a day or two she was attacked by the skin infection that was to affect her for the rest of her life. 'The torture is such that one might fancy one's head was filled with boiling lava, and one's head and face get so distorted that no trace of features remains.' They left for England on 18 April, Anne wishing it were but a *mauvaise quart d'heure*.[13]

Emily and her mother were at Victoria Station to meet them. Emily had slimmed down since their meeting two years before and become an attractive young woman. She and Judith decided to form an 'anti-Souls' society which they would call the Pawsoff and Rude Club. Emily spoke of Anne's relationship with Judith. 'One thing I like so about Lady Anne is that she enters into all Judith's jokes and encourages her to enjoy herself in her own way. No doubt youth does seem idiotic to age, but so long as youth is happy in a harmless way, what can it signify?' In August the Lyttons arrived at Crabbet from their Chelsea home and Emily wrote: 'I love Judith more and more, and feel much more at ease with Mr Blunt. It is nice to be where I am spoiled.'

Next morning she met Blunt on the stairs and he summoned her to the library. He said he would take her for a walk in the woods. She confided that Judith and she were writing a novel which as yet had no plot, but that he was to be the villain. He took her hand. 'Won't you let the villain love you, the villain does love you and will you love the villain?' More talk and they came to a bench and sat on it. 'He at once took my hand and kissed it and stroked it, said he adored me, which I told him I was very glad of, as one did not get adored every day.'

The suitor, now in his mid-50s, became more and more urgent in his entreaties. The insatiable lover began to look no more than a common lecher, but Emily was too overcome to care about the distinction. She told her Reverend all and he replied: 'Your letter is a delicious specimen of the minute truthfulness with which you spread out your entire life for my inspection. I am accustomed to it, but delight none the less in each fresh instance of your habit.'[14]

With Cupid's darts flying all round her, Anne concentrated on the horses and an almost permanent visitor to the stud, the Hon. Miss Etheldred Florence Lee Dillon, whose wealthy Irish family owned a famous Arab by the name of El Emir.[15] Miss Dillon was usually represented in correspondence and diaries as 'E.D.' or occasionally as 'Barbarian'. The Blunts were for once united in their

19. 'Hamid's mare, Kihefet Ajouz', undated watercolour by Lady Anne Blunt

20. Drawing of 'Faris' by Lady Anne Blunt, March 16, 1878

25. The 'Pink House', Egypt, 1900, watercolour by Lady Anne Blunt

26. 'Desert Days', January 31, 1900, watercolour by Lady Anne Blunt

*27. 'Esmafiha', undated coloured drawing by Lady Anne Blunt*

condemnation of Miss Dillon's breeding methods and of her criticism of the Blunt approach. Anne had fired off a terse reprimand to Miss Dillon in November 1892 on behalf of the entire family, but had had second thoughts. The Irish woman was stone deaf and Anne admitted afterwards, 'I always grieve for her.' In any case, by the time the rather technical dispute reached a climax, a more agreeable aspect of Anne's equine obsession had taken over.

In 1892 she had published her first and most affectionate translation from classical Arabic, *The Stealing of the Mare*, one of a cycle of tales forming the *Romance of Abu Zeyd*, a celebrated and popular work for more than 800 years in the Islamic world but little known in the west.[16]

Anne had worked on her translation for the past year or more, a test of her now fluent Arabic and a welcome refuge from the cares of Crabbet and Wilfrid's womanising. In fact, with Wilfrid as her versifier, she began to see yet again hope of a marital *modus vivendi* via a meeting of minds through work. In December 1891 she had written in her diary of Wilfrid reading aloud his poem of the legend of the golden-tongued rogue Abu Zeyd and the mare of Akeyli Jaaber. 'He had got as far as the descent of A.Z. from the tree and his slaying of Zohwa and Sahleh when he said his throat hurt him from reading.' She dedicated the work to Charles Doughty 'in recognition of his knowledge, the most complete among Englishmen, of Arabian things.'[17] The work conveyed a good sense of the language by which Abu Zeyd charmed his way through a gullible world, reminiscent in some ways of Burton's translation of the *Thousand and One Nights*, but like Burton's work, Anne's translation was too literal and Wilfrid's verse too formalised to capture the subtleties of the original Arabic: 'In the name of God the Merciful, the Compassionate! He who narrated this tale is Abu Obeyd, and he saith: The Emir Abu Zeyd the Helali Salame was sitting one morning in his tent with the Arabs of the Bani Helal and the Lords of the tribe.'

Thence to the vision of the beautiful Ghanimeh, oppressed by fate and in heed of the emir's thoughts and plottings. There was characteristic concern for the meaning of every inflexion, but her insistence on faithfulness to the original seemed to constrain Wilfrid's verse. The work was well received by Arabists but was hardly a literary sensation. As usual, Anne regarded her achievement lightly, recording the publication in her diary but never seeking praise or approval. She soon reverted to bleak domestic affairs.

After their last meeting Emily and Blunt had agreed to correspond and meet at his Mount Street 'bachelor flat'. They also vowed to spend a week together in Paris. But a bid to visit her in her bedroom at Crabbet fell flat. She refused his advances. Then in August she wrote him a love letter: 'I wear your ring and it is lovely. Whenever I see or feel it I think of you, and as there are little sharp points on it which stick into my fingers when I press them together I have to think of you very often.' She signed herself, in terms of unmistakable familiarity, 'Your affectionate adviser'.[18]

Belatedly, the Reverend Elwin tried to warn her of the danger of her attachment. Blunt was a villain and she must see no more of him. The clergyman might have been less concerned had he known that at that moment Blunt had invaded Arthur Balfour's gathering of intellectual 'Souls' given to cultural pleasures, Bible reading and *Morte d'Athur*, and where 'every woman shall have her man but no man shall have his woman'. Blunt was currently wooing one of its leading members, Margot Tennant.

At the end of October Emily was telling Elwin: 'Judith looks more beautiful than ever and more fascinating. She is as affectionate to me as I could want and we both revel in each other's company.' All the same, it was Judith's father who excited her emotions. 'I was suffering from a kind of nervous excitement which made it almost impossible to sleep, and quite unable to eat, and still more unfit to write.' She spoke of her 'infatuation' and was unable to think of him as a villain.[19] She was saved by the Blunts' invariable winter vacation. In November, Wilfrid went off to Egypt where the new building that they spoke of as the pink house was nearing completion.

During much of 1893 Emily agonised with her confidant in England while her lover visited Coptic monasteries and the scenes of ancient battles. 'If you could but know the burning shame with which I tell you of my weakness, or rather of my sin, for sin it is.' Elwin replied briefly to her long apologetic letter, telling her of the 'heaps' of love and praise he had for her and ending, 'you can wait for the rest, my dearest darling.'

In June 1894, Elwin virtually ordered Emily to cease seeing Blunt the 'demon', the 'Satan personified'. After a month's consideration she wrote to Blunt, threatening to tell her mother if he did not leave her alone. Blunt thought her letter could have been more graciously worded, but he promised to avoid her. 'Take care of your precious life and make those who love you happy,' he wrote. He wondered where to turn next to find his own happiness.

The theatre had largely escaped both Wilfrid and Anne in their adult lives, but as the century neared its close they brushed shoulders with the stage at two of its extremes. On his way back to England in 1893, Blunt had visited the royal stables at the Yildiz Kiosk in Istanbul, where he met and was much impressed by Sarah Bernhardt.[20] He was reminded of the time when, travelling with Anne some six years before, they had met the famous lady's 'monster' of a theatrical agent. On the latest Egyptian journey, Anne had travelled with a theatrical party on the way to Cairo. 'The ruck are in the 3rd class, poor wretches'. A prima donna sat at the Blunts' table; 'fat, fair and American... she speaks French well'. It was as close to the theatre as they got in their life together.

The last few years of the nineteenth century were to prove the nadir of Anne's married life, as her husband embarked on a last desperate bid to find that 'perfect love' which he had sought throughout his adult life with all the pent up force of the frustrated romantic.[21] Anne ceased for long periods to keep the detailed journals that were intended to give her daughter a private first-hand account of her life, to pass on to future generations of her family her unique knowledge of the Arabian horse which she had done so much to perpetuate, knowing that it faced hybridization and even extinction as a recognizable breed in the land of its origin. In the misery of those years her day-diaries reflected her dejection, often containing only the occasional shopping entry or household accounts. Even her father's demise went unrecorded. Lovelace died at Horsley Tower on 29 December 1893, in his eighty-ninth year. He had grown ever more remote from the family which he and Ada had relished and then virtually abandoned. But Anne did not share the bitter animosity of her brother Ralph, who succeeded to the title.[22]

The constant calls on her capital caused by Wilfrid's extravagance and his mismanagement of the Crabbet stud became the cause of increasing concern. In March 1894 she wrote to Ralph from Sheykh Obeyd to assure him that she had no plans to use her inheritance to pay off charges that had been incurred by Crabbet.[23]

As for her writing, she sought no literary recognition in her lifetime, though her travel books would endure as landmarks of their kind, with their genealogies and notes on such leading Arab dynasties as the Al Rashid of Hail becoming standard references for students of central Arabia the world over. Neither did she seek fame in posterity. She even regretted putting her name to her books on the Arab lands. When a bishop praised her works at a dinner party, she was embarrassed and wished that she had published anonymously. In the years that brought her married life to a close, she kept her innermost thoughts even from the journals that had been the anchor of her sanity for so long.

Wilfrid's preoccupations were much more tangible. There was still fun to be had in a social circle which Anne found repugnant, and none more than the Souls.[24] Balfour's freewheeling circle intrigued him, especially Mary, Lady Elcho, whose hand he had kissed in the autumn of 1894, after Emily's final note, and whom he had thought the most beautiful woman in the world when he met her at her family home. A dinner party at Margot Tennant's, attended by a sparkling group which included Wilde and Blunt's cousin Bosie, took Wilfrid's mind off women for a moment as he reflected on the young Lord Alfred Douglas's relationship with Oscar Wilde, the man Anne had found 'repulsive'. But the Blunt libido was as hungry as ever. Mary Elcho was lined up to provide the next grand passion.

Work on the new building at Sheykh Obeyd was now complete, its apricot exterior blushing in the sunlight, its two storeys and many windows testifying to the need for servants in plenty and accomodation fit for the lovely thirty-two-year-old woman who was shortly to arrive 'like a captured bird' in his hand. The new building was officially named El Kheysheh and Blunt had decorated it to be worthy of her. He occupied the main residence along with Anne and Judith.[25]

On 5 January 1895, Mary arrived with her three children Ego, Guy and Cynthia and the governess Miss Jourdain. Hugo, Lord Elcho was not with them.[26] His mistress, Hermione, Duchess of Leinster, was dying and Mary had insisted that he should be at her side. Wilfrid took his guest to the tomb of Sheykh Obeyd, hidden by trees beyond the garden gate, and there he offered up a silent prayer 'for good fortune with her'. Old Obeyd must have listened because on the fourteenth of the month she succumbed to his advances. She was alone in the Pink house when Wilfrid called, the shutters discreetly drawn and a large envelope addressed to Arthur Balfour at her bedside. He wrote: 'Then the others came in, and I went away and have gone about since like one distracted with my happiness'. There followed a series of expeditions with the children to sand dunes and camping excursions in which Anne and Judith joined. Wilfrid was almost always with Mary and frequently went to her tent at night.

Mary Elcho was the 'fairie queen', and when he was not reading poetry to her in the garden or making love to her, he listened while she explained her tangled life; Hugo and she lived happily together, though they went their separate ways. She had a 'friend', Arthur Balfour, to whom she was pledged far more than to Hugo. At the end of the month she received urgent pleas from Balfour and her husband (among others) not to fall for Wilfrid. In February the two families went on what Wilfrid called his 'desert honeymoon'. Anne and Judith rode with them for the first day and then turned back. The Elcho party and Wilfrid, with their Bedouin companions, camped in a different wadi each night, and most nights Mary came to his tent. 'I think the Arabs with us knew that we were lovers – indeed, they must have known it, for there were Mary's naked tell-tale footsteps each morning'. Mary was dressed in Arab costume, 'my true Bedouin wife'.

Soon the mood of the party changed. Mary had admitted her dalliance to Balfour, and now he wrote to her to protest. Worse, Hugo had been released temporarily from his mistress's sickroom and was on his way to join them. And there was another piece of news: Mary was pregnant. She was now determined to go home before further troubles came her way. For Wilfrid it was 'a pure gift from heaven'.

Lord Elcho, appearing at that crucial moment in a billycock hat and leading a chow dog, cast a further shadow over the proceedings. And there was one more bizarre twist to the tale. At camp, Wilfrid found Lord Elcho's hat in his tent; 'it moved me to anger. I feel that she has brought a stranger into my tent.' Adding insult to injury, Mary told Wilfrid that she and Hugo had a long-standing pact of reconciliation to take effect when his mistress died. All the same, Wilfrid insisted while they were in the desert his 'Bedouin wife' could not sleep with her real husband; the 'Arabs would not hear of it'.

Elcho returned to his mistress, aware of his wife's pregnancy, and the families went on towards the monastery of St Antony and the Gulf of Suez . Despite Anne's presence Wilfrid went to Mary's tent night after night, and before the journey's end he lit three candles (in a wadi) for Mary, as he had for Anne when their son was expected more than twenty-five years before.

When they all returned to England, he went to Mount Street expecting to find a love letter on the mat. In the event, Mary told him that he had tried to destroy her life. The only thing that prevented her from being 'utterly angry' was her belief that he 'did care for her, in a way'. Hugo was more forthright:

> You have wrecked the life and destroyed the happiness of a woman who a spark of chivalry would have made you protect. She was thirty years younger than yourself. You have known her from childhood. She was your cousin and guest. She was a happy woman when she went to Egypt, and her misery now would touch a heart of stone.[27]

Blunt was enjoined to silence, but foolishly told his daughter Judith everything. She wrote in her diary of the 'happy days before Mary Elcho and that child came to ruin my life'. At first Judith consoled her father, walking with him in the woods. He tried to submerge his sense of guilt and despair in writing a romance but could not finish it. He could no longer face life at Crabbet, with all its memories, and so moved to Newbuildings, the home he had once lent the Pollens, taking Anne and Judith with him. Judith was in the midst of a crisis of her own.

Stephen Pollen, her childhood sweetheart (though his brother Arthur had believed he was the chosen one), had proposed to her, but she turned him down; her 'childhood fancy' was no longer there. Blunt was pleased, but he had problems of his own. It was apparent that an Elcho boy sired by him would complicate the inheritance of the Wemyss title and fortune to which the Elchos were entitled. In any case, Mary told him, she was convinced that her own children would die, 'as punishment to me'. Even as the birth of Mary's child approached and the reconciled husband promised kindness to mother and baby, the incorrigible natural father welcomed both Emily and Janey Morris back into his fold.

Soon after saying goodbye to Mary, for the moment at least, he accepted an invitation to join the Lyttons at Cromer. There was a day of 'almost innocent' love, which he did not feel was disloyal to Mary. Anne no longer came into the reckoning, but the eternal lover was forgetting about his daughter, who cared a great deal; indeed, her devotion to Emily was greater than his. Emily locked her bedroom door and listened in the night as Blunt quietly turned the handle and then went away. Next morning, pitying him, she kissed his hand, 'which I always think a true sign of love'.[28]

Passionate love letters followed. As Mary's child neared Blunt took refuge in Emily, and in so doing fuelled a lifetime's resentment on the part of the one person whose opinion he valued, Judith. His daughter became jealous of Mary and turned on Emily in revenge.

Blunt, having confessed everything to Judith and having used her as his go-between with Mary, ran away from it all, leaving alone for old haunts in Paris and Poland, on to the Ukraine and Armenia, and then Egypt.[29] With unimaginable loyalty Anne saw him off from Newbuildings with what can only be regarded as misplaced devotion. 'Goodbye my beloved,' she said as he departed. Meanwhile Judith had learnt from Emily of a plan for her and Wilfrid to elope to Paris, and she wrote of the intention as 'a crime for which I have forfeited my birthright and my blessing.'

In Egypt, now under what amounted to permanent occupation by Britain, Blunt stayed with his cousin Philip

Currie, who was now ambassador to the Porte and married to Angelina Singleton, their dinner table chatter cementing the bond forged between them, that 'great bond between men who have loved the same woman'. At the start of his journey Wilfrid had received a last note from Emily, 'The night before you left I cried myself to sleep'. The enchanted recipient wrote, 'it is sweeter to be loved even than to love'.

From Sheykh Obeyd he wrote to Anne, depicting himself alone at their Cairo home, 'like a white blackbird in a cage'.[30] When he returned from a journey upriver to Aswan a message from Judith told him of the birth of a child to Mary, 'a splendid girl with thick black hair'. Affecting the Arab preference for male children, he had a pang of regret and then said that he hoped it would be called Zobadayah.[31] George Wyndham told him it would be called Mary, 'the family baby'. Blunt saw his daughter at ten months and kissed her, recalling pitch-black eyes following him with a friendly stare. Now, Mary was pregnant again and Blunt thought it must be Arthur Balfour's child, unless he, Arthur, was 'something more or less than a man'. Blunt could not understand a relationship that was not overtly sexual. In the event, the new child was a boy, Ivo, almost certainly Elcho's as it turned out.[32] In his attempt to fill the void left by Emily, the disillusioned Blunt now returned indefatigably to Janey Morris.

At the end of October 1896, following the death of William Morris on the 3rd of that month, the family was off again to Sheykh Obeyd. The funeral of Morris had provided another opportunity for Wilfrid to meet Janey and to rekindle the old flame.[33] He asked her to spend a few days at Newbuildings and she obliged most willingly. She turned up with her daughter May. On top of the funeral, the circumstances seemed to Blunt to militate against high jinks. He invited them both to Cairo, where things would be different. They could put up at El Kheysheh, the rose-pink retreat so recently dedicated to Mary Elcho. On 7

November, Anne rode over to El Kheysheh to prepare for the arrival of the Morris women. When they did turn up, the visitors were like fish out of water. Janey, Wilfrid's exact contemporary, was putting on weight alarmingly and, according to Anne, admitted to turning the scales at thirteen stone. May was taciturn, neither could ride, and they were taken on daily excursions by somewhat overburdened donkeys. A despairing Blunt, at his wits end to know how to amuse them, observed that he 'could not make love to either of them, and what else is there to be done?' The passionate affair that Rosalind Howard had brokered as an 'act of friendship', that had blossomed amid Pre-Raphaelite pranks, died with the high priest of that ruthlessly intrusive aesthetic movement. Janey observed that she enjoyed herself in Wilfrid's bed 'only too much'.

In August 1897 Emily found herself the husband she craved. She met the young Edwin Lutyens, who would build New Delhi in years to come, and he fell for her instantly, attracted by her 'cross and unhappy look'.[34] Blunt gave her a present of a moonstone necklace and she thanked him, 'Dear Mr Blunt'. Judith would never be consoled. Her father wrote of his resentment at her treachery and lack of affection, 'for the jealousy is not about me but about Emily... I am left like Adam when Cain had killed Abel, alone at my fireside'.[35] There was consolation of a sort for Anne. In July 1896, before the annual visit to Sheykh Obeyd, she had entered Mesaoud, Rosemary, Anbar and Mejliss in the Crystal Palace horse show.[36] Webb was in charge and she was pleased to find her groom-factotum sober before the event began. That night at dinner she received a telegram from Webb announcing that Mesaoud had won first prize, Mejliss second, and Rosemary had been commended 'in reserve'. Miss Dillon had expected to win the major prizes – 'It's comic, but also pathetic in a way'. Anne returned in a short-lived mood of optimism to Newbuildings and the horses.

## Chapter Thirteen
# Thirty-Two Years' Waiting

Much of Anne's story has been told thus far in tandem with her husband's. It could not be otherwise. Her adult life, her marriage, her work and achievements, were bound indissolubly to his domineering personality, to his demand for self-gratification and the willingness of others to satisfy that demand. Her achievements were many but she lived in his shadow; and there she has remained ever since.

What manner of man was he, this vain, sensitive, arrogant Adonis who wrecked a marriage which promised so much? Narcissus. Libertine. Petty philanderer. Misunderstood artist. Shunned philosopher, seeking a role at the margins of anarchism or radicalism. Opportunist revolutionary perhaps – Gladstone described him as 'mad' in politics – as much at odds with himself as with society.[1] He was, in part, all of these things, and more besides. He made little effort to conceal his faults, or excuse them. His accusers and apologists, within and outside his family, seem rather to plead a special case. Such good looks! Such irresistible charm! As if these qualities, allied to an artistic temperament, explain everything. In his favour, his remarkable compendium of sexual conquests was accompanied by a considerable output of work. His two dozen or more books and pamphlets, poetry, political essays and panegyrics represent a body of work between the years 1875 and 1914 of which many a writer might be envious. That is as a good an excuse as any.

His case has been made over and again, by himself and his admirers. But the wife's? How, it must be asked, could she have been so mistaken, so misled by her own instinct – the wife for whom no one had a critical word, who looked on him from the outset as the single star in her firmament, who saw in their marriage a perfect unity of mind and intellect, and the hope of enduring loyalty and love? Could the daughter who witnessed her father's seduction of her own best friend really be accused of unjust recrimination? The latest intrigue had taken place under the eyes of her mother, and when rancour had run its course Judith would write that her father had played havoc with her mother's heart, 'wrecked her life, and, jealous of her intellectual gifts, appropriated the credit of her brains to himself with shameless arrogance.'[2]

If Judith's verdict is unfair, as one of Blunt's biographers has maintained, it can only be because he would have been regarded more favourably by his family and society if he had been born at a less censorious time.[3] That same biographer, Elizabeth Longford, says in her magisterial *Pilgrimage of Passion*, '[his] vanity was widely accepted as a weakness', and she cites in evidence of this understatement a male exchange at a party. Lord Newton (a distinguished biographer of the day) mentioned Parnell's good looks to a guest, and Blunt, who overheard, chimed in, 'I do not suppose that any two men have been mistaken for each other so frequently as I and Parnell.' He was not quite the lion of his own estimation, but here, indeed, was a strutting peacock.

Fiona MacCarthy, William Morris's biographer, explains his attraction from a woman's viewpoint: 'To judge from Blunt's own diaries he had a real interest in women, the interest one finds in men who are pursuers: a fascination with women's histories, psychology, the details of their lives. He was inquisitive where Morris was so diffident. He understood precisely how a woman's body works. Blunt, assuming Morris's sexual disengagement, commented in his diary that Morris talked to women in exactly the same manner as he addressed a journeyman carpenter: the description rings true.' The same writer also remarks that, 'Blunt had in abundance what Morris lacked, not in his poetry but in his everyday behaviour; the imaginative quality in love.'[4]

Perhaps so, although he made little attempt to apply the same imaginative quality to his relationship with Anne, in or out of bed. What then of Anne, curiously immersed in her violin, her horses, her writing and Arabic studies, while her family life collapsed about her? How might she have responded if Wilfrid had treated her more sensitively? She was a woman of natural humility who thought little of having written two classics of Arabian travel and history, translated with genuine scholarship some of the finest of Arabic poetry, rescued the thoroughbred Arabian horse from near extinction, and won respect and admiration for her travels in regions where no European woman had ever before ventured? Was she blameless, this brave, rich lady of secluded childhood and advantaged youth, endowed with all the gifts of material security and self-confidence that aristocratic birth and inherited wealth could provide?

The questions are irresistible, but they can be answered only with reference to her own time. It is profitless to judge past generations retrospectively, to look back wisely – or impertinently – from an age of female emancipation and legislated sexual equality, and say, 'She was a whimpering fool to endure his conduct, his demands, his studied insults'; or to misplace her within the context of earlier times of easy morality. In Chaucer's time Wilfrid would have been no more than an ordinary roisterer of average capacity in bed, and she a lady who piously neglected the benefits and opportunities of privilege. During the Restoration or the Regency Period he would not have been thought outrageous or even much of a wag. But the pairing was unequal and the anachronism of time and place ran deep. He was out of his time, a creature of an age not so far off, when empire had resourced the extravagance of the court and the well-to-do, and patriotism and loyalty were worn on the sleeve. Born too late, he chose to rebel politically at the high point of his country's imperial splendour, and to flout publicly the moral constraints of the age.

She, on the other hand, was essentially a child of Victorian England, imbued with her mother's eccentricities but none of her wilfulness, harnessed to Lady Byron's sense of rectitude and virtue yet, unlike her grandmother, infuriatingly acquiescent and forgiving; a woman of much charm but little humour, trapped in a male-dominated world, loyal, stubborn and a little inclined to primness. It is easy to imagine Anne's grief at the treatment she received at the hands of this man whom she worshipped unreservedly, but her own compliance may have contributed to the frailty of the relationship. They held together through more than 30 tortured years because he could not see that there was anything wrong and she, as women of her day were expected to do, forgave, as she forgave the young tribesmen of the Ruwalla when they attacked her on the way to Al Jauf in 1879: 'In spite of their rough behaviour we could see that they were gentlemen. They were very much ashamed of having used their spears against me.'

Grief began to give way to subterfuge. Apprehensive of the dangers inherent in Wilfrid's spendthrift attitude to the stud as well as to other matters, Anne began to breed her horses in secret, at locations which she did not even name in her diaries, confiding them only to her daughter.[5]

Anne was in Cairo with Wilfrid in March 1896 when he and her maid Cowie received letters from Judith, who was at Luxor at the time. When she asked about their contents Anne was told the letters were private. She thought the secrecy 'alarmingly suggestive of proposals and sons in law.'[6]

The 'Emily affair' had proved the last straw for Judith.[7] After she had confronted her father in May 1896 with her knowledge of the plan to elope to Paris with her dearest friend and reminded him of the bedroom door incident at Cromer. He took the only course open to him and went on the offensive. He told her she was a fool to interfere, and boasted that what he had had in mind would have done Emily all the good in the world. He added ungallantly that Emily 'wasn't pretty enough to get much of a husband, and wasn't likely to get such a chance again.' Blunt's extraordinary responses to his daughter's accusations included an attempt to marry her off to Lord Alfred Douglas, soon after Bosie had delivered Oscar Wilde into the custody of Reading Gaol. He had in mind as well several other 'eligibles' including an ancient French marquis. He suggested to his daughter that there was nothing wrong with marrying a 'respectable dummy' and waiting for the right man to appear later.[8]

At Newbuildings in May, Anne was 'educating' the young horses while Wilfrid sorted out one of his mounting problems, the future of his son Berkeley Sumner.[9] The boy turned up in June, a handsome blond sailor, and, at the suggestion of George Wyndham, his natural father arranged to settle his debts and allow him £250 a year, in return for Berkeley's renouncing 'the Sumner money'. Thus he was able to enjoy a son at last, announcing that he had done with Judith as 'an eldest son'. He told Anne about the new arrangement, and according to Blunt's testimony she kissed the boy and said that she had 'long done fretting about such matters'. Disillusion soon crept in however. Blunt found his son 'a good fellow but a fool'.

William Morris had given Wilfrid a Kelmscott copy of *Morte d'Arthur*, and soon after their return to England in 1897 Anne's brother Ralph handed him the 'forbidden' Byron letters. Blunt began to see himself in a dual role, as a latter-day Sir Lancelot and as the romantic poet who 'never could love but that which loves.' Meanwhile, for Anne, Egypt had become a haven where she could find at least temporary deliverance from Wilfrid's world of amorous adventure.

Realpolitik began to assert itself in Cairo three years before the turn of the century, when Anne wrote in her diary: 'While we were sitting on the roof Freiherr Max von Oppenheim and Prince Aziz were announced – the former is attaché to the German Minister here. He is very spy-like.'[10] It was a perceptive observation. Max von Oppenheim, a talkative half-Jewish aristocrat from a German banking family, had led an archaeological dig at Tal Halaf in Mesopotamia and written a book about his travels in the Arab lands and Persia. He turned up as Kaiser Wilhelm's spymaster in the Middle East as Germany challenged the hegemony of the British empire. He was also a scholar of note and a wealthy bon viveur.

Throughout December, Anne was occupied with the 'tragedy' of Ali Pasha Sherif's declining stud.[11] She was told by one of the Pasha's sons that the remaining horses did not number more than 30, and some of those were probably half-breeds. In order to make sure that no desirable animals were overlooked, Anne listed all the horses she could find, 17 in all, with notes chiefly for Judith's future guidance. For example: Ibn Nura Seglawi Ibn Sudan, 'flea-bitten fine but v. old magnificent head'; Abuha Ibn Nura, 'v. promising. Dam died, brought up by hand'. There was a note at the end of her summary: 'Send to APS [Ali Pasha Stud] asking for particulars of breed and age and price of 9 of the horses seen.'

On 14 December she handed over a cheque for £350 for five of the best horses, and then rushed from Sheykh Obeyd to the centre of Cairo to place £400 in her Ottoman Bank account in order to be sure that the cheque was met. On the 19th of the month, eight days after her appraisal of the horses, she noted: 'Letter received by Wilfrid. A legal letter... demanding the mares and colt we have bought from Ali Pasha on the plea that the Pasha had no right to sell them.' Ali Pasha had been made a ward in Chancery some time before, but had continued to sell his horses and pocket the money. The matter was ironed out but Anne was unhappy. 'It was on Wednesday 30 December,' she wrote, 'that I saw the poor remnant of APS Stud tethered out in the garden of one of the Pasha's palaces... there were about a dozen of various ages, and in 4 loose boxes in a yard were the 4 old white horses'. By 20 January 1897, she had secured the larger part of what remained of the stud: 13 horses.

In February, Wilfrid set off accompanied only by Egyptian guides on a trip to the Western Desert, 'somewhere in the Senussi kingdom'.[12] It was the month of Ramadan and it was unlikely that the zealous Senussi tribesmen who inhabited the border desert between Libya and Egypt would be active. However, Blunt concealed his identity. He wore Arab dress, carried three guns and £55 in cash, and rode the mare Yemama. After losing himself several times on the journey – his guides proving practically useless – he arrived on the 26th day at the Senussi monastery of Zaytun at Siwa. The day after his arrival a desert raid took place. Blunt and two faithful servants were left by his other attendants to face 200 armed men. Blunt was hit over the head and his cheek gashed before he could claim sanctuary with the words, 'I am your prisoner'. He was hauled before the governor of the region and forced to admit that he was an Englishman travelling in disguise.

He arrived back at Sheykh Obeyd on 17 March after 40 days. He had experienced a small taste of Islam rampant and had begun to doubt the wisdom of fanatical movements. 'The less religion in the world perhaps, after all, the better.'

It was a judgement that some, including his first biographer Edith Finch (the future wife of Bertrand Russell), regarded as his final word on religion.[13] In fact, it was no more than a passing response to personal danger. Anne did not comment on the affair although there were signs that she was becoming impatient of his ambivalent search for love in both God and Woman – depending on the mood of the moment – and even more so of his rabid anti-British stance on almost any issue. As Judith was to write, her 'instinctive patriotism' rebelled against his 'heedless iconoclasm'.[14]

Within eight days of his return to Cairo, Wilfrid went ahead of Anne and Judith to bid at auction for the last remaining horses of Ali Pasha Sherif's stud. The impoverished owner had died in the meantime. On 26 February Anne had reported that her messenger Ahmad had met crowds of civilians, police and soldiers on his way back from Cairo, and been told that Ali Pasha was 'dead and being buried'. 'Poor Ali Pasha', wrote Anne, economically, for he had been her closest local collaborator in the purchase and listing of Arabs from the great Egyptian studs.[15]

Blunt would not let the Siwa incident rest. He called on Cromer and demanded to know why Britain claimed sovereignty over the Libyan dominions of the Senussi.[16] Cromer replied just as assertively that Blunt had no business to be in the territory, that if he went at all it should have been in English clothes and not in disguise, and that he had done harm since the Senussi were traditionally well disposed towards Britain.

Blunt was now suffering from attacks of indigestion which came upon him with increasing frequency. He was sick on the way home in April. Anne spoke of the ailment as 'regular', a mysterious pain which occurred after food or from want of food. He had lost some four stone in weight during the visit to Egypt. As Anne's impatience grew more and more apparent, he began to seek the traditional solaces of age. 'The thought of dying does not trouble me,' he wrote in May, 'but the pain of it is wearisome and I am glad of any relief.' The doctors began to prescribe morphia. Having alienated his daughter, Wilfrid settled for Anne's quiet company at Newbuildings and at a workman's cottage they had purchased near Crabbet and called Caxtons. But Anne was no longer the doting and devoted wife. At the end of April she observed that he was very ill after breakfast one day, but was later well enough to ride around the stud.[17]

While Wilfrid nursed his ailments, Anne went to nearby Southwater to receive the latest equine arrivals from Egypt. Two of the new horses, Badia and Bint Nura, stampeded on the journey home but arrived safely. Others had died on this and previous journeys. Anne was not pleased when Webb told her that as long as they were insured it did not matter.[18]

Both husband and wife were becoming increasingly eccentric in their behaviour. Wilfrid almost invariably received guests in his preposterous Arab garb, setting himself up as the great expert on Islamic questions and giving advice freely whether or not it was asked.[19]

He had re-entered the Wyndham-Elcho set by 1897, and had re-occupied the throne of the 'Court of Love' in the Arthurian terms now in vogue with the Souls. In June he had formed a 'ring' with Arthur Balfour, Edward Burne-Jones and Mary Elcho. Now it was cousin George Wyndham who was in love for the umpteenth time, telling Wilfrid that he had never been so happy.

Blunt's income had now reached £3,300 a year, only £200 less than his wife's. He was at last the self-sufficient squire, though it was later to transpire that he was overspending on Crabbet, and using Anne's capital to the extent of £2,000 a year to make expensive gifts to his ladies. He applied to the Somerset heraldic office for permission to represent the Scawen family (going back to the early 18th century) as well as the Blunts.[20]

As for Anne, devotion to horses had reached the stage, according to Emily Lytton, of going to bed in full riding habit – including top boots – so that she would be ready for action in the early hours of the morning. Outright eccentricity would show itself a few years hence when the Hilaire Bellocs moved close to Newbuildings and noticed that 'after her Eastern experience she thought it wrong to be without a hat or turban, even in her bedroom. Thus in bed she would wear a small Irish fishing hat and mackintosh, instead of a nightdress, to go with it.' Belloc quoted her future son-in-law Neville Lytton, saying she lay against her pillows 'dressed as though for a southwest gale in the channel.' More alarmingly, she insisted on calling the vet rather than her physician when she needed medical attention.

Sheykh Obeyd in November was intended to provide Wilfrid with another emotional diversion. Gay Windsor, the lady his cousin George had been wooing somewhat ineffectually, had asked him about Mary Elcho's visit to his Egyptian home and had half promised to make the same pilgrimage. He had discussed with her the merits of friendship as opposed to love between the sexes, and he had decided – in a moment of candour which threw light on his relationship with Anne – that 'Friendship plain and simple with a woman is to me an impossibility.' He wrote in his diary afterwards: 'If I do not make love, I don't know what to do or say and she is bored and I am bored and insensibly the friendship and all else withers away.' The couple agreed to meet at his Mount Street flat and later at Sheykh Obeyd but she turned up on neither occasion.[21]

The events of 1897 renewed the fire of rebellion that was always smouldering within Wilfrid. It was the year of the

Queen's Diamond Jubilee. On the day of the official celebrations, 22 June, he retired to his 'Egyptian' tent, his temper soured by the fact that a few days before he had arranged to meet Mary Elcho in Hyde Park but had been prevented from seeing her by a seething throng of 'ridiculous sightseers'. Love and politics became entangled. He was convinced that the Queen was behind the whitewashing of Cecil Rhodes over the 'scandalous' Jameson Raid. It turned out that George Wyndham had been instrumental in forcing Chamberlain's hand in support of Rhodes, and persuading the 'ridiculous MPs', both Tory government and Liberal opposition, to support Rhodes's policy.

By February 1898 the Blunts were together again at Sheykh Obeyd and Anne was going through another phase of remorse. Before retiring to bed one night with indigestion and a sore head, Blunt had asked her to book a passage home for him on 11 March, telling her pointedly that he did not wish the family to accompany him.

> I don't like his being alone but he will do as he pleases and it is no use trying to stick to people who don't want one. Of course not to be wanted is mortifying, but I ought to be used to that after so many years... To see this suffering and be powerless to help – there is the rub.

On 13 March she wrote:

> The words "final departure" ring in my memory. There is something more in them than appears and it is inexpressibly mournful. The new volume of life beginning with this farewell, how will it go on, where will it take us? In this illness there seems to me to be some mystery, something behind – mental suffering as well as physical.[22]

His illness, whether psychological or physical, was to trouble him increasingly, and the treatment, ever heavier doses of morphia, exacerbated his already choleric temper. Political events, coming on top of the family disunity that he had done so much to bring about, did nothing to ease the tensions of life at Newbuildings. He took refuge whenever he could at Mount Street and Caxtons, and left Anne to deal with the increasing burden of the stud, now split between Crabbet and Newbuildings.

The year 1898 saw Kitchener's avenging of Gordon at Omdurman and the exclusion of the French from Fashoda. The 'unspeakable slaughter' of the dervishes by Kitchener's army and the death in that war of Hubert Howard, correspondent of *The Times* and son of Lady Carlisle (Rosalind Howard), brought a characteristic letter from Blunt to that newspaper, written in blazing anger. To his surprise it was published. On the Fashoda question he denounced Britain's 'imperial plunder' but conceded that France was as bad, the difference being as between two highwaymen or card sharps. The tide of popular patriotism, of national pride in Kitchener's victory, was not turned back, however, by the impassioned protests of a man who likened his country's imperial battles to blood sports, while boasting of his own prowess with the gun.[23]

While political controversy raged again in the Blunt household, Anne continued her private war with Miss Dillon, who was still writing abusive letters to Wilfrid, criticising the Crabbet stud and boasting of her own purchases. Even Miss Dillon was set aside at the end of 1898, though, when the engagement of Judith to Neville Lytton was announced.

In the summer of 1897, while her mother was basking in the success of her horses at the Crystal Palace, Judith had shared in the family joy, writing cryptically 'I seem to be lucky with horses whatever I may be in love!' Tall, attractive but a little too athletic, and perhaps too pronounced in her opinions to appeal broadly to men, she had admirers none the less. She pined for serious devotion, and found it with Victor, heir to the earldom of Lytton after his father's death, and godson of Queen Victoria. Anne and

Wilfrid were both opposed to an engagement, though their reasons are not clear from correspondence or diaries. Emily had done her utmost to bring her elder brother and her devoted friend together, and perhaps that had something to do with parental opposition. In the end, Edith Lytton's opposition was decisive. She had become a lady-in-waiting to the Queen and considered that her son's career would be damaged were he to marry a Roman Catholic. Judith's version of the story, however, was that the Queen did not want the daughter of a revolutionary at court. Whatever the truth, after this sudden end to her hopes Judith turned down several suitors, including Hubert Howard before his death in the Sudan. Soon after, Victor's younger brother Neville, an art student in Paris, declared his undying love. Judith, never one to mince her words, tried to head him off with a message that could hardly have been misunderstood: I've got a code of honour in spite of my parentage!... So – KEEP OFF THE GRASS.'

The die was cast however, at the Lovelaces' London home, Wentworth House in Swan Walk Chelsea in July 1898, when Ralph's wife Mary decided to throw a party for Judith and several interested young men. Judith turned down three suitors on the spot before Neville Lytton appeared. He had proposed many times before, and now he put his head on Judith's shoulder and wept. Unmoved, Judith said she would think about it. Unfortunately for her, she told Anne who delightedly told Wilfrid. He promptly sent an engagement notice to the press.[24]

'HF has put a match to gunpowder,' said Judith. She was not in love with young Lytton and had even declared that there was something about his face that repelled her. After the announcement had been made and congratulations poured in, she told her future husband, 'you must make me love you.' Anne's shortcomings as a mother, though far from being unique, were magnified by her daughter's predicament. Judith had heard of the depraved atmosphere in Paris at the time of the Lytton embassy and feared she might find herself mixed up in it. She was even more terrified by the idea of childbirth, and wondered how to prevent that eventuality. She asked Anne, who stuttered in confusion and told her daughter she had better ask the doctor.

A letter to Wilfrid from Edith Lytton, arriving on 15 October, contained, according to Anne, 'all, and more than all, that could be wished.'[25] The same day a telegram arrived from Balmoral confirming the Queen's consent to the marriage. Ten days later Anne went to the Lyttons' new home at Bloomsbury Square.

> The door was opened by Edith Lytton herself who folded me in her arms with a welcome more delightful than words can describe. She told me she had 30 letters to write to smooth over huffed people who saw the newspaper notice before being told. But there was just time for the Queen to be told before seeing it... fortunately Mrs Mallet who was going out driving with H.M. was able to inform her. Then she sent for Edith to her own room and they talked and Her Majesty showed herself deeply interested. Of course she is interested in all the Lytton children...[26]

Wilfrid had insisted that Anne should raise the matter of a settlement on the bridegroom, 'a guarantee of £1,000 a year'. As one mother to another, Anne told Edith that her daughter was keen on Neville's chosen profession, portrait and landscape painting, and would be happy for him to continue in Paris for the next two or three years. Judith would also like her fiancé to join the family at Sheykh Obeyd for the Christmas period. A Cairo wedding was suggested by Blunt.

Edith didn't object to her son being married in Egypt but thought it would look odd if Wilfrid was not there to give his daughter away; Wilfrid had already decided that declining health would prevent his going. The presence of a new lady on the scene, Madeline Wyndham's niece Dorothy

Carleton, may have had rather more to do with his reluctance.

When Anne and Judith arrived in Paris on their way to Egypt, a letter was waiting from Wilfrid containing the surprising suggestion that Lord Cromer should give the bride away.[27] Anne called it 'astounding'. Everyone was asking, 'Why Cairo?' not least the bride and bridegroom. But 'asking of Lord C. (who has been treated as a personal enemy)' to give away his daughter was too much, although, as usual, Blunt had his way and Cromer agreed to take the bride's arm.

Neville breakfasted with Anne and Judith on 9 November. The next day Judith broke off the engagement. The mothers were not so easily blown off course, however. They had agreed between them that the wedding would take place on or after the couple's joint birthday, 6 February, in the following year, when Judith would be 26 and Neville 20. In fact, the date was eventually fixed for 2 February.

Anne began preparing Sheykh Obeyd to accommodate the wedding guests. Ever practical, and just as worried as his fiancée about conception, Neville asked the advice of a Cairo doctor and was given some strange devices called French letters.

On 2 February 1899, Anne wrote to her absent husband:

My dearest Wilfrid – My first thought must be of you and my first act on getting home after the marriage of Judith and Neville must be to begin a letter to you. Not but what many thoughts perpetually turned towards you during this day and the ones preceding it, and many regrets that you were not on the spot to enjoy as well as take part in the proceedings. I wish I felt capable of describing them, but in fact I feel just the contrary though I will try. The marriage created as much sensation as you could have desired and the scene at the church [the Roman Catholic church of Zaytun] was one to remember not only on account of the crowds of people but for itself. There were carpets spread and a profusion of beautiful flowers on the altar... what music there was being mostly soft would not have thrust any imperfections in it on your notice... Outside Colonel Harvey Pasha had supplied some mounted police to keep order among the carriages. The signatures after the wedding were interesting as, besides mine, there were Lord Cromer's, M. Cagordan's and General Talbot's... The wedding dress from Mme. Joyeuse was worthy of her fame. Judith looked most perfectly beautiful – it is a way she has and she now looks very well in health – and Lady Lytton's lovely veil that had been worn also by Betty [Balfour] & Emily [Lutyens] as a wedding veil, suited admirably. 'His Lordship'... was waiting on the carpeted steps outside the church when we arrived...The church was full of people, but no confusion in consequence of Mr Dormer's excellent management. I forgot to say that the chief landowner of Zaytun had planted in honour of the occasion an avenue of those feathery trees that grow so fast which look most festive. The newly married couple drove off in Lord Cromer's brougham with the splendid kavass on the box and the smart runners in front. I came back with Lord C. in his open carriage with a pretty pair of chestnuts, good steppers (Arabs)... I never saw the like of the flowers offered yesterday to Judith. They had to be brought away by special carriage & filled a compartment in the train. The luncheon and party were a great success, and it was with considerable difficulty that Judith and Neville got away by the 3.30 train. Waiting at the Ezbet an-Nakhle station was a body of horsemen from Abu Taul who performed evolutions while escorting them to the house. The equestrian performance has been continued this morn. It was the sequel to a feast I had provided. About the feeding of the poor it was managed by giving a certain number of sheep and some rice to each of the four villages...[28]

The wedding fell at Ramadan but Blunt's old friend Muhammad Abdu came straight from a sitting of the court over which he now presided, breaking his solemn duty as a Muslim.[29] Among other Muslims present the barrister Yusef

Bey Mubarak sat down to luncheon. The Khedive had been away on an official visit, but within two days of the wedding Anne was discussing with his secretary the new English thoroughbreds imported to his stables. She noted that he was carefully preserving the Arab strain, though she feared that it would eventually be neglected.

Anne's matter-of-fact account of Judith's wedding was reminiscent of her diary essay at the time of her own marriage. Queen Victoria telegraphed to Cromer through the Foreign Office, 'I hope the marriage of young Mr Lytton and Miss Blunt has gone off well today.' Cromer wired back to her majesty: 'Marriage duly performed.' Cowie, who had stayed behind to look after Blunt, was shown a photograph of Judith leaving the church; there was no husband in evidence. Neville had gone off to meet Rowland Baring, his best man, who had failed to turn up at church, and had not stayed to be photographed. Cowie observed to Blunt that his daughter's face looked black; 'not that you will be sorry, as you think all black people more beautiful than white.'[30]

Blunt lived out the remaining months of the 19th century in a state of almost perpetual political agitation. The last rites of Omdurman came first – the dispatch of the Mahdi's head to the Royal College of Surgeons in London and the preservation of his fingernails for White's Club – and then the Boer War, which he hoped might result in the final destruction of the British empire. Kitchener, when he turned up in England, was described by Blunt as 'a big brutal fellow fitly representing modern British soldierdom'. For Blunt it had been a 'poor wicked century', and he bade it a none-too-fond 'Farewell!'[31]

In May 1898 Blunt had taken on a new secretary, the brilliant Sydney Carlyle Cockerell, admirer of Ruskin and disciple of William Morris. He was a socialist of the kind that appealed to Blunt. He was the living embodiment of words he had once heard Ruskin utter: 'Of course I am a

Socialist – of the most stern sort – but I am also a Tory of the sternest sort.' The thesis was later extended by Bernard Shaw, who found in Blunt the inspiration for some of his best-known character studies and in Cockerell a bond with Morris whose essay on communism he edited for the Fabian Society. Shaw wrote: 'All Socialists are Tories. The Tory is a man who believes that those who are best qualified by nature and training for public work, and who are naturally a minority, have to govern the mass of the people. That is Bolshevism.'[32] It was a theory which explained Blunt's political stance almost exactly. At the end of 1899, Blunt ventured from his sick bed in order, with Cockerell and his recently acquired nurse, Elizabeth Lawrence, to visit Mount Sinai. Their ship foundered in the Gulf of Suez and they were rescued by the gunboat HMS *Hebe*.

With Judith married and already expecting a baby despite the precautions taken on medical advice, there was now nothing but horses to keep Anne's body and mind in trim. At 62 she rode as much and as expertly as ever. Everyone who came to stay at Newbuildings commented on her courageous and immaculate horsemanship. Her morale was not, however, in such good shape. On 31 December 1899 she, on the annual visit to Egypt, wrote in her diary: 'Last day of the year. Wish I could have spent it better. Sleep will be the wisest ending now.'[33]

On the journey home to England in March 1900, Anne caught a severe chill. Her throat was badly swollen and her head ached for days on end. Apart from her repeated miscarriages, she had never known ill health: her hardy upbringing at the hands of Lady Byron had stood her in good stead physically. This present sickness was diagnosed as severe bronchitis, and it augured a weakness that was to show itself at intervals for the rest of her life. She arrived at Victoria Station on 23 March, where Judith and Neville were waiting.

The couple insisted on her going with them to their Cadogan Gardens home, though she had wired from Vienna telling them that she was too ill to stay in London and would go straight to Newbuildings. She returned to her Sussex home on 2 April. On the 7th of that month she recorded, 'Judith's son born 11am.' The previous evening she had had a telegram from Neville: 'Judith ill all night do come.' She caught a train from Horsham at 12.35 the following day, and the porter at Cadogan Gardens gave her the news of a son. 'Joy, Joy, Joy,' she exclaimed, 'after three months' tension. Everybody radiant.'[35] The boy, who weighed 13 pounds at birth, was christened Noel Anthony Scawen, and was always called Anthony. Wilfrid arrived on the scene from his Sinai venture nearly a month after the birth. The feud with his daughter was still active and Anne was of the opinion that he would stay away. She heard after the event from nurse Lawrence and Cowie that he had visited and had been in high spirits.

Immediately after the birth of Anthony, Anne threw herself into the preparation of the Crabbet horses for a Paris horse show in September. She had opposed their entry but Wilfrid had set his heart on it. When the moment came on 6 September, her fears were borne out. A telegram from Webb told her: 'Mesaoud 4 Bozra 5'. 'To be 4 and 5 is as good as nowhere,' she remarked acidly, blaming the English judges and Wilfrid's reputation for the fact that her horses had come behind three of the Sultan of Turkey's entries.[36]

At the end of 1900, Anne went with Cowie to Ashley Combe. The estate on the Devon-Somerset border, the fairyland of her girlhood, was now owned by Ralph as Earl of Lovelace, and Anne had not seen it since her disappointing honeymoon visit. She was delighted by Mary's alterations, and received a warm welcome from her brother and sister-in-law. Days spent in the fields and along the coast road to Lynmouth were 'heavenly'. Ralph walked while she rode a new mare and Mary an Exmoor pony. It was just the interlude she needed before the tribulations of the annual winter visit to Sheykh Obeyd, where the Blunts saw out the first year of the new century without mishap and without sign or hope of reconciliation.[37]

They had been back in England for less than a month when, in July 1901, Blunt was presented with a golden opportunity to belabour the Anglo-Egyptian authorities. He received news that a party of eight British officers had trespassed in the gardens of Sheykh Obeyd in pursuit of the silver foxes there, which were the particular delight of Anne, who went to great trouble to protect the handsome creatures. They roamed freely in the grounds and a prominent notice had been erected: 'Sport forbidden'. The officers, led by Captain Harman of the 11th Hussars, galloped into the estate, put up a fox, and were promptly set upon by the foreman Mutlak and two other Egyptians. The soldiers fled as the Egyptians attacked them with sticks. Press notices on 22 July headlined the news with, 'Natives beat British Officers.' The Egyptians were arrested and sentenced to terms of imprisonment ranging from three to six months. Blunt went to the Foreign Office and demanded of the permanent under-secretary, Sir Thomas Sanderson, that they be released. Sanderson told him to write to Foreign Secretary Lansdowne.[38]

Cockerell, with Blunt's help, concocted a letter which was circulated to several newspapers. It 'pitied' the unfortunate officers for the beating they had received and portrayed them as a bunch of cowards who had run away from three Egyptians armed only with sticks. Astutely, the letter referred to the danger posed by the raid to the Blunts' valuable breeding stock and to the desecration of the wildlife sanctuary at Sheykh Obeyd. Mary Lovelace was told by her sister Margaret Talbot that British officers in Egypt would never forgive Blunt the accusation of cowardice. The sentences on the Egyptians were cut drastically and Blunt received a promise that there would be no further trespass. A British government Blue Book was published on the incident in 1902, and Blunt asked Anne to translate for him the evidence of the court proceedings in Arabic. Her work enabled him to demonstrate in a letter to Lord Salisbury the inconsistencies between the evidence and the 'astonishing lies' of the Blue Book's version. The incident and its 'Uncle-Tom-Cobbley' roll of culprits gave rise to one of Anne's rare adult attempts at rhyming verse:

> *Oh for Kipling to sing of*
> *that glorious hunt*
> *Of July 21st in the garden of*
> *Blunt!*
> *Ryecroft, Rowe, Hartwell,*
> *Bradley, Buchan and Greer,*
> *'Master' Harman and Keyser –*
> *a name slightly queer...*

She presented a copy to Wilfrid on his birthday and on 17 August wrote in her diary: 'H.F.'s letter this morning contained the agreeable opening sentence: "I find your verses very amusing and congratulate you on having exercised at last your hereditary talent." NB. Thirty-two years I have been waiting – I may say – for a compliment!'

## Chapter Fourteen

# Exile and Death

Anne was coping with a very down-to-earth problem – an invasion of Newbuildings by an army of rats[1] – when Wilfrid took to his bed assailed by thoughts of terminal illness.[2] Vermin scampered across her bed and kept her awake but she somehow dealt with the matter while Nurse Lawrence looked after her sorrowful husband, who had kept up the pose of the 'great lover' long after he was deserted by those powers so necessary to self-esteem. As doubt assailed him, he became morose: 'Now, death I do not fear. But to be stricken helpless would be an evil fate and it has scared me.' His recurrent intestinal complaint had returned, and there were suggestions of prostate trouble.

Yet there was a brief note of optimism and family togetherness. Anne was looking for a site at nearby Three Bridges to build a home for Judith and Neville.

We rode at once into Blackwater and then on to Forest via Dench's [wood]. Of course, although there is a quite charming site near Half Smock Bottom close to the wood, the most beautiful, and perfect in itself situation for a house is the furthest off.

Eventually they decided to make alterations to the existing Forest Cottage, which the Blunts had used as a retreat from time to time. Anne adapted a newly imported Texan wagon so that it could be pulled by her Arab Shibine between Newbuildings and Crabbet and the site of her daughter's new home. Between times she coped with the 'Jodhpur' people who came in ever increasing numbers.

Wilfrid soon found familiar avenues of pleasure. Nurse Lawrence, making the most of the power given her by her admiring patient, had more or less usurped Anne's role as the lady of the house. Concern for the decline of his sexual powers didn't hold Blunt back for long. He had teamed up in a threesome, this time with Wilfrid Meynell and Adeline, the wife of his friend Sir Charles Russell, spending 'afternoons of love' with Adeline, and evenings on park benches imitating the ways of lesser folk who stretched out amorously on those municipal amenities. When Adeline returned to the arms of her lawyer husband, Blunt saw himself as the worker of the miracle of domestic peace. 'What wonder men are cynics who have made a study of the human heart.'

Another stirring of the human heart came to the fore at this time to take Wilfrid's mind off the women immediately to hand. Ralph had decided to publish, under the title *Astarte*, his vindication of his grandmother Lady Byron, an extended form of the private document he had circulated within the family in 1887.[3]

The bitterness with which Lady Byron had treated the memory of his grandfather was rivalled only by the animosity which Ralph and Lady Byron had shown towards his own father. Now he used the correspondence and diaries that had come into his possession on the death of his father to 'prove' the accusation of incest against Lord Byron and the goddess 'Astarte', Augusta. The provenance and selective use of the Lovelace papers gave rise to as much speculation as it was designed to quell. Not until 1941 did the papers become available to scholars and writers outside the family, and not until 1962, with the publication of Malcolm Elwin's *Lord Byron's Wife*, was it possible to examine with some objectivity both sides of a scandal which had intrigued generations of men and women and greatly affected the lives of all the poet's descendants, not least Anne's. Writing of Ralph's action, Elwin explained:

> Succeeding as 2nd Earl of Lovelace on his father's death in 1893, he found among his father's papers another box of Annabella's letters relating to her marriage and separation. He then compiled the first version of his book *Astarte*... Unfortunately he did not publish this version which remains in typescript among Lovelace's papers. In 1898 John Murray began to publish Byron's Letters and Journals under the editorship of R. E. Prothero... Lovelace had been on friendly terms with Murray and allowed him to copy some of Byron's letters to his wife and half-sister; on finding that Murray had allowed Prothero to publish these letters from what he regarded as confidential copies, he refused further co-operation with Murray, and instead of publishing the first version of *Astarte*, wrote the account of the separation which he issued in the privately printed edition of 1905.

Thus Anne and Wilfrid had seen the first and, up to 1905, the last versions of this persistent story. Blunt found the published edition more moderate than the first, a fact which he attributed to his own efforts in persuading his brother-in-law to avoid 'disparagement' of Byron, and to spare the poet 'morally' as far as the facts would allow.[4] The impression the book made on discerning friends may be judged from the reception given it by Ralph's friend

Gertrude Bell and the latter's stepmother, Florence Bell. On 13 January 1906, Florence wrote to thank him for his 'excessively interesting book', which had been taken from her and eagerly devoured by Lady Stanley, who was staying with her at the time. Three weeks later Gertrude Bell wrote in similar vein to Ralph, whom she nicknamed 'Signor Conte'. They shared an enthusiasm for mountain climbing, especially in the Swiss Alps, and had corresponded regularly on mountaineering matters for some four years: 'I have read *Astarte* & must congratulate you upon a magnificent piece of work. The difficult task has been performed so admirably that I cannot think that any unprejudiced reader can doubt that the ghost has been set forever at rest.'[5]

Gertrude Bell was interested to see that the *Observer* newspaper had taken a pro-Byron line, expressing anger 'at the injury done to the fair name of literature by the writing of such a charge on our greatest poet.' She was inclined to think that others would take the same view. So was Gertrude's friend Eugenie Strong, wife of the House of Lords' librarian.

Irish nationalism was once again Blunt's preoccupation. Under Balfour's Conservative administration, Ireland was in the hands of George Wyndham, who appointed Blunt his unofficial ambassador in dealing with the agrarian problem and negotiating with John Redmond and other Irish leaders. But Anne had little concern with such matters. Her life was separate from his, and her daughter and the stud were all that mattered.[6]

Most friends and tutors from the distant past had gone. Florence Nightingale and Joachim were still alive but old and frail. In fact Anne had seen little of the companions of her youth since marriage and travel had taken possession of her life, and as with her own father, their passing seems to have left her largely untouched.[7]

A new generation of desert explorers and Arabists had come on the stage, and in May 1904 she met Gertrude Bell for the first time, the young woman whom Ralph had corresponded with for some four years and who was destined to succeed Anne as the 'Lady of Arabia'.[8] Neville and Judith had heard Ralph and Mary sing the praises of the scholarly and intrepid Gertrude and invited her to lunch. Anne was invited too, and discovered that Gertrude's stepmother was the daughter of Sir Joseph and Lady Olliffe who had entertained the Blunts and the Lascelles in Paris before the Prussian army arrived in 1871. And Sir Frank Lascelles was Gertrude's favourite uncle. There was plenty for the women to talk about, but Neville thought his guest, who had recently visited Persia with Uncle Frank and had just begun to skirmish with the desert and the sown, inclined to show off her learning. Anne paid her a typically generous tribute: 'she is naturally energetic and fond of talking and very physically vigorous and "full of go", and many-sided.'

One death at this time touched Anne profoundly: Isabella Cowie, the maid her husband had picked up at a railway station as a young girl looking for work 30 years before, was taken ill before she and Wilfrid left for Cairo in the winter of 1902, and it was decided that she should not face the journey. She was put in the care of Judith and Neville at Forest Cottage. On 6 February 1903, a telegram came from Judith, 'Cowie dying probably live fortnight.' Next day Anne sent a messenger to the Catholic church in Cairo with £3 to have fifteen Hail Marys said for her. On the 12th a telegram arrived: 'Cowie died today.' The loss of the hard-working, simple and loyal maid affected Anne deeply. Cowie's last letter, written in January, had said simply, 'I believe I am wore out.'[9] Wilfrid's response to her death in a letter to Judith was not without honesty: 'I feel that my home life is broken up in a way which cannot be mended.' He found compensation, however, in the attendance of Nurse Lawrence.

Soon after there was another death which affected Anne almost as much as Cowie's. In August 1903, her favourite horse met its end. 'Poor Bozra suffered much as she was perpetually lying down and getting up and looking round at her left side. I am glad she died of her own accord. To have to hasten the fatal moment always gives me a pang.'[10]

Judith was pregnant again and Anne was trying to persuade her to occupy rooms at Newbuildings and give up Forest Cottage.[11] There was already a second child, Anne, a year old, while Anthony was now three and a half. Relations between father and daughter were strained once again. Wilfrid had begun to feel neglected. Judith and Neville failed, it seems, to make him welcome when he called at their home, and Anne spoke of domestic 'crisis'. Judith told her mother with tears in her eyes that when she showed affection her father was 'as a rock unmoved'. Daughter and mother quickly admitted defeat, agreeing that the disagreeable husband and father had not enough love for them and his other women. Even in conversation with Judith, Anne concealed the full force of her feeling' but her diary became bitter. 'He wastes his regard on his poetesses and other admiring feminine acquaintances – friends I will not call them. But he might leave some crumbs for those who really do care for him and really are more capable of appreciating him than these people who amuse themselves with him.'

Perhaps Anne and her daughter made the mistake of believing that good intentions were enough to win over the sympathy, if not the declared affection of this hedonistic ingrate. He would almost certainly have responded more positively to indifference and a suggestion of competition. For all her natural high-born charm, Anne had too expertly inhabited a world of male endeavour and perhaps had forfeited the love that sits more easily with passivity. Anger welled up where for so long there had been only pain.

There was a last hopeless attempt at that unity of minds which Anne had long sought in place of the physical union that was as foreign to her as it was delectable to Wilfrid.

Her own scholarly inclinations and her admiration for his versifying powers led to a last literary synthesis – a translation and rendering of the *Seven Golden Odes*, the *Mu'allakat* of pagan Arabic verse.[12] The result was published in 1903: 'Translated from the original Arabic by Lady Anne Blunt. Done into English Verse by Wilfrid Scawen Blunt.' There was an introduction telling of the authorship of Imr el-Kais ibn-Hejr, 'earliest and most interesting of the Poets of the Ignorance... Of the noblest blood of the Arabs, being descended from the Himyarite Kings of Kindi. The *Golden Ode of Antar* told of the poet's love for the girl Abla. It was, Anne thought, the *Iliad* of pre-Islamic Arabic poetry. In her notes, she wrote of 'the slur of illegitimacy' and of the author's 'obscure similes'. Blunt added a note on 'the thrill of Arab poetry', of the 'sudden and unexpected pleasure caused by the cadence'. In places they achieved in tandem some of the qualities which they had analysed in the original. But in the main they were faced with the almost untranslatable subtleties and inflexions of the Arabic text:

> *Weep, ah weep love's losing,*
> *love's with its dwelling-place*
> *set where the hills divide*
> *Dakhali and Hanmali...*
> *Here it was I watched her,*
> *lading her load-camels,*
> *Stood by these thorn trees*
> *weeping tears of colocynth...*

As in the Koran, the true beauty of Arabic resists most attempts at rendering in European tongues. The Blunts' effort, like so many, was commendable, but only occasionally convincing. Their earlier translation was somewhat more satisfactory.

Judith's third child, Winifred, was born in 1904. Her grandfather's indifference was anticipated. 'I don't know why you should suppose me dissatisfied with your female baby, which no doubt will be an interesting addition to the family, especially if it has black hair and eyes,' HF told his daughter. By now melancholia had set in with the irascible Blunt.[13] While at Sheykh Obeyd in December 1904, he had been attacked by malaria which eventually affected his spine. When they set off for home in March 1905, Anne expected to accompany her invalid husband and Nurse Lawrence at least to the Ramleh rail station. When they were ready to depart, Nurse Lawrence announced, 'Her ladyship can look after the luggage, I cannot leave him.'[14]

Thus put in her place, Anne decided to stay on at Sheykh Obeyd with Judith and Neville and Sydney Cockerell in order to meet Auberon Herbert – 'a singular apparition'[15] – and Princess Zeynab, the Khedive's maternal aunt. On her subsequent way home she drew Mount Etna, and Cockerell liked the sketch so much she gave it to him. When she arrived in England she discovered that Wilfrid had nearly died at Venice, and was more than ever under the thumb of his nurse. He smoked hashish constantly and his hands trembled. Anne showed signs of self-chastisement. She blamed herself for deserting him. 'I quite understand HF feeling inclined to visit his anger upon us but hoped he would forgive us as he must be glad to see Neville and Judith.'

A few weeks later in London, he was apparently recovered and had good reason for keeping Anne at bay. 'I believe she has been in London most of the time and is hurt at my prohibition. But last time she was constantly wandering about the house and this drives other women away.' He had just refused to have an operation on a lung said to be tubercular. Like Anne, he had come to rely on the veterinary surgeons who treated their horses when he needed medical attention – not altogether a wise choice as by no means all the horses survived into old age.

In December 1905 Anne was asked to review in *The Speaker* a book entitled *The Thoroughbred Horse*, by a well-known writer on such matters named William Ridgeway. Her essay was uncharacteristically savage in its criticism. The writer had gathered all kinds of 'historical evidence' for his proposition that the English thoroughbred was of Libyan origin. The very idea, according to most experts, was palpable nonsense, and a red rag to Anne if ever there was one.

> And to a commonplace intelligence the author appears to jump to conclusions with so acrobatic an agility that the ordinary mind is left hopelessly behind. To keep up with his erratic progress one feels in need of the wings of that Pegasus whose reported mythic birth in Western Libya, near the shores of the Atlantic Ocean, he cites in support of the dark Libyan horse (not the upstart Arab) being the genuine article...

She pursued the author back to pharaonic Egypt, attacking both his precepts and conclusions. Finally:

> We rise from its perusal impressed by the magnificent but confused vision of the all-pervading presence of millions of splendid dark Libyan horses with stars on their foreheads overrunning the world, and turning all other breeds inside out from the Equator to the North Pole, yet haunted all the while by a sense of the unreality of the scene.[16]

Her reputation in equine matters was sufficient by now for her to take on any of the world's experts, and she relished the task, especially when she was defending the Arab against its persistent denigrators.

If her public conflicts were invariably intellectual and usually esoteric, her husband's political battles could be relied on to hit the headlines. An event in 1906 embroiled Blunt in a lurid affair and brought him into close alliance with the Fabian Socialists, particularly with Shaw who had a dramatist's liking for his colourful debating skills. Once again Blunt found himself in bitter opposition to his fellow Conservatives over Egypt. The infamous Dinshawi incident occurred in May, when a party of British officers echoed the Sheykh Obeyd affair with much more serious consequences. They went out to shoot pigeons belonging to some Egyptian peasants near Tanta in the Nile Delta. According to the evidence subsequently produced, the villagers rushed forward to protect their tame birds, and to give the offenders a piece of their collective mind. One fellah woman and four men were promptly injured with gunshot. The officers were then attacked with sticks. One of the officers, Captain Bull, was coincidentally affected by sunstroke and collapsed while trying to escape. The villagers tried to revive him but he died. In the aftermath, four of the fellahin were sentenced by the courts to death by hanging, two to life imprisonment, six to seven years' servitude and others to flogging.[17]

Much of the British press was on Blunt's side, describing the punishment as 'outrageous'. He wrote a pamphlet called *Atrocities of Justice under British Rule in Egypt* in which he asked if there was no MP with courage enough to say publicly to Cromer, 'J'accuse!' Shaw asked Blunt for more information on Dinshawi for use in the preface to *John Bull's Other Island*. Sir Edward Grey, foreign secretary in Asquith's Liberal administration, was the minister chiefly responsible and Shaw suggested to one Cabinet member, Burns, that he should hang Grey out of a Whitehall window and leave him there until he repented.

Anne was at Sheykh Obeyd at the time of the incident, dealing with financial problems caused by Wilfrid's sale of land and properties. When she turned up at Newbuildings in June it was to find that Wilfrid had sold a number of horses to representatives of the Indian government but had ignored her advice to sell the colt Rifaat, for which a large sum had been offered. She also found the stud in poor condition. Land drainage had been stopped by Wilfrid in order to implement a crackpot notion that the estate should be restored to 'heath and marsh'. She marked as she always did the anniversary of her wedding, 8 June, 'memories of some joys and many sorrows'. Anne was unwell with symptoms which suggested to her that she might have been poisoned, although it is more likely that her condition was psychosomatic. She was mentally exhausted by Wilfrid's activities and still fuming with anger and guilt over the Nurse Lawrence affair when Dinshawi took over the household in July.

But it was the future of the stud which became the decisive element in the ultimate dispute. On 20 June, Blunt had handed Anne a document 'purporting to be a historical sketch of the Stud winding up with his ideas of an agreement.' It was not, wrote Anne, something she could accept. 'I said I would look at it but would not enter into the matter now... I will have no more partnership – what I have must remain mine and mine only. I believe it could be managed, but it will be difficult to have separate ownership.'

Then, six days later:

A new idea occurred to me but I do not suppose H.F. would agree. I mentioned it however to Guy [Carleton, stud manager and brother of Dorothy, Blunt's current mistress], and we discussed whether I should have any conversation with H.F. before going to London on Saturday – I must decide tomorrow. My sole wish being for the success of the Stud and its permanence, and I do not especially covet the management if that success could be better secured otherwise. With H.F.'s ideas and practice about breeding – the system he had adopted I mean – I am convinced that it must perish. I wondered whether he would agree to making it over to Judith.[18]

She finished her diary entry for the day and left Dorothy Carleton reading to her husband from the writings of her late aunt, Hester Stanhope.

On 9 July: 'He spoke in no hostile spirit... but it was probably because in this proposed division he has seen the opportunity to get rid of my presence as after reading his papers he said that of course I ought to be "domiciled" with my half of the stud (to which I have no objection only I must have time to find a place to inhabit). He was so evidently pleased at this prospect that I am nearly sure it weighs much with him in coming to an arrangement.' As they both had to go to London, he to gain 'emotional refreshment', she to see her solicitor, she asked if they might travel together. He replied, 'I will not have this sort of thing. I shall have to go away somewhere under a feigned name to escape.'

'What sort of thing?'

'I will not be followed about. If I had to choose one of you, I should certainly choose Miss Lawrence.'[19]

By 14 July he was asking her to help him write his pamphlet on Dinshawi. 'It is amusing his making use of me while longing to be rid of me!'[20]

She took Judith to her solicitor on 19 July to finalise the separation and the division of the stud that Wilfrid's conduct had forced on her. 'For as I finally leave Wilfrid things must be on a strictly business footing.'

July 29: 'Of course both J[udith] and N[eville] are greatly disappointed at the failure of my negotiations as to the ultimate fate of the Stud and I am afraid Judith will decline to do any managing, but I could not help having to accept an arrangement short of what I wished. Wilfrid now said he wanted £15,000 for Sheykh Obeyd Garden without El Kheyshi's [house]... To think of my efforts in gaining money for H.F. being rewarded by his asking me to pay a large price! I shall calculate the sums I have sunk in the garden... and as to the outside land I shall begin by the price and interest on that price for the years since it was paid.' On 1 August she wrote the epitaph of her marriage: 'Lovely day the last at Newbuildings where almost all traces of me will be effaced... So all is done. I paid Mrs Macquire's books – Annie and Fanny's wages I paid to next Friday Aug. 3 and Monday Aug. 6 – and so no complaint can be made – and there are stores, candles and the like to go on with. Farewell to Newbuildings after 37 years!'

She went to her daughter's cottage at Three Bridges, taking Judith's bedroom. 'It seems that H.F. has expressed surprise at not hearing from me,' she wrote on 21 August. 'But I have had my congé and accepted it. I have considered that it is an accomplished fact.' What Anne did not know was that at the very time she was preparing to leave and was tying up the legal loose ends of the stud, Wilfrid was anxiously awaiting the outcome of a meeting hurriedly arranged between Dorothy Carleton and Lady Gregory's young son Robert in Ireland.[21] The Wyndhams, acting as matchmakers, hoped the couple might fall in love. Wilfrid hoped devoutly that they would not, otherwise his latest dalliance would suffer and he feared he might have to return to Anne. At their remote hideout at Coole in Ireland, Dorothy and Robert listened to Yeats reciting Wilfrid's verse and delivering a eulogy on the 'handsome' poet. Dorothy flirted with both Yeats and young Robert. 'There is much of the charlatan in Yeats,' wrote Blunt. He was relieved to learn that Dorothy had decided to return to his embrace.[22]

When he was confronted with Anne's decision to leave home, Wilfrid wrote to her, 'only let the separation be a friendly one and not a quarrel, I can still go to stay with you as a guest and you with me. Only we shall have our separate establishments.'[23] He recorded his belief that Anne had 'entirely agreed', and so the whole thorny question had been 'settled in half an hour'. It wasn't quite as simple as that however.

Just before Anne's move to Forest Cottage, Judith had written in her diary, 'My Father has turned Mother out of the house and she has taken lodgings at Three Bridges. She cannot put up with Dorothy and H.F. won't give D. up.'

No sooner had the matter been resolved, however unsatisfactorily for the women of his family, than Wilfrid began to have second thoughts, claiming not to understand Anne's phrase about being given her 'congé'. He wrote to her, 'It was... rather your proposal than mine, for, until you pressed the division of the stud and of all common financial arrangements, I was averse to any change.'

In the margin of the letter Anne wrote, 'Humbug'.[24] And she told Ralph, 'I am fighting against the Powers of Evil and am striking out as it were in the dark, against one who is a match for almost any lawyer.'

Blunt's latest theory was that Ralph was responsible for his sister's change of attitude from a 'friendly' one to hostility. What Anne had not bargained for was that within eight days of her writing her valedictory letter to Wilfrid, Ralph was to die unexpectedly. Her younger brother went suddenly on 29 August, at the age of 67.[25]

Ralph had inherited a large part of Ada's fortune and a third of Lady Byron's estate. He left it all to his wife Mary, Lady Lovelace, and after her to his sister Anne and his niece Judith, ignoring the daughter of his first marriage, Ada Mary, who succeeded to the Wentworth title. During the long battle between Anne and Wilfrid, Ralph had been Blunt's most formidable opponent as a shareholder in the stud, and had proposed before his death to challenge in the courts the settlement that was being forced on Anne, and to obtain for her a divorce, despite her own Catholic reservations. Blunt was now released at last from the dangers inherent in his attempts to be rid of Anne and to gain ascendancy in the disposal of the stud. All the same, he began to blame Ralph and 'his perpetual memories of the old Byron separation' for his own position. Three months after the separation Wilfrid wrote a pamphlet extolling the stud. For Anne, the hurt her husband was prepared to inflict on her was endless, yet she lacked the will or the instinct to repay him in kind.

Her diary exhibited irony, but not the anger and disdain that might have flowed naturally from a less ladylike pen:

By the way last night I read H.F.'s pamphlet on the C.A.S. [Crabbet Arabian Stud] in which he is glorified and I am ignored. There is an account of how Mr Blunt went and bought horses from the Bedouins and how later Mr Blunt bought up what was left of Ali Pasha Sharif's stud! His portrait of Shieha adorns the work as frontispiece.[26]

In November she left for Sheykh Obeyd, where she was to spend most of the rest of her life. Before leaving she received a message from Judith to say that Dorothy Carleton had moved into Newbuildings and was to be adopted as HF's 'niece'. Miss Lawrence was said to be furious. Dorothy had only just been installed when his 'Bedouin wife' Mary Elcho reappeared. Blunt felt guilty 'for Dorothy's sake.'

Anne had had lunch with her daughter and Neville on 5 November, 'a happy party of 4 notwithstanding sadness and sorrow.' The fourth member of the party was Cowie's successor Jennie Richie. They talked of Wilfrid's latest scheme, land sales in Egypt, where land prices were booming in consequence of the spread of suburban Cairo and the construction of a railway close to Sheykh Obeyd. Like many protectors of the weak and oppressed, Blunt was not above making a profit from their misfortunes. Anne had plans of her own for preparing part of the Egyptian estate for Judith and Neville.[27] She proposed to let off part of the extensive garden and to sell a slice between it and Al Kheysheh, the house that had been dedicated to Mary Elcho, 'by which means I should be able to supplement my claim and get enough to buy the outer strip.'

Among her first visitors was Gertrude Bell.[28] 'Her visit was really delightful to me, there is so much we both care about... I was regretful when she left.' The friendship of the older woman for her successor as a woman explorer in Arab lands was generosity itself. And whenever Gertrude was in the vicinity she repaid the compliment by making Sheykh Obeyd her first port of call.

For the time being Anne shuttled back and forth between Cairo and Three Bridges, dividing each year almost equally, with the inexpressible joy of regularly seeing Judith and the grandchildren. She refused now to meet Wilfrid. 'The first object I saw as I came down the park was my grandchild Anne perched on top of Berak!' she noted in September 1907. 'Yesterday Anthony informed me that "Daddy" had told him he might have a horse.' Her daughter and now her grandchildren were set to carry on her family's equine tradition and her satisfaction was obvious.

The following year she returned to England to discover to her surprise that Judith had decided to move into Crabbet from Forest Cottage. Judith had discussed the matter with Wilfrid, having invited him to come for two days and talk, and signing herself with the familiar name he had given her in childhood, 'Bibi'. She told her father she did not want to make changes at Crabbet without consulting him, and offered him a room of his own, the 'hermitage' he had often spoken of.[29] But daughterly appeals to his better nature were no more effective than wifely stratagems. There was a barrage of angry correspondence between Blunt, Neville and Guy Carleton about the accommodation of Dorothy at Crabbet. Blunt insisted that if Judith could not be polite to Dorothy she must not expect him to visit her. 'Judith has no real right to set up as my censor of morals.' Neville explained that Judith's attitude was based not on moral grounds but on loyalty to her mother. She wanted to remain neutral. Why could he not keep his affair with Dorothy away from the family? Blunt decided to force the issue, announcing that he would be calling in with Dorothy and could they be given lunch. Judith caved in, and the couple arrived on 13 April. Blunt was far from contrite.

> I slept in the big bedroom in the east front where I have spent many a happy night in former times with loves that are gone to their graves. Now I am installed there in an old man's way with my nurse next door to me. I find Judith

most anxious to make things agreeable to me; and I am sure I was right in showing my teeth about Dorothy.[30]

Judith, conscience-stricken at having betrayed her mother, wrote to tell Anne how 'inimical' the whole visit was. Anne was shocked and angered. She wrote to Wilfrid and Judith, telling both of her indignation and accusing him of 'immorality', 'premeditated insult' and 'revolting conduct' in dragging his daughter into his sordid affair. Wilfrid promptly accused Judith of treachery: 'You are too hard, too self-interested, too double tongued, to be trusted... Enjoy Crabbet for the future in your own filial way, I will never set foot inside its doors again. Wilfrid Scawen Blunt.'

Guy Carleton had the last and perhaps most telling word: 'I don't think you and Dorothy know what scandal you have caused. You and she see only a very small set of people and do not know what is being said. You may explain till you are black in the face but the world at large will not take your view of the matter.'[31]

Writing one political tract after another in between angry disputes with all and sundry, Blunt became ill again, this time with a hernia and a tubercular abscess in his throat. When Judith refused henceforth to meet her father in the house, though willing to discuss stud matters in the open, he noted that hers was 'precisely the kind of letter Lady Byron might have written in answer to a message from her husband.'

Anne, still incensed, returned in June from Sheykh Obeyd. On 4 June she wrote to her sister-in-law Mary, Lady Lovelace:

It is really a joy to see Crabbet lived in by Judith and Neville and the delight they and the children take in it. Everything they have done in the house is admirable, the library, which was so dull, is their own private writing room – one at each end – and by slight alterations in the bookshelves, and painting in white the room now looks lovely.[32]

Anne had acquired a motor car in 1908 and was taken to London in it. She visited Lewis's store in Oxford Street to buy a whalebone hairbrush and was confronted by a portrait of Wilfrid with 'hair ébouriffé [ruffled] so that you could not see its quantity', with an advertising claim beneath to the effect that it was all the result of 40 years of hair care at Lewis's. But visits to England were devoted increasingly to arguments with Blunt, conducted through Guy Carleton, about the sale of bloodstock. Her husband had begun to feel sorry for the woman he had induced to share his old age. 'Up to this moment I have not really felt my years, having it still in my power to make a woman I love happy. I can hardly hope any more for this, and the thought is depressing.' In 1909 he told Neville that going round the stud with Anne and Holman (the groom) with umbrellas raised against the English weather was not attractive to him. 'I closed the door on that portion of my life once again, not to knock more at it,' he said. Yet he would again hold out a deceptive olive branch.

On 22 September 1908, Anne's diary read: 'My seventy-first birthday!!! Really it feels quite impossible. I don't understand being old, especially so old, a bit!'

In Egypt Anne spent more and more time in the desert among her Bedouin friends. She was usually accompanied by her Cairo stud manager Mutlak al Batal, and two or three tribal guides. The sheikhs were always delighted to see her and were astonished that her riding skill and agility had not diminished. She had been taught by the Bedouin of central Arabia many years before, the skill of jumping on to her horse without a stirrup, and how to ride without bridle or bit, only a rope halter. Even at 70 she could, at a pinch, still mount as they mounted and ride as they rode. The desert and the Arab horse were her abiding passions, as enchanting as they had been when, as a child, she had listened to stories of strange and distant lands. Most of her time was spent talking of horses with the great men of desert and town, especially since she had decided to enter one of her favourite steeds, Saadun, at a future Heliopolis race meeting in March 1913.[33] It had been trained by a wealthy Greek by the name of Michaelides who thought it unlikely to win. In fact it was last but one. A visitor in December 1912 had been Muhammad al Bassam, wealthy merchant and powerful supplier of guides and horses in the Arab lands, who had helped her and her famous predecessor Charles Doughty on their way to central Arabia. He carried good wishes from Faisal al Duwish, supreme sheikh of the powerful Mutair tribe of Najd and leader of a fanatical warrior sect known as the Ikhwan (brotherhood).

Al Duwish's tribesmen and the Muntafiq of Ibn Saadun, traditional enemies, had recently made common cause against Sheikh Mubarak of Kuwait and Ibn Saud of Riyadh, and had lost many of their best horses in the enterprise, which had caused some concern to Britain. When she heard the news, Anne decided to rename her horse Abeyan, calling it Saadun after the distinguished Shia family of the Iraqi Muntafiq and its warrior chief.[34]

Lord Kitchener, Britain's resident in Cairo at the time, was another frequent visitor to Sheykh Obeyd. He wanted to purchase Anne's beautiful filly Ghadia but she refused to sell. Her great hope at the moment was that her investments in Egypt would provide an income of £1,000 a year, so that in the event of her death Judith could maintain the home and stud at Cairo.[35]

Late in 1913, while in England, Anne wrote optimistically of a visit by Judith to Forest Cottage, where she had lunch with her father. 'H.F. spoke of liking Neville better than anyone else in the world! So much the better.'[36] She was overjoyed to learn that her grandson Anthony was to go to Downside School and was more than happy to pay the fees. But Anne had another reason to visit the cottage at Three Bridges. At Woolborough nearby she had for three years been attempting to buy a 'charming' horse breeding establishment presently occupied by a tenant, Lilywhite, of whom she had the highest opinion. With the aid of Judith she intended to set up a new stud to take the place of Crabbet, where horses could be protected from Blunt's erratic and unpredictable methods.

Before returning to Cairo in November she learnt that Wilfrid wanted to rewrite the 'horse book' she had been compiling in Cairo (sending him sections for comment from time to time). She was not flattered. 'Whatever I do I will be responsible for, and it shall be mine alone. I being the worm that turned.'

All the same, she was pleased in her seventy-eighth year, to receive an invitation from Wilfrid, by way of Judith, to visit Newbuildings.[37] Dorothy would be absent, he said. Almost two years before, in October 1912, she had confided to Mary Lovelace that she 'lamented separating' and hoped that there might still be the possibility of reconciliation. She had found Wilfrid's tone 'not such an unkind one' in communications that had passed between them. But since the arrangement still held with Dorothy,

I should have to stipulate that going [to Newbuildings] did not imply approval of being displaced by her. That was one anxiety. Another, that I fear H.F. if he actually met me would again have that sense of irritation my presence had caused for several years before I was told to cut myself adrift. Otherwise I should like to accept, I should not like to refuse and lose the chance of breaking down the barrier between us. H.F. is the one person in the world to whom I ought to be nearest, the very pain of seeing him again is caused by that. For through him came all that made life worth living for me – even through him I got religion (though he opposed it) for it was praying for him as he lay ill on the ground in S.W. Persia that caused the window to open in Heaven; not half open but wide so that had I then backed out it might be shut forever.

A luncheon party was arranged for 12 May 1915, 'My brother Byron's birthday – he would have been 79 had he lived', not at Newbuildings but at another of the Blunt homes nearby, Worth Manor. Judith had prepared for the meeting with military precision, driving her mother in a carriage without servants so that no one but she would witness her parents' greeting. They kissed and were soon discussing stud and other horse matters animatedly. Judith herself was now 42 and entered fully into the spirit of the 'really gay' reunion. Anne described in her diary how Wilfrid came towards her with a look of kindness in his eyes such as she had not seen for ages.

Wilfrid wrote: 'I have never been more impressed with her intellectual superiority and the pleasantness of her conversation... the threads of life seem drawn together again, to the extent that it seems strange there should ever have been any quarrel.'

There were further meetings throughout the summer that Anne stayed at Caxtons.[38] The Blunts decided in their propinquity to reorganise the stud at Wilfrid's suggestion. They would jointly revoke a deed of 1906 giving him day-to-day control, he would assign the ownership and management entirely to her while she lived, and it would revert to him if he survived her. When she left in October she received what was surely the kindest letter he had ever written her:

> Dearest Anne: It has been a very great pleasure seeing you... and it seems a pity it should end so soon... You have made Caxtons a very perfect little hermitage... I wish I was going with you... I shall expect you back about Christmas time, perhaps before. And so goodbye and God bless you. Your affectionate W.S.B.

Anne left for Egypt in despondent mood, despite the pleasure she felt at a partial reconciliation with Wilfrid. Great care had been taken to ensure that Anne did not meet Dorothy, but Judith's blood was up, and she was determined to force the intruder from the family home. She was so angry on one occasion that she threatened Dorothy with physical violence after her father's mistress had ill-advisedly taken the children to the dentist without her permission.

Despite considerable financial help from Anne, the Lyttons found it hard to meet the expenses of Crabbet and Judith dismissed Caffin her agent and stud manager, accusing him of embezzling £14,000.[39] Even worse, in the course of her stay Anne had begun to see her daughter's generation go the way of all the others. 'Neville left after 5 o'clock – to go to theatre in London. He does not care one straw for home except to get what worldly honour and glory he can by a show of it – it is terribly humiliating to see him thus,' wrote Judith.

Judith had written on a letter she received from Anne in 1913 a note that Wilfrid had 'thrown cold water' on her mother's latest work. None the less, it was that work, the horse book, that kept Anne and Wilfrid in touch.

'I think I have nearly finished the horse book; what was one chapter of it has become three with chronological sequence.'[40] It was the most precious of Anne's life's works, and the one destined never to be completed. With its echoes of the nomadic tradition in Najd and inner Arabia, of romantic fable in Islam and the east, it was a tribute above all to her first love, the Arab horse. There were chapters of deep and sympathetic scholarship on the 'Life of the Desert Horse', the 'Golden Horsemen of Arabia', the 'Poets', 'The horse in Verse', 'The Tribes' and 'The Strains'. The final chapter traced the pedigree of the Arab horse from its most ancient origins to the great modern studs. Judith, as the 16th Baroness Wentworth, would eventually inherit the papers and write her famous book, *The Authentic Arabian Horse* (first published in 1945), vindicating her mother in equine and many other respects. Anne continued working on it for the rest of her days. After her death, the work was to be the cause of further dispute between her husband and the daughter who inherited it.

A few days after her return to Egypt, Anne wrote to tell Wilfrid she had almost completed the project. The last day of 1915: 'The enclosed rose leaves were waiting to be sent to you, almost since Christmas Day... They were so glorious in colour but, poor things, have shrunk woefully.'

In February 1916 her faithful retainer at Sheykh Obeyd, Mutlak, began to sink into oblivion, 'his face, sharpened and drawn seemed to me to have the peculiar refinement of death – and so it was... the end has come as I feared and knew must be. A preparation for myself.'[41]

The unending tradition of family feud began to involve her in disputes with her beloved Judith. On 11 September 1916 she told of two letters from her daughter containing 'much ill-natured gossip'. Eight months later, on 28 May 1917, she wrote to Wilfrid:

> As to the frame of mind, so suspicious and pervaded with the idea of having 'enemies' through which I see Judith passing, I have been thinking that it came on that calamitous visit to America. She and N[eville] were never the same after that and I have suspected the loss of large sums of money there, in the going and returning and the stay there, of which we shall never hear the true story – or perhaps any story at all. I hope it will not continue always, especially as I am told 'You are siding with my enemies (plural).'[42]

Neville was an outstanding tennis player and in 1911 had become amateur champion. He and Judith had gone to America early in 1915 with their tennis coach Geoffrey Covey, and had returned wiser and poorer to renew the conflict with Wilfrid, who had become addicted to morphia. There was an hysterical climax just before Christmas 1916, when Blunt shouted at his daughter, now known as 'Jack' to her children, who were present, that her head should 'hang with Cromer's on Traitor's Gate'.[43] Judith henceforth refused her children permission to visit

Newbuildings, and in her anger decided to auction parts of the Crabbet estate that had been her birthright. It was that threat which must have alarmed Anne as much as it did Blunt. When Blunt heard of the plan he accused Judith of extravagance and told Anne of her wickedness. Judith replied, 'What has been your example as a Father?'

She tried to rescue her father from the clutches of his 'immoral paramour', using a local priest, Father Lawrence, as an intermediary. Blunt told the priest that he was an atheist in no need of priestly succour and that he loved Dorothy 'more than wife, child or grandchildren'. The priest told Judith, 'He is a most dangerous and most wicked man. He is determined to get hold of Anthony, and he will stop at nothing, mind you, nothing, in order to do so. He would get you certified as a lunatic to get the boy.'

Judith feared that she was becoming paranoid. She was convinced that her father had planted spies everywhere at Crabbet, and on one occasion thought she had caught one of them, a maid, red-handed. The maid had, she decided, stolen clothes, rings, and a bottle marked Sexual Pills, intended for Judith's dogs (she was a leading light of the Kennel Club and presumably an enthusiastic breeder). 'I hope she took them,' said Judith with singular lack of charity. She told Dorothy that for years her relationship with her father had been common talk; 'now my Father's age has turned the gossip into ridicule. All this is gall and misery and horror to my Mother and me.'

Anne's life in Cairo continued in the growing belief that the war had reduced her means drastically, – a belief which was without foundation, – and that she must economise in every possible way.[44] She was visited frequently by the members of the Arab Bureau, a military intelligence section billeted at the Grand Continental Hotel. First among them was Gertrude Bell, who in 1914 had followed Anne's path to Hail in Najd, where the once-proud Rashid dynasty had fallen into the hands of the boorish young Prince Saud, son of Abdul Aziz ibn Rashid. Gertrude went off to Basra early in 1916 at the instigation of Lord Hardinge the Indian Viceroy to head the Arab Bureau there. Sheykh Obeyd became a favoured refuge for that brilliant bunch of academics and intelligence agents who gathered together to foster the Arab revolt against the Turks and to keep an eye on the Arab chiefs – Hogarth, Fielding, Lawrence, Gertrude Bell, Storrs and others. On 16 November 1916, Anne had recorded a visit from David Hogarth and Everard Fielding, and she noted with satisfaction: 'Certainly the Intelligence Dept. as to Arab matters is now very well served. He [Hogarth] told me Miss Bell has done most valuable work in Basra.'

In the belief that she was close to insolvency, Anne temporarily cancelled Judith's allowance of £4,000 a year, and began to walk rather than use the horses to save money on their fodder and, incidentally, to help the war effort. She collected wood in the grounds and reduced it to charcoal in order to provide fuel. And she hurried to finish her book. What she enigmatically called the 'most embarrassing' chapter, 'Hira and Ghassan', was, she noted on 1 February 1917, 'almost finished'.[45]

Anne was feeling weary and working by candlelight at night, though still taking cold showers, a habit she had acquired as a girl in the stark regimes of the Byron and Lovelace homes. She learnt from Judith that Crabbet was being auctioned – the stud remained intact through the agreement reached with Wilfrid – and she was informed that her husband thought she should know lest she 'wasted good hopes and prayers'. Anne was inclined, when she heard, to blame her daughter as much as Wilfrid. 'I suppose the utmost one can hope for W. is that his own soul should become safe, he and J. are so alike in their absolutism'.

As she viewed the break-up of Crabbet, she faced with as much distress the thought that she might have to dispose of Sheykh Obeyd. But she could not envisage a future without the horses; 'when one's mind is sorrowful a sight of the 4 legged friends is most soothing – an affectionate welcome in which there is no guile and then the contemplation of extreme beauty and distinction!'

On 19 June 1917, she received a telegram from Wilfrid telling her that her niece 'Molly' (Ada Mary), 14th Baroness Wentworth, had died. Now, just before her eightieth birthday, Anne became Baroness Wentworth. 'Strange,' she wrote, 'that something over two centuries ago an "Anne" of my ancestors was also compelled to inherit the title from a generation below. The reverse of the order of nature'.

On 22 September she celebrated her eightieth birthday, 'alas 4/5 of a century...What a remarkable birthday – it is a happy one too, in spite of many anxieties, as such delightful friends surround me and also I have I do believe got the preparation for death well established – if only H.F. could be shown what I was shown and Judith could see what is the only right course towards him.'[46]

The next day her beloved Saadun died. 'The end came rather suddenly, he seemed rather dazed and like one with a severe headache. A great loss'.

Two months earlier, on 31 July, she had written to Wilfrid telling him again of the 'Glory which may not be described':

> ...the sight of which for more than a few seconds no human being as we are now could behold and live. I may not put into words what I saw but it was such that further doubts were out of the question. I knew. When we got to Simla I ought to have been received into the Church but a shyness held me back. I knew not how to set about it, so I waited till we were in England, uneasy all the while as it was conveyed to my mind that the window would never open again. To write at all, or even to speak, of this or anything that stirs me deeply is hard – most of all what touches depths unfathomable. I should not do so now but that if I put it off I may never tell you.[47]

Anne's last days were tormented by the unidentified skin disease that increasingly disfigured her. She still had the affection of her daughter and grandchildren and she was adored by the staff at Sheykh Obeyd. And while the husband for whom she still cared wrote sonnets to the worshipping Dorothy, Anne wrote again, with that clipped candour which characterized her diaries from start to finish, of her 'Indian Summer', lived in the shadow of that immeasurable Persian experience: 'The afternoon heavenly, the sun set in blaze of fire followed by that strange return of a brilliant radiance. My ride was so delightful, I feel as if I had never ridden before! What a joy to have such a pleasure before I die.'[48]

A week before, she had received her last recorded letter from Wilfrid discussing the disposal of some of the horses from the depleted English stud. 'I feel it too for one can't make breeding successful with numbers too restricted,' she wrote. Next day she was visited by three old friends from the Arab Bureau, Lieutenant Commander Hogarth, her most devoted admirer in Cairo's military intelligence hierarchy MacIndoe, and 'Everard himself'.

November 2: 'A day of clouds, rather warm, in any other country one would think a storm brewing but it only ended in a splendid red and fiery sunset.'

November 7: 'The chill that began on the night Sun-Monday is rather bad – internal upset, no rest night or day but I managed to be about all Wed. afternoon... this is Saturday 10 am & am a shade better but no Mass for me on Sunday.'

On 26 November 1917, her friend and joint executor Philip Napier wrote to her sister-in law Mary:

Dear Lady Lovelace, I have been asked by Lady Anne to write and tell you she has been ill and is unable to write letters. It began with a chill on the stomach, which would not yield to home treatment, so a very good doctor was called in, who persuaded Lady Anne to go into the Anglo-

American hospital, which she did and there everything is being done for her. The doctor calls it dysenteric-diarrhoea. This has left Lady Anne very weak, but she is able to take nourishment and is slowly regaining her strength. She wants for nothing and is particularly anxious that none of her family should endeavour to make the journey to Egypt. In a younger person the illness would not be serious, but with Lady Anne's advanced age it is serious and I will not disguise from you that we have had an anxious time. I have written to Mr Blunt and to Judith, but was somewhat guarded in what I said and did not mention that Lady Anne was in hospital as I was particularly asked not to cable and as letters take so long now I said to her, I hope by the time she receives my letter that Lady Anne will be well again... I hope very soon to be able to write you better news... Believe me, Sincerely yours, Philip Napier.

Anne felt separated irreconcilably from husband and daughter. Napier and his wife Gabriella, and her own devout faith, were her comforters in the last days. She died at the hospital on 15 December 1917.[49]

# Chapter Fifteen

# Requiem

Anne was buried at the nuns' cemetery on Jabal Ahmar, Red Hill, looking out across the plain of ancient Egypt to Heliopolis.[1] Wilfrid designed a headstone for her grave and had inscribed on it the simple legend:

Here lies in the Egyptian
desert which she loved
LADY ANNE BLUNT

Beneath her name was the title she had held for only six months, 'Baroness Wentworth'. Judith succeeded to the title; her father feared that it would make her more arrogant than ever.

Not until 14 June 1917 had Anne drawn up her last will and testament and put her signature to the document which gave power of attorney to Philip Henry Napier of the Ministry of Finance in Cairo, and the Public Trustee, and which in the complexity of its wording was to give rise to family disputes after her death as tempestuous as those of her married life. Wilfrid called it 'a wicked will'.[2]

After the customary minor bequests to family and servants, she disposed of her property, fortune and life's work:

'I bequeath all my stud books and papers relating thereto to my husband Wilfrid Scawen Blunt of Newbuildings Place in the County of Sussex.' That was all. There was no further mention of the man who had assumed that he would inherit the goodwill and the fortune of the woman who had accepted voluntary exile in Egypt so that his 'niece' by adoption could occupy the marital bed and his nurse dictate the running of her household. He should not have been surprised, but he was, and was outraged.

To Judith, she left 'a stand of four tin boxes painted white, presently at Caxtons Worth in Sussex... and the contents thereof and the manuscript of my book "Fragments on the Horse of Arabia", together with all books, manuscripts, papers and writings of what kind so ever in any way relating thereto.'[3] She went on to explain that she had made no financial provision for her daughter, 'first because ample provision has been made for and is secured to her by marriage settlement... to a sum of twenty eight thousand four hundred and seventy pounds and nine shillings such estate and sum having been left by my grandmother Anne (sic) Isabella Noel Byron Baroness Wentworth upon trust... and secondly because my said daughter has been in receipt of an ample income from her marriage settlement from the Crabbet Park Estate a gift to her from her father... and has received from me the portion of £20,000 (Twenty thousand pounds) which came to me under the marriage settlement of my mother Augusta Ada Countess of Lovelace and thirdly because I have given to my said daughter all my jewellery [etc]... as well as sums of money amounting in aggregate to not less than £31,000 in fifteen years.' There was a hint in the lawyer's language that her daughter's interests had not been entirely neglected.

If the bequest of the 'horse book' manuscript to Judith took priority over other weightier matters, it proved to be the daughter's most precious possession. Her mother's notes were the substance of her sumptuous work *The Authentic Arabian Horse,* published in 1945. Judith claimed that after her father had discouraged her mother's work she destroyed important parts of the manuscript in 1913. But when David Hogarth visited her just before her death she arranged her 'book portfolio' for him to see, and there is no evidence that anything was lacking. After Judith had used the manuscript for her own purpose, it disappeared.

In a cascade of unpunctuated and almost unintelligible legal jargon, the will went on to leave the land Anne had acquired at Sheykh Obeyd and its thoroughbred stock together with her 'private' breeding centre at Woolborough near Three Bridges (which she had finally purchased in September 1916 after six years' negotiation) and 'all my other estate both real and personal' to her trustees to hold or convert into cash on behalf of her granddaughters Anne and Winifred Lytton. On the death of either granddaughter 'without issue', her share was to be disposed of at the discretion of Cardinal Bourne, 'or other the head for the time being of the Roman Catholic Church in England', for the benefit of a suitable home or hospital for disabled sailors and soldiers, or 'failing such appointments', to the Royal Sussex Hospital at Brighton.

The effect of the will was to ensure that there was no surplus of money for Blunt to lavish on the very costly studs at Crabbet and Newbuildings, of which he now believed himself the sole owner according to the deed of partition drawn up with Anne in 1906.[4] In fact, the 1906 agreement had been revoked by Anne in 1915, and the whole ownership transferred to her. Blunt was convinced that Anne had been 'got at' by his enemies. He considered her death an unwarranted intrusion into his plans for the sunset of his life.

Matters soon came to a head. In February 1918, while
the rest of the world awaited with bated breath the outcome
of the last decisive battles of the Great War, Judith fired the
first shots in another conflict, claiming through her
daughters' trustees part of the stud and certain horses of
which the most important was named Riyala. These were
among the horses Anne had bred secretly at Woolborough
and elsewhere in order to prevent Wilfrid from selling or
racing them indiscriminately, and Judith had staked her
claim almost ten years before, when in June 1909 Anne had
promised the mare to the cosmopolitan American inventor
and breeder of Arabs, Colonel Spencer Borden. 'J[udith] is
still harping on my having let Riyala be bought by Borden,
and she says Riyala is of the whole stud the mare she would
choose,' Anne had noted.

Despite the Married Women's Property Act of 1882, the
law was heavily biased in favour of inheritance through the
male line and the Public Trustee intimated to Blunt that he
could probably sustain a case for total ownership of the
stud. Nevertheless, the lawyers' view on balance was that
he should allow his daughter the horses she claimed her
mother had given her and her grandchildren. But Blunt
refused to countenance the claim. He intended to stand firm
against his daughter and grandchildren 'even at the risk of
litigation'. He quickly transferred all the horses to
Newbuildings and waited as if for an impending siege.

In early April his fears were realised. Judith descended
with her three children, her coachman and gardener and
raided the loose horseboxes. Riyala was in a closed box and
Judith ordered her son Anthony to break the lock.[5]

What followed was described by Blunt. As the tall
athletic Anthony forced open the horse box, the
Newbuildings groom Holman and his daughter Dulcie ran
from their cottage to prevent the raiders from getting at the
mare. With characteristic hyperbole Blunt described
Anthony as an expert at 'garrotting'. In fact, like his mother

and sisters, he was practised at judo, and he was very muscular. Holman was left with a bleeding hand and a torn-off finger nail, as Riyala was led away in triumph, the entire Holman family screaming abuse as they went.

According to Elizabeth Longford, Wilfrid's biographer, Judith described the event somewhat differently in her manuscript autobiography *Myself and Others*. After the mare had been securely locked up at Crabbet, Judith and her cohorts returned to Newbuildings in pursuit of Riyala's foal. The ageing Holman grasped the foal's head while Anthony held on to its tail. Then Holman flung himself at Judith who, with Anthony's help, pinned him against the railings. After a bloody battle Judith and her daughter Anne, carrying the torch of her namesake grandmother, marched at the head of the column as it made its way back to Crabbet, the cry 'You pack o' savages!' echoing at the rear. 'Possession is nine points of the law,' shouted Judith to the outraged Holmans. The conflict had hardly begun for a family hardened by history and upbringing to public brawls. The armistice on the Western Front was celebrated by Blunt giving permission for the horse Regiz to be shot and its flesh consumed at Newbuildings in a celebratory feast, so that his daughter could not claim the animal.

The Paris peace conference was going about its interminable business by the time the infirm Wilfrid and his progeny faced each other in court. The Public Trustee, Sir Charles Stewart, had tried to avoid litigation by suggesting to Blunt that he leave the whole stud to Judith after his death. That official was, according to the new Baroness Wentworth, 'a dear old fossil, not used to dealing with explosives.'

In the end, Stewart was forced to bring the dispute to the courts in order to establish the ownership of what had become one of the world's most valuable collections of thoroughbred horses. Blunt's London hairdresser had been sent for to ensure that he looked his best in court. Philip

Napier was called as a vital witness to the intentions of Anne, expressed so vaguely in her will. Judith averred that she 'gave it to him hot and strong in the neck'. She was put under a savage cross-examination by her father's counsel. While the legal acrimony flared, the press flocked to Crabbet and Newbuildings. As the drama unfolded an Egyptian diplomat rushed from one stable to another brandishing an open cheque, while Prince Kamal ad-Din instructed his agent to buy the entire stud and not to leave a single horse behind. They in turn were pursued by an American commission agent on a motorcycle wielding a knuckleduster and other offensive weapons.

When it was Blunt's turn to give evidence the court was convened at Newbuildings and a High Court judge and counsel for all sides repaired to Blunt's bedroom. Predictably, the aged HF as Judith still called him, wore gold-embroidered scarlet robes and reclined, like the actor he was, on the four-poster bed that had witnessed so many nocturnal adventures, surrounded by Morris tapestries and the paraphernalia of his Arabian days. He was savaged.

At Newbuildings and at a subsequent hearing in the High Court there were frequent questions about his life with Anne, her exile, and the last of his mistresses, Miss Carleton; ammunition astutely assembled by Judith and just as astutely fired by her counsel. Judith commented dryly, 'He has had his past put to him pretty mercilessly.' Her counsel told her that her father 'showed his fangs in a way which did him no good.' As the case dragged on, another compromise was suggested. He would have half the stud, on condition that he left it to his granddaughter Anne on his death.

But Blunt scented at least partial victory and was in no mood to make concessions. All the same, on 5 March 1920 he was told by his lawyers in a telegram: 'Decision against you with all costs but you allowed cost of keeping all horses that you had from January 1918.' Judith's legal advisers were more succinct: 'Game, set and match.'[6]

Blunt accepted defeat, if not with good grace at least with resignation. 'The duty of preserving the Stud now goes to my grandchildren,' he said, 'and they may or may not be found worthy of it.'

By November 1920 he had brushed aside such matters, beset as he was by ill health and the renewed calls of Egyptian nationalism, now pursued by Saad Zaghlul Pasha, who had risen from the ashes of the 1882 debacle to become the country's Prime Minister under Field Marshal Allenby's post-war regime. But Blunt was by then too sick to take part in the latest protest against British occupation; there was not even strength enough to write letters to the press.

Some ten years earlier, Blunt had experienced the piercing pain of the 'old man's' disease, a swollen prostate. Youth had finally deserted him and he felt his impotence keenly. Dorothy was happy nevertheless with her Newbuildings haven, without the passion and carnal pleasures that had for so long permeated its rooms and gardens.

The writer Desmond MacCarthy recalled the reminiscent dreams of youth exalted by the aged WSB in the hall at Newbuildings:[7]

*What has my youth been that I*
*love it thus,*
*Sad youth, to all but one grown*
*tedious,*
*Stale as the news which last*
*week wearied us,*
*Or a tired actor's tale told to*
*an empty house?*

'As I murmur that quatrain I shall remember the old man who wrote it; a very handsome vain old man, with spreading beard and eagle nose, and a voice sinisterly soft, whom I used sometimes to watch when talk had stopped, nid-nodding in Arab robes beside a pile of smouldering branches in the wide fireplace of a stone-paved panelled hall.' There were reminders of joyful days spent with Anne in the desert and in the Sussex countryside before all turned sour. Ostrich eggs, blue butterflies, bunches of immortelles; 'the Botticelli tapestry as fresh in colour as when it came off William Morris's looms'; that white marble hand, too, ('From what woman was it modelled? Why was it there?'); the freakish and fastidious collection of books.

He compared Blunt's work with Byron's. Blunt would have liked that, just as he would have enjoyed the singular praise and the acceptance of his imposture as the authentic picture of an Arab sheikh.

Others came to honour him and sit at his feet, but few spared a thought for Lady Anne, though it was she who had written the books which brought them, man and wife, the world's recognition for their achievements in the Arab lands, she who was always bravely at his side and had won the admiration of the Arabs of the desert; she who had rescued the Arab horse from near-extinction by breeding and codifying the pure strains discovered in their native habitat and rescued at great cost in money and labour. It was she who had given him that sense of compatability with her maternal grandfather that he savoured. For his part, he was at best a good poet, at worst an affected versifier and a vain, ungenerous man. Yet, in posterity, his was to be the fame.

He entered a second childhood in his last years. The man in whom Bernard Shaw had found the substance of Captain Shotover and Hector Hushabye was coddled and fussed over by Nurse Lawrence, propped up in bed, washed and dressed and undressed, gurgling with delight at his helplessness.[8]

A new generation of Arabophiles came to pay homage, led by its *enfant terrible* T.E. Lawrence and the self-appointed protagonist of the Saudi Arabian cause, Harry St. John Philby, father of Kim.[9] But it was Winston Churchill, just turned fifty and back in the political arena after the disasters of his wartime initiatives at the Admiralty who, next to Sydney Cockerell, became the closest of the friends of his dotage. Even in the immediate aftermath of Gallipoli, Winston and Clemmie had enjoyed dinner with Blunt, his grandson Anthony Lytton and Hilaire Belloc, and had marked the occasion by attacking the War Office (which had opposed the Gallipoli scheme at the outset). As colonial secretary in 1921-22 it had fallen to Churchill to resolve the nationality questions in Egypt and the Arabian peninsula which resulted from the break-up of the Ottoman Empire after nearly 500 years of dominion, and it fell to Anne's friend Gertrude Bell, Al Khatun of the Arabs, to help draw the new frontiers and explain Britain's policy to the emergent nations.

On the 5 September 1922 Churchill listened to the dying Blunt as the anti-imperialist demanded the return of Zaghlul, exiled by Britain like his predecessor Arabi Pasha. With that demand, Blunt effectively bade farewell to men and politics. Five days later, on the 10th, he died as Nurse Lawrence tried to restrain him from rising to look out of the window at Newbuildings. His last command was that Judith should not be told of his death until Cockerell arrived, perhaps to protect his secret memoirs and other papers.

Two years before his death, Blunt had received a message from Neville Lytton announcing his impending divorce from Judith. A loveless marriage came to the same bitter end as her great-grandparents' and her own parents'.

Their daughter, Lady Anne Lytton, who inherited her grandmother's personality and most of her wealth and property, was able to celebrate the centenary of the Crabbet Arabian Stud in 1978, and to show in her old age that she could ride with the same instinctive skill, and carry with the same affection and understanding, the stewardship of those brave and beautiful creatures which the first Lady Anne had bred from native stock.

Newbuildings was inherited by Dorothy Carleton. Judith died in 1957. She left the greater part of her estate to her godson Cecil, son of the international tennis player Geoffrey Frederick Covey who had become the tennis coach at Crabbet in 1915, and her estate manager Gladstone Moore.[10]

Judith penned her last words on the family in her work on the Arabian horse. Her mother and great-grandmother were saints; her own rocky marriage had helped to convince her of their innocence and of the culpability of generations of men. She recalled the occasion when Lord Byron threw himself at Annabella Milbanke's feet in a fit of remorse and begged her to forgive him. Seeing her moved by his grief he sprang to his feet and mocked her. 'That she ignored all subsequent protestations has been held against her as proof of vindictive coldness. More probably, like her granddaughter Lady Anne, she had learnt her lesson. She dreaded risking a second heartbreak which she felt unable to face and, treacherously disillusioned, consumed her own heart to ashes.' It was a subjective judgement, but it was not without substance. When Judith addressed more recent events, her bitterness spilled over and she was not entirely truthful:

Blunt's crowning heartlessness was the deliberate suppression of her last urgent message requesting him to tell her daughter of her approaching end. He never did so. Unselfish to the last, Lady Anne allowed herself to be taken to hospital, and there alone she died, waiting in vain for an answer which never came, believing herself forsaken by those she loved, to whom her death is a never-ending tragedy. For herself peace has come. In the desert sands of Egypt she lies for ever under an Eastern sun in the land of her heart, where her memory is held in honour by the natives who make pilgrimages to her tomb. To them she is the 'Noble Lady of the Horses', the friend of the nomad tribes... The dumb things that cannot speak shall speak for her as long as the Arabian horse exists... [and] somewhere in another world she may know it and be glad.

Yet her mother's own wish, conveyed in Napier's letter to Mary Lovelace, was that Anne had asked that her immediate family should not be encouraged to journey to Egypt.

Echoing the anonymous obituary writer of *The Times*, almost certainly David Hogarth, Judith added: 'To the end of her life she had the heart of a child, the brain of a scholar, and the soul of a saint.'[11]

# END NOTES

## BIBLIOGRAPHIC ABBREVIATIONS

BL     *British Library, Wentworth Collection*
LP     *Lovelace Papers (Dept Lovelace/Byron), Bodleian Library*
SP     *Somerville Papers, Bodleian Library*
FM    *Fitzwilliam Museum, Wilfrid Scawen Blunt Collection*
*The principal archive used in writing this book is the Wentworth Collection, consisting of:*
*Vols I - CCXIV Diaries of Lady Anne Blunt from 1847 - 1917 BL53871 - 54030*
*Vols CCXV - CCXLV Sketch books of Lady Anne 1850 - 1900 BL54031 - 54061*
*Vols CCXLVI - CCLII Notebooks and papers of Lady Anne c.1850-1947 BL54062 - 54068*
*Vols CCLIII - CCLXIV Diaries, sketchbooks etc., of Wilfrid Scawen Blunt BL54069 - 54080*
*Vols CCLXV - CCLXXII Miscellaneous papers BL54081 - 54088*
*Vols CCLXXIII - CCCXIII Correspondence BL54089 - 54129*
*Vols CCCXIV - CCCXXXII Horse Breeding/Crabbet Arabian Stud BL54130 - 54148*
*Vols CCCXXXIII - CCCXXXIV Lady Wentworth selected papers BL54149 - 54155*

# END NOTES

## Introduction

1.  Quotation, Wentworth, Judith Lady, *The Authentic Arabian Horse*
2.  Britain, Turkey and Greece. Kinross, Lord, *The Ottoman Centuries*, London 1977; Anderson, M.S., *The Eastern Question 1774-1923*, London 1976.
3.  Byron in Greece, see Moore, Doris Langley, *Lord Byron, Accounts Rendered*.
4.  Inter-family relationships of Noels, Milbankes, Melbournes, Byrons, Blunts, and their successors. See Elwin, M, *Lord Byron's Wife*; and by the same author, *The Noels and Milbankes*, and *Lord Byron's Family*. See also, Moore, Doris Langley, *Ada Countess of Lovelace*, Longford, Elizabeth, *A Pilgrimage of Passion, The Life of Wilfrid Scawen Blunt*, and Finch, Edith, *Wilfrid Scawen Blunt*.
5.  Medora to Lady Byron, Langley Moore, op.cit., Appendix 5.

## Chapter One

1.  Anne's birth, Official Register of births, Vol 1, Page 60, July-Sept 1837: 22nd September 1837, King, Ann Isabella Noel, St James's, Westminster.
2.  Quotation, LP, September 1836, in Moore, Ada, Countess of Lovelace.
3.  Anne's recollections, BL54809 and Moore, op.cit.
4.  Ada, Lady Byron, Babbage. Ibid., and Woolley, Benjamin, *The Bride of Science*.

5.  Ada, Babbage. BL54809; and see Moore, op.cit, and Woolley, op.cit.
6.  Miss Lamont, governesses; Ada's and Lovelace's attitude to children. BL 54089; and see Moore, op.cit.
7.  Education, ibid.
8.  Lovelace. ibid. Elizabeth Fry, see De Morgan, Sophia, *Threescore Year and Ten*. Fanny Kemble, see Wright, Constance, *Fanny Kemble and the Lonely Land*.
9.  Lady Byron and her entourage. BL54089. And see De Morgan, op.cit.
10. Mrs Fry and Lady Byron at Clapham Common, ibid.
11. De Fellenberg, Pestalozzi and Lovelace children, BL54090, and LP, November 1834, quoted by Moore op.cit. p55f.
12. Anne's first letter, to mother, BL54091.
13. Dr Carpenter, LP, November 1843, quoted by Moore, op.cit. p193f. In *The Bride of Science*, the latest biography of Ada and with regard to her mathematical and scientific work by far the best, Benjamin Woolley says p286; 'Annabella [Lady Byron] recommended to William [Lovelace] that he appoint Dr Carpenter as the new tutor of the Lovelace children. What she did not tell her doting son-in-law was that she had also instructed Dr Carpenter to see what he could do about Ada, a mission that the doctor embarked upon with enthusiasm...' Woolley adds: 'He [Carpenter] discovered a woman in a state of frustration and confusion.'
14. Mr Frederick Knight, Moore op.cit, p160f. Local newspaper, 'unidentified'.
15. Ada and Crosse, Wheatstone, Babbage, BL54090, and Moore, op.cit, p220f.

## Chapter Two

1.  Diary, 1 July 1847, BL53817.
2.  Quote, BL54090.
3.  Lady Millicent, BL53817.
4.  Ada to Lady Byron re. Boys and Ruskin, ibid and LP43. Lady Byron's address at this time, 21 Dover Street, London. Also see Collingwood W.G., Life of John Ruskin, p21, T. Boys described as an engraver and one of Ruskin's drawing circle.

5. Birthday, Wednesday 22 September, BL53817.
6. Mr Scott, BL54090.
7. Lady Byron, Ada to Lady Byron re. Miss Lamont, LP 43.
8. Fraulein Waechter, LP43. And see Moore, op.cit. p280.
9. Ada's health. ibid.
10. Letter from Ashley Combe, ibid.
11. Ada and Anne's education, BL54089; quote Ada's children, LP60, letters Ada to Lady Byron 1848-50.
12. Letter from Ashley Combe, BL54090.
13. Anne's letter, BL54089.
14. Anne's letters and diaries, LP167 and BL53817.
15. Stradivarius. Moore, op.cit., remarks that instrument known in musical circles by solecism 'The Lady Blunt'.
16. Betting, debt and blackmail. LP 43.
17. Germany LP 60; and BL53817 (Tuesday 6 July 1850 et seq.), and BL54090.
18. Anne to GM, BL54090.
19. Anne to her parents, 12 Nov 1850, BL54090.
20. Ada to Anne. LP 43.
21. Horse racing activities, ibid.
22. 'Consolation of her life', quoted by Moore, op.cit.
23. Ada to Lady B and Anne; Lovelace and children, LP 43.
24. Journey to France, ibid, and BL53818 (15 Aug-6 Sept 1851).
25. Miss Waechter, LP177.
26. Ada to GM, BL54091.
27. Ghost from the past. See Moore, op.cit., p103f.
28. Betting saga. Floodgates of dementia. LP 167. Moore, op.cit. p300 notes that at about this time Lovelace admitted that he had given Ada a letter authorising her 'tremendous betting' at Epsom. Moore observed 'it strains credulity [yet] the evidence that he did so is conclusive.'
29. New Year's Ball. BL54089.
30. Ada on deathbed. BL54091, and Moore, op.cit. quotes Lovelace's journal of wife's illness in SP. Lovelace's journal entries herein, BL54089.
31. Wilkinsons. Ibid.
32. Ockham, Miss Waechter. BL54091.
33. The last days of Ada. BL54089. Pages from Lovelace's journal, 'copied from his own hand by Lady Byron', see Moore, op.cit.

## Chapter Three

1. Correspondence and quotes, BL54090.
2. Correspondence and quotes, BL54090.
3. Lovelace to GM, LP 60.
4. Ockham, ibid.
5. Nightingales at Horsley, BL54090.
6. Lt Arnold, ibid.
7. Nightingales, ibid.
8. Ockham, Moore, op.cit. p.359.
9. Grand tour, BL53820.
10. Ruskin, Rawdon Brown, Norton, et al. See Ruskin, *Praeterita*, and Abse, *John Ruskin, the Passionate Moralist.*
11. Nightingales, Newstead Abbey, BL53820.
12. Presentation at Court, ibid.
13. Ockham, ibid. And see Stowe, Harriet Beecher, *Lady Byron Vindicated.*
14. Father and daughter, BL 53820 & BL54091.

## Chapter Four

1. Ball at Horsley, BL53821, 17/18 June.
2. Social whirl. BL53821/22.
3. Lessons from Ruskin and Hallé, ibid. Wilkinson, Layard, ibid.
4. Nightingales, Verney, Monckton Milne, ibid.
5. Noels and Ockham, ibid.
6. Emma Vischen, 'Nobody', ibid.
7. European tour. Ibid.
8. Ashley Combe, BL53823.
9. Auberon Herbert, Fitzherbert, *The Man Who was Greenmantle.*
10. Grandmama. BL53823.
11. Correspondence with father BL54091. Lady Byron to Lovelace, ibid.
12. Death of Lady Byron, LP 78, June 1860.
13. Lady B's friends. Moore, op.cit. p361.

14. Ockham's death, ibid, p360. Central Registry, September 1862; and see Complete Peerage, vol 8; Mary Countess of Lovelace in Memoir of Ralph.

15. GM, Last will and testament of the Rt. Honourable Anne Isabella Baroness Noel Byron, proved at the High Court, 1st August 1860. Principal Registry.

16. Relentless attacks, BL54091; Anne on GM, SP, 19 June 1860, quoted Moore, op.cit., p.362; bitterness, de Morgan, Sophia, op.cit., p178.

17. Olympia Usedom. She was the daughter of Sir John Malcolm, British ambassador in Tehran.

18. Accounts for Hertford Street, BL53826, 26 Jan 1863.

19. Friendship with Joachim. BL53826 & BL53827, from March 1863

20. Visit to Germany and Italy, ibid.

21. Milan, June 1866, BL53828/54100. And see Longford, Elizabeth, *A Pilgrimage of Passion*, Chapter 3, 'Vita Nova'.

22. Olympia, 'nice rich wife', ibid, p57.

23. Blunt's impressions of Anne, ibid.

24. Anne's 29 years, ibid. Elizabeth Longford, p58, remarks that Blunt always said that Anne was his senior by two years, whereas she was three years older all but a month.'

25. Blunt and Skittles. See Blyth, Henry, *Skittles - The Last Victorian Courtesan*.

26. Quote: 'She thought herself...' Longford, op.cit.

27. Blunt's movements, ibid.

28. Blunt's letter to Anne, 2 July, BL54100; Anne to Blunt, ibid.

29. Correspondence, ibid. And see Longford, op.cit.

30. Wedding, Register of Marriages, April-June 1869: Blunt, Wilfrid Scawen to Lady Ann Isabella Noel-King: Vol 1a, 525, St George's, Hanover Square. Account of wedding. BL53831 and BL54068 (Epitome of Marriage Settlement).
    Latter document shows settlement on Anne by Lovelace of two amounts of £10,000 each, and £10,300 in East India Company stock, 'hers in perpetuity, for her sole and separate use, free from the debts or engagements of Mr Blunt.' But bequest would revert to 'Mr Blunt' on her death.

31. Ella Baird. See Moore, op.cit. p70, reminder of Contessa Theresa Guicciola's intended appearance at her grandfather's wedding 34 years before.

## Chapter Five

1. The evidence of Harriet Beecher Stowe. See Elwin, *Lord Byron's Wife*.
2. Honeymoon, BL53831; and see Longford, *A Pilgrimage of Passion*, p71f.
3. Ralph's engagement, BM53831; Anne/Ralph correspondence, BL54092/3.
4. Wilfrid to Godfrey Lushington, Longford op.cit., p74.
5. Worth, Ashley Combe, Paris, BL53830.
6. Marriage of Alice and Nep, BL53831 (diary composed 'from memory' in 1871). And see Finch, Wilfrid Scawen Blunt, p58 and Longford op.cit. p73.
7. Corresp. Anne/Ralph, BL53829 July-Sep 1869; BL53830-31 Oct-Dec.
8. Anne's sickness, BL53831; and see Longford, op.cit.
9. Stowe, Macmillan's and Medora. See Moore, Ada, p180; and Longford, op.cit.
10. Alice and Blunt, BL53850.
11. Paris, BL53830; Torquay, BL54091.
12. Lord Lytton, Longford, op.cit. p77.
13. Anne to father, BL54091.
14. Letter, BL54091, 1870.
15. Sensible, practical. Longford, *A Pilgrimage of Passion*, p78ff.
16. Worth, Paris. BL53831. Anne's pregnancy.
17. Skittles. See Blyth, Henry, *Skittles*, p191f.
18. Wilfrid's letters. BL54100. And see Longford, op.cit, p79.
19. Olliffes. See author's *Gertrude Bell*.
20. Wilfrid's sickness, birth of son. BL53832; and see Longford, op.cit,p82
21. Portugal, BL53835.
22. Anne's pregnancy, BL53835.
23. Spain, Blunt and bullfighting, BL53836.
24. Blunt and search for 'true love'. Longford, op,.cit., p84.
25. Paris, Anne's confinement, BL53835.
26. Quote, Ibid.
27. Deaths of Alice and Francis, see Longford, op.cit., p90-92 and notes.

28. Birth of Judith, BL53835.
29. More European journeys, BL53836/7.
30. Marie Leigh and George Eliot. See Haight, Gordon S (ed) The George Eliot Letters, p314. And Marghanita Laski, *George Eliot and her world*. And Mayne, Ethel Colburn, *Life & Letters of Anne Isabella, Lady Noel Byron*.
31. Anne to Disraeli, Murray Correspondence, See Bibliography. Correspondence re. Byron memorial, BL54125.
32. Ralph. See Longford, op.cit. p93; Lady Longford describes quip as 'a cruel lie'.

## Chapter Six

1. Equestrian references, see Wentworth, Lady, *The Authentic Arabian Horse*.
2. Travels in Turkey, Algiers etc., BL53835/7 and BL54073 (Blunt diary).
3. Anne's maternal qualities, LP, Dep LB177, Anne to brother Ralph.
4. Anne's miscarriage, BL53835.
5. Ralph's appearance, BL54091. And Longford, op.cit., p98.
6. Blunt and Pollen ladies, ibid.
7. Miscarriage, BL53857; and see Longford, p103.
8. Anne, quote, ibid.
9. Dear Papa, BL54091.
10. Blunt and Dorchester letters, See Moore, Doris Langley, *The Great Byron Adventure*, p19f.

    An interesting aspect of a matter that is usually overshadowed by the charge of incest is dealt with by Janet Adam Smith in Appendix A to her biography of John Buchan, published in 1977. Here it is enough to state that Buchan in his own autobiography *Memory Hold-the-Door*, referred to an 'Opinion' which he and Henry James had been asked by Mary, Lady Lovelace, to give on an 'archive' at Ockham where the two men were staying. Mary was, in fact, the aunt of Buchan's wife Susan. In their *Opinion*, given in April 1910, the two distinguished writers stated: 'We can bear witness that they afford most weighty corroborative evidence of the truth of the story told by Lord Lovelace.'

But Janet Adam-Smith points out that Buchan's account was written nearly 30 years after Lovelace's (Ralph's) private publication of *Astarte* in 1905 in an effort to vindicate Lady Byron. The report he wrote with his friend James, she says, 'shows that the papers they examined were not the papers that had descended from Lady Byron to Lord Lovelace... but the Melbourne correspondence (then owned by Lady Dorchester, now by John Murray) of which Lovelace had taken copies.'

The Melbourne correspondence was published in 1922 by Murray, without expurgation. James had been shown the papers relating to Byron's relations with his half-sister Augusta when dining with the Lovelaces in 1895. The report was confused. A slip of memory.

Doris Langley Moore, referring to her early research among the Lovelace papers, observed that she 'recorded one document', which enabled her to correct a much-quoted but misleading impression given by John Buchan. Buchan had said that James 'never turned a hair' and that his only response to words of 'special vileness' had been 'singular' and 'most curious'.

Moore remarked 'Henry James never turned a hair and neither did the public'. The letters seem to have been more concerned with charges of sodomy and homosexuality than with Byron's relationship with Augusta. It is not clear whether Blunt showed them to Anne or discussed them with her in detail. (Author).

11. Blunt's own case. See Longford, op.cit, p106, and Finch, *Wilfrid Scawen Blunt*, p53.

12. Anne quote, BL53863.

13. Egypt, BL53865.

14. Summons, ibid.

15. Anne's plea, BL53876.

16. Suggested operation, BL53879.

17. Zouche divorce, ibid. For most detailed account, see Longford, op.cit., p115f.

18. Anne's diaries. Pages have been torn from the diaries of this period as if in anger. Elizabeth Longford noted that according to Judith, Minnie Pollen had 'commandeered' Anne's diary and was responsible for the exisions. (Author).

19. Skittles. See Blyth, *Skittles* etc. p207f.

20. Improper intervention of Prince of Wales, see Longford op.cit., p120.

21. Spiritual awakening, BL53876.

22. Gibralta, BL53863.

23. Anne at Crabbet, BL53887.

24. Journey to Arabia. Jan 9-Feb 22, 1878, BL53889 and BL54075. And see the Blunts' *Bedouin Tribes of the Euphrates*; and Archer and Fleming, *Lady Anne Blunt, Journals and Correspondence*.

25. Mesopotamia, Feb 23 to 29 March, BL53891.

26. Arab breeds. BL53892, Darley No.1 Keheilan Ras akl Fedawi, 30 Napoleons, etc. Also memo on Anezah [Anaiza] and Shammar tribes.

27. Syria, March 29 to April 15, BL53892.

28. Damascus, April 16-April 24, BL53893.

29. *Breeds of Arabia*, ibid, and Wentworth, *The Authentic Arabian Horse*, p88f.

## Chapter Seven

1. Forty-first birthday, BL53857.

2. Damascus, Lady Jane Digby. BL53893.

3. God and Christianity. Longford, op.cit., p132.

4. Wrote to John Murray, Murray Corresp.

5. Arabs and their Horses, Archer & Fleming, *Lady Anne Blunt, Journals and Correspondence.*

6. Inaccuracies, See Kelly, J.B. *Britain and the Persian Gulf, 1795-1880*, OUP 1968.

7. Founding of Crabbet stud, BL53894.

8. Wilfrid's finances, ibid, 28 June.

9. Last days at Crabbet; Molony portraits, BL53896.

10. Alarming news, ibid.

11. Departure and journey to Central Arabia, see Blunt, *Pilgrimage to Nejd*. And Anne's diaries BL53896/8.
    (pocket diary); Anne's sketchbook BL54808;
    Wilfrid's diary BL54076 and notebook BL54803. And see Longford, op.cit. (Chapter 6, The Children of Shem),
    Freeth and Winstone, *Explorers of Arabia* (The Blunts' Journey), and Archer and Fleming, op.cit.

12. Music notes, BL53898, Hamdan's song.

13. Al Jauf [often Jôf in Blunt]. BL53897/8 and sketchbook BL54048.
    Of known travellers, Wallin, G.A., 1845, and Palgrave, 1862, were
    the only European visitors before the Blunts.
    Vide, *Records of the Abdul Rahman Al Sudairy Foundation at Al
    Jauf*, and private communication to author from the late Colonel
    Colin Paddock, dated 27 March 1986, with reference to two
    English cannons at Jauf which the Blunts had seen there and
    which he thought may have come from one of Nelson's warships.

14. Cannons at Kasr. See note above. Similar it seems to the
    pair of weapons at Kasr Mitab ibn Rashid in Jauf, described by
    Anne as 'two twelve pounder cannons of English make... of no
    value.'
    And see Freeth and Winstone, *Explorers of Arabia*, chapter
    'Lady Anne Blunt'.

15. Quotes, BL53898.

16. Dressed in silk and gold. Anne's description in her diary changed
    somewhat when she came to write the book.

17. Mares of Hail, BL53900.

18. Visit to Harim, ibid.

## Chapter Eight

1.  Journey from Hail to Najaf; Blunt, *Pilgrimage to Nejd* and
    BL53898.

2.  'Fantasia of the Mares', BL53900.

3.  Ali Kuli Khan. See Blunt, Pilgrimage and BL53898/9, BL54076.

4.  Story of Prophet's son-in-law Ali, BL53898.

5.  Nixons and horses, see Archer and Fleming, *Lady Anne Blunt,
    Journals and Correspondence*, p84f.

6.  Journey to Baghdad and wild boar hunt, ibid, and BL53902/3.

7.  Journey into Persia. BL53903 and BL54076.

8.  Anne's vision and conversion to Roman Catholicism. See Longford,
    Elizabeth, *A Pilgrimage of Passion*, p148f.
    Lady Longford says in footnote p149, that the full story was told by
    Anne only to her granddaughter Anne Lytton, and that the nature of
    the vision was never known to Wilfrid.

9.  Bushire, quote, BL53900.

10. Visit to India. See Longford, op.cit., p151f and Lutyens, *A Blessed Girl*.

11. Lytton's confidences. Longford, op.cit., p153, quotes Lytton Papers in possession of the Earl of Lytton.

12. Blunt's red notebook, FM1190/1977.

13. Quote, Longford, op.cit., p156.

14. Horse dealer in Bombay. Archer and Fleming, Letter July 8th, p110.

15. Judith, 'Bibi', BL54109 Anne to Judith, 1875 to 1884; BL54100-8, Anne to WSB.

16. Minnie Pollen, BL53905.

17. Riding, Judith and Crabbet. See Archer and Fleming, *Journals* etc, p111f.

18. Anne's musical enthusiasms, ibid, note 56, p473. 'Lady Anne was a determined violinist'.

19. Mary Batten. See Longford, *A Pilgrimage of Passion*, p162.

20. Geographical Society, BL53905. And see Archer and Fleming, op.cit., and Longford, op.cit.

21. Visit to Palgrave, BL53905.

22. Spiritual rebirth, BL54100. See also Longford, op.cit., and Archer and Fleming, op.cit., p114 (March 5th).

23. Lord Stratford de Redcliffe, formerly Sir Stratford Canning, ambassador at Constantinople, ibid.

24. Cardinal Newman. BL54100.

25. Ralph, ibid.

26. Dinner with Tennyson, Browning etc., ibid.

27. Crabbet and Blunt's influence. Wentworth, Lady, *The Authentic Arabian Horse*, p69f.

28. Blunt and Angelina, Longford, op.cit., p162f. Angelina married Blunt's friend Philip Currie, ambassador to the Porte, in 1890.

29. 'I beg my wife to believe'. Longford, op.cit., p164. At the end of her life Anne would ask retrospectively and bitterly, 'You ask my love, what love then should it be, an aspiration, a desire?' BL54068.

30. *Pilgrimage to Nejd*, Murray Correspondence, Sept-Nov 1880.

31. Damascus, BL53913. And see Archer and Fleming, op.cit., p125f.

32. Journey home, ibid.

## Chapter Nine

1. Quote, diary BL53913. And see Archer and Fleming, *Lady Anne Blunt, Journals* etc. Chapter V.
2. Islington show, ibid.
3. Oppenheims and Rothschilds, ibid.
4. Blunt and Egypt. See Longford, *A Pilgrimage of Passion*, p170f
5. Egyptian nationalism.
   See Mansfield, Peter, *The British in Egypt*. Also see Baring, *Modern Egypt*, Colvin, Sir Auckland, *The Making of Modern Egypt*, Beaman, Ardern Hulme, *The Dethronement of the Khedive*, Malet, Sir Edward, *Egypt 1879-1883*; and Blunt's *Secret History of the English Occupation of Egypt*.
6. Visit to Ali Pasha Sharif's stables, BL53913.
7. Arabi, ibid.
8. Louis Sabunji, BL53913. Note: variously described as Sabinjie.
9. *The Times*, ibid.
10. *Al Ahram*, Arabi's disclaimer, ibid.
11. Malet, ibid.
12. Visits to desert. On 5 Jan. Anne noted in her diary 'Broke with civilized life...We're off with the camels...' ibid.
13. Colvin and Blunt, 'annexation'. Ibid.
14. Letters to Minnie, BL54121.
15. Gladstone, BL53915.
16. Quote: 'new leaf of life', ibid.
17. Quote: BL53916.
18. Wilfrid and Pollens. Ibid. Anne notes in diary 'it is impossible to follow his [Wildfrid's] movements.'
19. Interview with Gladstone, ibid. And see Longford, *A Pilgrimage of Passion*, p176f, 'twisted the impressionable Blunt around his finger'.
20. Molony, painting, fishing etc., BL53916. Diary contains several inserted sheets at this time related to equine and domestic matters, including lists of horses. See Archer and Fleming, *Lady Anne Blunt* etc., p150f.
21. Cockerell. At the outset, Mr W. Cockerell had shared his

colleagues' view. BL53916, 23 March 1882.

22. Palmer. BL53916, 'Mr Palmer... he does not like the title Professor...'

23. Naval manoeuvres, Arabi, Muhammad Abdu, and Sultan Pasha. Ibid, and see author's *Diaries of Parker Pasha* (Quartet, 1983), Chapter I, and Besant, Walter, *The Life and Achievements of Edward Henry Palmer* (Murray 1883).

24. 'Vicisti O Colvine! Longford, op.cit.

25. Pharaoh at Horsham. ibid26.

26. Riots in Alexandria and subsequent events, Cabinet Papers CAB37/8 in Public Record Office, and Command Paper Cmd 3494.

    In connection with Blunt's part in the events which led to the British invasion and annexation, Longford, op.cit., notes, p191, that a Russian biography of Blunt was published in Leningrad in 1970 by Alla Mihailovna Lynbarskaya, *Wilfrid Scawen Blunt: Life, Work & Struggle*.

    In reference to that book the editor of *Marxism Today* (August 1970) pointed out that just before his death Marx was making notes on Blunt's article 'The Egyptian Revolution' in the *Nineteenth Century*.

27. Palmer, Charrington and Gill in Sinai. See Winstone op.cit.

28. E.St J. Fairman, quote, BL53916.

29. Lady Gregory, ibid, and BL53917. And see Longford, op.cit., p174f.

30. Blunt and Gladstone, BL53917.

31. Anne and Gordon, BL53918.

32. Oscar Wilde, ibid.

33. Years of insult, ibid, and FM25/1975.

    See reference to copies of these notes on loose sheets in Blunt's memoirs and diary, in Longford, op.cit., p444.

34. 'I am tired...' BL53921.

35. Bobinsky, Potocki and others, ibid.

36. Paris, BL53922.

37. Voyage to India, BL53926.

38. Farewell breakfast, Longford, op.cit., 201.

39. Madras, Hyderabad, BL53930.

40. Anne quoted, 'Wilfrid begins...'; BL53937.

41. Quote, Anne's silent anger; ibid.

42. Edward Noel, ibid.

# Chapter Ten

1. Quote, Wentworth, *The Authentic Arabian Horse*, p74.
2. Judith, BL53950.
3. Mrs Georgie Sumner, Longford, *A Pilgrimage of Passion*, p207f.
4. Judith, BL53950.
5. Janey Morris, Longford, op.cit., p224.
6. Constrained to ask, quoted in Archer and Fleming, *Lady Anne Blunt*, etc.,p172, 6 Sept 1884.
7. Vienna, Cracow, Constantinople, BL53950.
8. 'Home rule for everyone'. For this and a colourful summary of Blunt's political views in general, see Wentworth, *The Authentic Arabian Horse*, p74f. A more dispassionate account is given in Finch, Edith, *Wilfrid Scawen Blunt 1840-1922*, and in Longford, op.cit.
9. Gladstone's handshake, BL53954.
10. 'A pedant...', Longford, op.cit., p215.
11. Hyndman, ibid, p212.
12. Lord Stanley, Auberon Herbert, Randolph Churchill, Irish Nationalism. See Longford op.cit.,p210.
13. Skittles. Ibid, p211, quotes letter from C. Walters (Skittles) to WSB in FM636/1976. And see Blyth, Henry, *Skittles - The Last Victorian Courtesan*.
14. Salisbury Club, Anne quote 5 June 1885, BL53954.
15. Horses and domestic animals, ibid.
16. Camberwell campaign.FM333/1975. And see Longford, op.cit., p221f.
17. 'In public life...' Ibid.
18. 'He has a way...' Wentworth, op.cit., p77.
19. Ireland and the land battle. See Blunt, W.S. *The Land War in Ireland*.
20. Rome, Longford, op.cit., p235.
21. Egypt, BL53958. And see Longford, op.cit., p240f.
22. Ireland. BL53958. And see Blunt, W.S., op.cit.
23. Wyndhams. LB177/156.
24. Mitchelstown shootings, Blunt, W.S. op.cit.

25. Dublin, Galway, ibid.
26. Anne and court proceedings, October 1887, BL53958/9 and BL54115. For Blunt's version, see his *In Vinculis*.
27. 'Political mania', BL53958.
28. Woodford proceedings, BL53964. And Blunt, W.S. op.cit.
29. Depford, BL53967.
30. *The Times*, 29 February 1888, quoted in Longford, op.cit. p263.
31. Oscar Wilde, see Pearson, Hesketh, *Oscar Wilde*, quoted in Longford, op.cit., p464.
32. Return to Ireland, BL53967; and Longford, op.cit., 265f.
33. Lady Byron and the Leighs. LB177, 26-7, 151-3, 156-66.
34. Blanche Hozier, Longford, op.cit., p271.
35. Anne, quoted: BL53972.


# Chapter Eleven


1. Lady Blanche Hozier, née Ogilvie. See Longford, op.cit., p271.
2. Henry Hozier, member of Lloyds and one of the founders of the modern military intelligence service. Ibid; and see author's *The Illicit Adventure*, p6.
3. Another domestic drama. BL54115, Blunt to Judith, September 1891. And see Longford, op.cit.
4. Pollen; 'the great eviction', Longford, op.cit., p275.
5. Anne and Judith, BL53968.
6. Judith's version. The essay *Myself and Others*, quoted extensively by Longford, op.cit., is an unpublished document, but I have been unable to trace it; it is not listed among Wentworth publications in her bibliography. (Author).
7. Greece, BL53969.
8. Cairo in 1889, ibid and BL53970.
9. Hungary and Venice, BL53970.
10. England and Crabbet, ibid.
11. London; Russell, Gladstone, ibid.
12. Blunt and the Morris ladies, FM1/1975. And see Longford, op.cit., p278f., citing other Blunt papers in Fitzwilliam Museum collection
13. Goodbye to Crabbet, BL53970.
14. Wilfrid's faith, Longford, op.cit., p280. Quoted passages are hers.

15. Rome held aloft, BL53970.
16. Cowie's illness. BL53978.
17. Anne, quote, ibid.
18. Blunt and Margaret Talbot FM31/1975. His religion, need for 'illicit love', see Longford, op.cit., and FM31 and 32/1975 (Secret Memoirs), and FM1 and 3/1975 (General Memoirs).
19. Wilfrid's poem to Judith, Archer and Fleming, *Lady Anne Blunt* etc, p207.
20. Lyrical words, ibid.
21. Mesaoud, ibid.
22. Collapse of new house, BL53984.
23. Chess banter, ibid. A slightly different version of this nonsense conversation is given in Archer and Fleming, op.cit., April 21st, p225. Their rendering of Anne's diary entries are generally meticulous, and their 'bolo' for my 'bobo' and 'stale mats' for my 'stale mat' may be correct, though I stand by my notes. (Author)
24. Lady Edmund Talbot, FM31/1975. And see Longford, op.cit, p287.
25. Lady Helena Carnegie, ibid.
26. 'Queenie' Grosvenor, ibid.
27. Anne, Crabbet and horses. See her notes in Chapter IX, 'Wentworth, The Authentic Arabian Horse', which she worked on at this time, 'Omnia praeclara sunt rara'. And see Chapter VIII, 'The Veiled Face of Truth', in Archer and Fleming, op.cit.
28. Anne, quote; BL53984.
29. Violin playing, ibid.
30. Crabbet, ibid. And see Longford, op.cit., p289f; and see Harris, Frank, *Oscar Wilde, His Life and Confession* (New York, 1918).
31. Anne, quoted, BL53984.
32. Princess Wagram, Longford, op.cit., p293.

## Chapter Twelve

1. Anne, quoted, BL53984.
2. Margot Tennant, Longford, *A Pilgrimage of Passion*, p295.
3. Anne heralded, BL53984.
4. Webb 'the lodger', and other Webbs, see Archer and Fleming, *Lady Anne Blunt* etc., note 69 p474.

5.   Review of Lytton's poems, ibid.

6.   'These are things', BL53985.

7.   Hozier divorce, Longford, op.cit,.p295.

8.   Rossetti, Margot Tennant, Blunt, Janey Morris, FM31 and 32/1975.

9.   Edith and Emily Lytton at Crabbet. See Lutyens, Lady Emily, *A Blessed Girl*.

10.  Anne's 55th birthday, BL53985.

11.  Esther and 'Skittles', ibid, and see Blyth, Henry, *Skittles* etc.

12.  Horsley Towers. BL53985.

13.  Sheykh Obeyd, Nov 1892 - April 1893, ibid.

14.  Emily, Elwin and Blunt, Lutyens, op.cit., p254f. And see Longford, op.cit., p306.

15.  Hon. Etheldred Florence Lee Dillon, see Archer and Fleming, op.cit., p409.

16.  Stealing of the Mare. See Blunt, W.S., *The Stealing of the Mare* (London 1892). For background on literary form the *maqama*, see *The Assemblies of Al-Hariri: Fifty Encounters with the Shaykh Abu Zaid*, retold by Amina Shah from the *Makamat of Al-Hariri* (London 1981).

17.  Anne, 22 December 1891, Archer and Fleming, op.cit., p234.

18.  Blunt and Emily, Lutyens, op.cit., Chapter Twelve.

19.  Emily to Rev. Whitwell Elwin, 9 July 1892, FM32/1975.

20.  Sarah Bernhardt, LB177/162 Anne to Ralph 16 March, 1894.

21.  'Last desperate bid'. Diaries almost ceased in 1893 and, apart from small pocket diaries with only occasional enigmatic notes, her own record of her life is not resumed until 1896. It is safe to assume that her demoralisation was complete by this time and the incentive to make a daily record of her married life, even with its obvious defects, had gone. For the next three years I rely primarily on the Blunt diaries and on Finch's and Longford's biographies of Wilfrid to follow Anne's movements. (Author)

22.  Death of Lovelace and succession of Ralph, *Burke's Peerage* and *Who Was Who 1897-1916*.

23.  Ralph and Crabbet, LB177/162 Anne to Ralph 16 March 1894; 'nor was subject ever referred to by Edward Chandler' [Blunt's solicitor].

24.  The Souls, see Longford, op.cit. p303f. And see Ridley, Jane, and Percy, Clzyre, *The Letters of Arthur Balfour* and Lady Elcho 1885

1917, London 1992, p42, 'poet and Byron worshipper'.

25. El Kheysheh, FM34/1975.
26. Mary Elcho and Blunt, ibid (Blunt's 'Secret Memoirs'); and Ridley and Percy, op.cit., p115f. And see Longford, op.cit., Chapter 16.
27. Hugo, quoted, FM34/1975.
28. Blunt and Emily, ibid.
29. Blunt's departure, Lutyens, op.cit.
30. Blunt to Anne, October 1895, BL54104.
31. Mary's child. FM35/1975.
32. Mary's next pregnancy, birth of Ivo, see Longford, op.cit. p320f
33. Death of William Morris, reunion with Morris women, ibid; and see MacCarthy, Fiona, William Morris, *A Life for Our Time*.
34. 'Ned' Lutyens, op.cit., p294.
35. Quote, 'left like Adam', Longford, op.cit., cites Blunt diary, Lytton FM, 15 Aug 1896.
36. Crystal Palace horse show, Archer and Fleming, op.cit., p253.

## Chapter Thirteen

1. Gladstone, Ridley & Percy, *The Letters of Arthur Balfour and Lady Elcho*, p113.
2. Daughter's verdict, see Wentworth, *The Authentic Arabian Horse*, Chapter III, 'A Stormy Life'.
3. One of his biographers, see Longford, *A Pilgrimage of Passion*, p.xiii: 'In Lady Wentworth's Authentic Arabian there is an extremely biased and unfair chapter on her father...'
4. Fiona MacCarthy, see her William Morris, *A Life for Our Time*.
5. Anne and secret stud arrangements. See Longford, op.cit., p362f.
6. Cairo and Judith. Archer and Fleming, *Lady Anne Blunt*, etc., p250f. By this time Anne had resumed in part her old habit of keeping diaries and journals but spasmodically. I have relied a good deal on the careful work of Archer and Fleming, op.cit., from here on.
7. The Emily affair. Lutyens, *A Blessed Girl*.
8. Judith's marriage prospects, ibid.
9. Berkeley Sumner, FM35/1975.
10. Freherr Max von Oppenheim, Archer and Fleming, op.cit., 27th

November 1896. And see author's *The Illicit Adventure*.

11. Ali Pasha's stud, 11 December 1896, Archer and Fleming, op.cit.

12. Wilfrid in Senussi territory, see Longford, op.cit., p328.

13. Final word on religion, ibid. A view shared by E.M.Forster and Edith Finch.

14. Her 'instinctive patriotism', Wentworth, *The Authentic Arabian*, Chapter III, 'A Stormy Life'.

15. Ali Pasha, Archer and Fleming, op.cit.

16. Called on Cromer, FM35/1975.

17. Wilfrid's health, ibid.

18. Latest equine arrivals at Southwater, Archer and Fleming, op.cit., May 31st, 1897; note, although seldom used, Southwater was the actual location of Newbuildings, described by Hilaire Belloc, who lived nearby, as a 'magnificent Charles II mansion'.

19. Anne's and Wilfrid's eccentricity. Lutyens, op.cit., and Wilson, Hilaire Belloc, p142.

20. Blunts' financial affairs, Longford, op.cit., p330f.

21. Wilfrid and Lady (Gay) Windsor, FM36/1975 (August 1897), and Longford, op.cit., p332.

22. Sheykh Obeyd, February 1898, Archer and Fleming, op.cit., p262f.

23. Blunt on Omdurman, *The Times*, 10 September 1898.

24. Judith's engagement, Longford, op.cit., p339, quotes Judith's diary and 'Myself and Others'.

25. Letter to Wilfrid from Edith, 15 October 1898, Archer and Fleming, op.cit., p267.

26. Bloomsbury Square, quote, ibid.

27. Surprising suggestion, BL54006.

28. Anne to Wilfrid, Archer and Fleming, op.cit., p268.

29. The wedding, Longford, op.cit., p341.

30. Cowie to Wilfrid, ibid.

31. Blunt on Omdurman, Kitchener, ibid.

32. Cockerell, Shaw and Socialism. See Bernard Shaw, *Collected Letters* (ed. Dan H. Laurence, London 1972), p111; and Shaw, *The Intelligent Woman's Guide to Socialism* (London 1928), Chapter 5.

33. 31st December 1899, Archer and Fleming, op.cit.

34. Judith's son born, ibid.

35. Telegram from Webb, ibid.

36. Ashley Combe, ibid.

37. The fox hunt, BL54009.

# Chapter Fourteen

1. Anne at Newbuildings, 14 November, 1902. Archer and Fleming, op.cit.
2. Wilfrid's fears, BL54009.
3. Astarte, See Elwin, *Lord Byron's Wife*, p19.
4. Blunt found..., FM374/1975 and LB432/20-25.
5. Gertrude Bell, LB432/20 - 25, Florence Bell to Lord Lovelace, 13 January 1906; Gertrude Bell to same, 10 January and 5 February, 1906.
6. Blunt and Irish nationalism, FM382/1975.
7. Anne's friends. Ironically, Arthur Balfour was telling Lady Elcho in March 1895, the time of Mary Elcho's frisson with Wilfrid, that he had dined with the conductor Sir George Henschel and Anne's old violin teacher Joachim.
8. Ladies of Arabia. Both Anne and Gertrude were known to the Arabs as 'Al Khatn', a term that translates roughly as 'Lady of the Court', or 'of high birth'. See author's *Gertrude Bell*.
9. Death of Cowie, Blunt to Judith, BL54115.
10. Death of Bozra, Archer and Fleming, op.cit., August 2/3, 1903
11. Judith's pregnancy, ibid
12. The Seven Golden Odes, see Blunt, *The Golden Odes of Arabia*, London 1903.
13. Blunt's melancholy, see Longford, *A Pilgrimage of Passion*, 353f.
14. Anne and Nurse Lawrence, BL54015. And see Longford, op.cit., p356f.
15. Auberon Herbert, Archer and Fleming, op.cit., Saturday January 9th, 1904.
16. Review 'The Thoroughbred Horse', see *The Speaker*, 23 December 1905.
17. Dinshawi [Denshawai] affair, see Mansfield, *The British in Egypt*. And see Laurence, *Bernard Shaw, The Collected Letters*, Shaw to R.B. Haldane and John Burns, Nov 1907.
18. H.F.'s [Wilfrid's] ideas on stud and breeding, Archer and Fleming, op.cit., p312f.
19. Nurse Lawrence, ibid.

20. Dinshawi, ibid. And Archer and Fleming, op.cit., p313.
21. Dorothy and Robert Gregory, Longford, op.cit., p365.
22. Yeats and Blunt, ibid.
23. Anne's ultimatum, ibid.
24. 'Humbug!', BL54097. On 21 August, Anne had written from Forest Cottage 'It seems that H.F. has expressed surprise at not hearing from me. But I having had my congé and accepted it have considered that it is an established fact.' Archer and Fleming, op.cit
25. Death of Ralph; financial consequences, Longford, op.cit., p367f.
26. 'H.F.'s pamphlet', BL54018, 24 October 1906.
27. Plans for Judith and Neville, ibid. Note: 'I see that if I can give the £30,000 it will be a joy to Judith and Neville...'
28. Gertrude Bell, ibid.
29. Judith and 'H.F.', Longford, op.cit., p377.
30. Blunt quoted, ibid; quotes Tennant Papers 'formerly in possession of Dorothy Carleton'.
31. Guy Carleton, ibid.
32. Anne to Lady Mary Lovelace, BL54019-54030. Note, from here on notes in Anne's diaries (or journals) become so dispersed that in my notes I have telescoped the remaining documents. For an accessible rendering the reader is recommended to refer to Archer and Fleming, op.cit.
33. Heliopolis meeting, ibid.
34. Saadun. Named after Sadun Pasha ibn Mansur, thought to have been murdered by Turks in 1912. See author's *Illicit Adventure*
35. Her great hope, ibid, 26 November 1912.
36. Visit by Judith, BL54019-30.
37. An invitation from Wilfrid, ibid.
38. Further meetings, Longford, op.cit., p404f.
39. Caffin, ibid, p405.
40. The Horse Book, BL54019 - 30. And see Wentworth, *The Authenic Arabian*.
41. Death of Mutlak, 16 February 1916.
42. Anne to Wilfrid, 28 May 1917 from Sheykh Obeyd, BL54108.
43. Hysterical climax, Longford, op.cit., p407f.
44. Cairo in wartime, See author's *Illicit Adventure*, Chapter 9, 'The Intrusives'.
45. Horse book, BL54108.
46. 80th birthday, BL54019-30.

47. Anne to Wilfrid, 'The Glory', BL54108.
48. Last days, disposal of horses, BL54019-30.
49. Death, 15 December 1917: Registry: Consular Returns 1916-20, vol 14, page 343, Anne Isabella, Cairo, age 80.

## Chapter Fifteen

1. Burial site. Her remains were moved to the Roman Catholic section of the Abbasiya cemetery after the Second World War.
2. Last Will and Testament, Anne Isabella Noel Blunt (commonly called Lady Anne Isabella Noel Blunt), probate granted to Philip Henry Napier of Ministry of Finance, Cairo, by Provincial Court Cairo, 26 January 1918.
3. Judith and manuscript, Archer and Fleming, Lady Anne Blunt Etc., note 123, Notes to Journals.
4. Effect of the will, BL54028.
5. Judith descended. Longford, *A Pilgrimage*, p412f.
6. Court proceedings. See Archer, Pearson and Covey, *The Crabbet Arabian Stud*.
7. Desmond MacCarthy, see his Portraits I, London 1931.
8. Shaw and Blunt, see Laurence, Dan, *Bernard Shaw Collected Letters*.
9. New generation of Arabophiles, LB436/11-12, May 1920, Gertrude Bell to Lady Mary Lovelace. And see Longford op.cit., p418, and author's *Illicit Adventure*.
10. Judith and Newbuildings, see Longford, op.cit. Chapter 22, 'The Unconquered Flame'.
11. *The Times*, obit, 29 December 1917.

# BIBLIOGRAPHY

## PRIMARY SOURCES

REGISTRY, LONDON
*Birth*: King, Ann Isabella Noel, Vol 1, page 60, July-
September 1837
*Marriage*: Blunt, Wilfrid Scawen, Vol 1a, page 525 April-
June 1869
*Death*: Anne [sic] Isabella, Age 80, Consular Returns,
Cairo, 1916-1920, Vol 14, page 343
*Last Wills and Testaments*:
Rt Honourable Anne Isabella Baroness Noel Byron,
dated 21st July 1860, with codicil dated 1st August 1860
Anne Isabella Noel Blunt, commonly called Lady Anne
Isabella [Annabella] Noel Blunt, filed in Provincial Court,
Cairo, 25th January 1918. Probate granted to Public
Trustee, 14th November 1918.
Rt Honourable Judith Anne Dorothea Baroness
Wentworth, dated 15th September 1954, with codicil
dated 23rd October 1956.


PUBLIC RECORD OFFICE
*FO 633 series (Cromer papers)*
*Cabinet Papers 1880 - 1900, CAB37/2-37/51, Egyptian,*
*Irish and Indian affairs*


BRITISH LIBRARY
*The Wentworth Bequest: Letters, notebooks and diaries of*
*Lady Anne Blunt*
This is the principal source for text and illustrations,

consisting of 339 volumes. The relevant documents are:
Vols I - CCXIV: Diaries of Lady Anne Blunt, files
BL53817 - 54030 (1847-1917)
Vols CCXV-CCXLV: Sketchbooks of Lady Anne Blunt,
BL54031-54061 (1850-1900)
Vols CCXLVI-CCLII: Notebooks and Papers of Lady
Anne Blunt, BL54062-54068 (1850-1917)
Vols CCLIII-CCLXIV: Diaries, Sketches, etc. of Wilfrid
Scawen Blunt, BL54069-54080
Vols CCLXV-CCLXXII: Miscellaneous material,
BL54081-54088
Vols CCLXXIII-CCCXIII: Correspondence BL54089 -
54129 (1843-1917)
Vols CCCXIV-CCCXXXII: Selected Papers of Lady
Wentworth BL54149-54155

BODLEIAN LIBRARY, OXFORD
*Lovelace Papers (Dep. Lovelace Byron)*
*Somerville Papers*

ST ANTONY'S COLLEGE, OXFORD (ME LIBRARY)
*Diary of Lady Anne Blunt 1 Jan 1882 - 18 May 1882*
(Copy of part of BL Add Mss 53914 - 53916)

FITZWILLIAM MUSEUM, CAMBRIDGE
*The Blunt Papers*

CAMBRIDGE UNIVERSITY LIBRARY
*Sedley Taylor Collection* (Letters of Lady Byron)

MURRAY ARCHIVE
*Correspondence examined at John Murray
(Publishers) Ltd:*
*Letters to John Murray:* 5 July 1875 re. proposed letter
to *The Times* from Lady Anne and Miss Leigh concerning
a Byron memorial sculpture: 'I am now writing a private
letter to Mr Disraeli', signed A N Blunt; 8 July 1875, from
Thomas's Hotel, Berkeley Square: 'I enclose copies of the
two letters to *The Times*... I enclose my note to Mr
Disraeli, A N Blunt'; 31 July 1875, inviting Mr Murray to
Crabbet Park; 5 October 1876 from Crabbet, Three
Bridges, Sussex; inviting Mr Murray to visit to meet M.
Gobineau, 'a man of the world and of letters'; re Byron
memorial; 28 August 1878; re publication of *Bedouin
Tribes of the Euphrates*, with suggested alternative titles; 2
October 1878 from Crabbet, same subject; 20 November
1878 'Please send proofs of 2nd volume to Lord
Wentworth', recommends friend Mlle de Lagrené as
translator; 'leaving tonight for Alexandria and Beyrout';
26 May 1879 from Simla, still awaiting letter and copies
of *Euphrates* book, 'supposed to have been sent to Col.
Nixon, Consul-General Baghdad': 'an interesting journey
to Nejd'; 11 September 1880, from Crabbet, propose to
call on you Monday with a letter from French
Geographical Society. Huber ('a botanist I believe') has
gone to Jof [al Jauf] anxious to proceed to J. Shammar the
way we took'; 15 September 1880, 'glad you approve of
our volume' [*Pilgrimage to Nejd*]; 5 October 1880 from
Crabbet, suggested titles for new book; 19 November
1880, Hotel du Nil, Cairo, request for copy of book 'as
soon as it is out'; travel plans via Suez; dedication, 24
May 1881 Crabbet, 'Mrs Pollen informs me that Hachette
wish to translate'; cannot attend party, 'my little girl is ill';
18 August 1884 Crabbet, various concerns, husband still
suffering from fever; 21 July 1886 Crabbet, plans to visit
Albermarle St., fell through 'owing to circumstances
unseen'; 20 August 1891, received cheque 'with great
pleasure', looks forward to introducing daughter.

# BOOKS BY LADY ANNE BLUNT

*Abu Zaid al-Hilali. The Celebrated Romance of the Stealing of the Mare*, London, 1892

*The Seven Golden Odes of Pagan Arabia,* also known as the Mu'allakat, done into English verse by W.S.B., London, 1903

*Bedouin Tribes of the Euphrates*, ed. W.S. Blunt (2 vols), London, 1879

*A Pilgrimage to Nejd, the cradle of the Arab race. A visit to the court of the Arab Emir, and our 'Persian Campaign'*, (2 vols), London, 1881

*Voyage en Arabie. Pelerinage au Nedjed, berceau de la race arabe.* Ouvrage traduit... avec l'autorisation de l'auteur par L. Derome. Contenant 1 carte et 60 gravures... dessinees par G.Vuillier d'apres les aquarelles de Lady Anne Blunt. Paris 1882

'The Thoroughbred Horse' review in *The Speaker*, 23 December 1905

# OTHER KEY SOURCES

Archer, Rosemary, and Fleming, James, *Lady Anne Blunt, Journals and Correspondence 1878-1917*, Cheltenham, 1986

Archer, Pearson and Covey, *The Crabbet Arabian Stud*, Cheltenham, 1978

Blunt, Wilfrid, *Cockerell*, London, 1964

— *Desert Hawk - Abd al Kader etc.*, London 1947

Blunt, Wilfrid Scawen, *Sonnets and Songs by Proteus*, London, 1875

— *Proteus and Amadeus, A Correspondence*, ed. Aubrey de Vere, London, 1878

— *The Future of Islam*, London, 1882

— *Ideas about India*, London, 1885

— *The Stealing of the Mare*, London 1892

— *The Poetry of Wilfrid Blunt*, selected by W.E. Henley

and George Wyndham, London 1898
— *Satan Absolved*, London, 1899
— *The Golden Odes of Arabia*, London 1903
— *Secret History of the English Occupation of Egypt*, London, 1907; Reprinted 1969
— *Gordon at Khartoum*, London, 1912
— *The Land War in Ireland*, London, 1912
— *My Diaries, Part One (1888-1900), Part Two (1900-1914)*, London, 1919/1920
Cecil, Lord David, *Melbourne*, London, 1955
De Morgan, Sophia Elizabeth, *Threescore Years and Ten*, London 1895
Elwin, M, *Lord Byron's Wife*, London, 1962
— *The Noels and the Milbankes*, London, 1967
— *Lord Byron's Family*, London, 1975
Finch, Edith, *Wilfrid Scawen Blunt 1840-1922*, London, 1938
Freeth, Zahra and Winstone, HVF, *Explorers in Arabia*, London 1978
Irwin, Robert, *Night & Horses & The Desert, An Anthology of Classical Arabic Literature*, London, 1999
Longford, Elizabeth, *A Pilgrimage of Passion, The Life of Wilfrid Scawen Blunt*, London, 1979, paperback edition 1982
Lovelace, Ralph, 2nd Earl of, *Astarte*, London, 1905; a new edition (ed. Mary Countess of Lovelace), London 1921
Lovelace, Mary Countess of, *Ralph Earl of Lovelace: A Memoir*, London, 1920
Lytton, Anthony (4th Earl), *Wilfrid Scawen Blunt - A Memoir*, London, 1961
Mayne, Ethel C., *The Life and Letters of Anne Isabella, Lady Noel Byron*, London, 1929
Moore, Doris Langley, *Ada Countess of Lovelace*, London, 1977
— *The Great Byron Adventure*, Philadelphia, 1959
— *The Late Lord Byron*, London, 1961
— *Lord Byron: Accounts Rendered*, London, 1974

Ridley, Jane and Percy, Clayre (eds), *The Letters of Arthur Balfour and Lady Elcho 1885-1917*, London 1992

Shah, Amina, *The Assemblies of Al Hariri: Fifty Encounters with the Shaykh Abu Zayd, Retold from the Makamat of Al Hariri*, London 1981

Stowe, Harriet Beecher, *Lady Byron Vindicated*, London, 1870

Wentworth, Judith Lady, *Flame of Life*, London, 1930
— *The Authentic Arabian Horse*, London, 1945

Wentworth, Lord (2nd Earl of Lovelace), *Lady Noel Byron and the Leighs: Some Authentic Records etc.*, '*Strictly Private*', 1887
— *Astarte*, see Lovelace

## GENERAL BOOK REFERENCES

Abse, Joan, *John Ruskin, the Passionate Moralist*, London, 1980

Adams, W.S., *Edwardian Portraits*, London, 1957

Alexander, C., *Baghdad in Bygone Days*, London, 1928

Amery, Julian, *The Life of Joseph Chamberlain*, London, 1969

Amery, L.S., *My Political Life, 1896-1940*, London, 1953-5
— *The Leo Amery Diaries, Vol. 1 1896-1929*, Ed. Barnes and Nicolson, London, 1980

Anderson, M.S., *The Eastern Question, 1774-1923*, London, 1966

Asquith, Cynthia, *Haply I May Remember*, London, 1950

Asquith, Lord Oxford and, *Memories and Reflections*, London, 1928

Asquith, Margot, *Autobiography*, (2 vols), London, 1920-22; new edition ed. Mark Bonham-Carter, London, 1985
— *Off the Record*, London, 1943

Babbage, Charles, *Passages in the Life of a Philosopher*, London 1864

Balfour, AJ, *Chapters of Autobiography*, ed. Blanche

Dugdale, London, 1930

Balfour, Lady Frances, *Ne Obliviscaris*, 2 vols., London, 1930

Baring, E. (Lord Cromer), *Modern Egypt* (2 vols), London, 1908
— *Ancient and Modern Imperialism*, London, 1910
— *Political and Literary Essays*, London, 1914
— *Abbas II*, London, 1915

Beerbohm, Max, *Seven Men*, Oxford, 1919

Bell, Lady, (Ed.) *Letters of Gertrude Bell*, London, 1927

Bell, Moberly, *Khedives and Pashas*, London, 1884

Blyth, Henry, *Skittles - The Last Victorian Courtesan*, London, 1970

Burckhardt, JL, *Travels in Syria and the Holy Land*, London, 1822

Burne-Jones, Georgiana, *Memorials of Edward Burne-Jones*, (2 vols) London 1904

Canning, Stratford (Viscount de Redcliffe), *The Eastern Question*, London, 1881

Carne, J, *Syria and the Holy Land, Asia Minor* (3 vols), London, 1836-38

Carruthers, ADM, *Arabian Adventure to the Great Nafud*, London, 1935

Carson, Gregory, *Abu Zayd: the Rogue of the Golden Tongue*, in *Ur*, magazine of the Iraq Cultural Centre, London, Vol 3, 1981

Chapple, JAV and Sharps, John Geoffrey, *Elizabeth Gaskell: A Portrait in Letters*, Manchester, 1980

Chardin, J, *Voyages du Chevalier Chardin en Perse, et autres lieux de l'Orient* (ed. Langles), Paris, 1811

Chesney, FR, *The Expedition for the Survey of the Rivers Euphrates and Tigris* (2 vols), London, 1850

Chirol, Sir VI, *Indian Unrest*, London, 1910

Churchill, Winston, *Great Contemporaries*, London, 1937

Collingwood, W.G., *The Life and Work of John Ruskin* (2 vols), London, 1893

Colvin, Sir Auckland, *The Making of Modern Egypt*,

London, 1906

Curzon, George (Marquis of Kedleston), *Persia and the Persian Question* (2 vols), London, 1892
— *Tales of Travel*, London, 1923

Curzon, Grace Elvina (Marchioness of Kedleston), *Reminiscences*, London, 1955

Dugdale, Blanche, *Arthur James Balfour* (2 vols), London, 1936

Dussaud, R, *Missions dans les Regions Desertiques de la Syrie Moyenne*, Paris, 1903

Egremont, Max, *The Cousins*, London, 1977
— *Balfour*, London, 1980

Eliot, George, *Letters*, Ed. Gordon S. Haight, Oxford, 1956

Euting, J, *Tagbuch einer Reise in Inner-Arabien* (2 vols), Leyden 1914

Faulkner, Peter (ed.) *Jane Morris to Wilfrid Scawen Blunt*, Exeter 1968

Fitzherbert, Margaret, *The Man who was Greenmantle*: *Life of Aubrey Herbert* London, 1983

Fraser, D, *The Short Cut to India*, Edinburgh, 1909

Gérin, Winifred, *Elizabeth Gaskell*, Oxford, 1976

Glubb, Sir John B, *Britain and the Arabs*, London, 1959

Harris, Frank, *Oscar Wilde, His Life and Confessions*, New York, 1920

Hilprecht, HV, *Explorations in Bible Lands during the Nineteenth Century*, Edinburgh, 1903

Hitti, Philip K, *History of the Arabs*, London, 1937
— *History of Syria*, London, 1951

Hobhouse, JC (Lord Broughton), *Contemporary Account of the Separation of Lord and Lady Byron*, London, 1870
— *Recollections of a Long Life*, ed. Lady Dorchester (6 vols), London, 1909/11

Hogarth, David George, *A Wandering Scholar in the Levant*, London, 1896
—*The Nearer East*, London, 1905

— *The Penetration of Arabia*, Oxford, 1922

Hogarth, Janet, and Courtney, W.L., *Pillars of Empire*, London, 1918

Hourani, A., *Arabic Thought in the Liberal Age, 1798-1939*, Oxford, 1962

Huber, C, *Voyage dans l'Arabie Centrale*, Paris, 1885

— *Journal d'un Voyage en Arabie*, Paris, 1891

Hurewitcz, JC, (ed.) *Diplomacy in the Near and Middle East: a Documentary Record*, New Jersey, 1956

Kelly, JB, *Britain and the Persian Gulf, 1788-1880*, Oxford, 1968

Kent, Susan Kingsley, *Sex and Suffrage in Britain*, Princeton, 1987

Kiernan, RH, *The Unveiling of Arabia*, London, 1937

Kinross, Lord, *The Ottoman Centuries*, London, 1977

Knight, Frida, *University Rebel, The Life of William Frend*, London, 1971

Lambert, Angela, *Unquiet Souls*, London, 1984

Landow, George P, *Past Masters (Ruskin)*, Oxford, 1985

Lane-Poole, Stanley, *Life of Stratford Canning*, London, 1888

— *The Story of Cairo: History, Monuments and Social Life*, London, 1893

Laurence, Dan H, (Ed.) *Bernard Shaw, Collected Letters 1898-1910*, London, 1972

Layard, Sir Henry, *Early Adventures in Persia etc,* London, 1887

— *Autobiography and Letters*, London, 1903

Leslie, Anita, *Edwardians in Love*, London, 1972

Leslie, Sir Shane, *Men Were Different*, London, 1937

Lindsay, Jack, *Turner*, London, 1973

Longrigg, S.H., *Four Centuries of Modern Iraq*, Oxford, 1925

— *Iraq 1900-1950*, Oxford, 1953

Lufti as-Sayyid, Afaf, *Egypt and Cromer: A Study in Anglo-Egyptian Relations*, London, 1968

Lutyens, Edwin, *Letters to His Wife Lady Emily,* ed. Percy and Ridley, London, 1985

Lutyens, Lady Emily, *A Blessed Girl*, London, 1953
— *The Birth of Rowland*, London, 1956
Lutyens, Mary, *The Ruskins and the Grays*, London, 1972
Lytton, 4th Earl of, *The Desert and the Green*, London, 1957
MacCarthy, Desmond, *Portraits I*, London, 1931
MacCarthy, Fiona, *The Simple Life, C.R. Ashbee in the Cotswolds*, London, 1981
— *William Morris, A Life for Our Time*, London, 1994
Mackail, JW, and Wyndham, Guy, *Life and Letters of George Wyndham*, London, 1925
Mackay, Charles, *Medora Leigh: A History and an Autobiography*, London, 1869
Mackenzie, Jean, *Children of the Souls*, London, 1986
Malet, Sir Edward, *Shifting Scenes*, London, 1901
— *Egypt 1879-1883*, London, 1909
Mansfield, Peter, *The British in Egypt*, London 1971
Marlowe, John, *Spoiling the Egyptians*, London, 1974
Marshall, Dorothy, *Fanny Kemble*, London, 1977
Meynell, Viola, *Alice Meynell - A Memoir*, London, 1929
— (ed.) *Friends of a Lifetime: Letters to Sydney Carlyle Cockerell*, London, 1940
— *The Best of Friends*, London, 1956
— *Francis Thompson and Wilfrid Meynell - A Memoir*, London, 1952
Milner, Alfred (Viscount), *England in Egypt*, London 1892
Moore, Thomas, *Letters and Journals of Lord Byron*, London, 1830
Nicolson, Harold, *Small Talk*, London, 1937
Palgrave, William Gifford, *A Year's Journey through Central and Eastern Arabia 1862-1863* (2 vols), London 1865
— *Essays on Eastern Questions*, London, 1872
Philby, H. St. J., *Arabia*, London, 1930
Pollen, Anne, *John Hungerford Pollen*, London, 1920
Porter, JL, *Five Years in Damascus* (2 vols), London, 1885
Richmond, Lady (ed.) *The Earlier Letters of Gertrude Bell*, London, 1937

Rose, Kenneth, *Curzon, A Most Superior Person*, London, 1969
— *The Later Cecils*, London, 1975
Ruskin, John, *Praeterita*, Oxford, 1978
Schmidt, Margaret Fox, *Passion's Child – The Extraordinary Life of Jane Digby*, London, 1976
Shaw, George Bernard, *Collected Letters*, Ed. Dan H. Laurence, 1972
— *John Bull's Other Island*, London, 1908
Smith, W.R., *Kinship and Marriage in Early Arabia*, London, 1907
Sykes, Sir Mark, *Through Five Turkish Provinces*, London, 1900
— *Dar ul Islam*, London, 1904
— *The Caliph's Last Heritage*, London, 1915
Turney, Catherine, *Byron's Daughter, London*, 1974
Upton, Peter, *Desert Heritage – An Artist's Impression of the Original Arabs Imported by the Blunts*, 1979
Weintraub, S, *Victoria*, London, 1987
Winstone, HVF, *Gertrude Bell*, London, 1976; (revised edition), London, 1993
— *The Illicit Adventure*, London, 1982
— *Uncovering the Ancient World*, London, 1985
Wright, Constance, *Fanny Kemble and the Lonely Land*, London, 1972
Woodham-Smith, Cecil, *Florence Nightingale*, London, 1983
Young Kenneth, *Arthur James Balfour,* London, 1963
Zeine, Z.N., *The Struggle for Arab Independence*, London, 1960
Zetland, Marquess of, *Lord Cromer*, London, 1932
Zwemer, Rev SM, *Arabia: Cradle of Islam*, London, 1900

# GLOSSARY

| | |
|---|---|
| *abba* | cloak, outer garment |
| *abd* | slave |
| *abu* | father |
| *aga* | headdress cord |
| *agheyl* | official guide in Ottoman Arabia |
| *akhawat* | fee for passage, money paid to guide |
| *allah, illah, ullah* | God |
| *Allah akbar* | God is great |
| *arfai* | pasture bush, firewood |
| *ausaj* | thorny bush |
| *bab* | gate |
| *bedouin* | desert nomad; more correctly, *badu* (collective), *badawi* (singular), *badawin* (plural) |
| *birka, birket* | cistern, artificial reservoir |
| *boum* | sailing boat |
| *burga, burqa* | face mask on woman or hawk |
| *burghul* | crushed wheat |
| *dakhala, dakhilak* | sanctuary, binding promise of protection |
| *darb* | road, path |
| *dhalul, thalul* | female riding camel |
| *dhow* | sailing ship |
| *dira* | pasture land, tribal homeland |
| *dishdasha* | male's white gown |
| *diwaniya* | living quarter, rest room |
| *dowla* | official, authority |
| *fali* | hollow between sand dunes |
| *fatihah* | opening verses of the Koran |
| *fi aman illah* | Go in the peace of the Lord |
| *ghada* | succulent tree, camel fodder |

| | |
|---|---|
| *ghaz(z)u, badu* | raid |
| *hajj* | pilgrimage to Mecca |
| *hakim* | wise man, doctor |
| *hamd* | praise; also pungent shrub |
| *hanash* | snake |
| *haramieh* | thieves |
| *Haram* | holy precinct of Mecca |
| *Harem, harim* | women's quarters |
| *harra* | volcanic terrain |
| *Hejira, Hegira* | 'flight' of Prophet to Madina, marking the beginning of the Muslim era |
| *ibn* | son of; colloquially, *bin* |
| *imam* | religious leader |
| *jabal* | mountain or prominent hill |
| *jambiyah* | dagger |
| *jemader* | camel minder |
| *jihad* | holy war |
| *kadhi* | magistrate |
| *kaffiya* | Arab head cloth |
| *kahawa, qahawa* | coffee, entertainment room |
| *kaimaka, qaimaqam* | local governor, mayor |
| *kalima, kelam* | to speak God's word; the holy slogan of Islam |
| *kasr, qasr* | fort or palace |
| *kavass (Turkish)* | armed servant or guide |
| *kayf, kayif* | pleasurable contemplation, solace |
| *khabra* | share; also pond |
| *khanjar* | curved dagger |
| *khatih* | preacher |
| *kiswa* | black-and-gold cloth on Kaaba at Mecca |
| *leben* | butter milk, soured milk |
| *lisam, litham* | badawin face mask |
| *madrassah* | school |
| *mahmal* | ceremonial camel litter |

| | |
|---|---|
| *majlis* | assembly, council |
| *mafrash* | carpet for tent floor |
| *maktub* | 'It is written'; common badawin response |
| *Mamluk, mamluke* | Circassian slave dynasty of Egypt |
| *mashab, mehjan* | camel stick |
| *mattrah* | mattress |
| *mereesy* | dried milk cake |
| *mizrak* | primitive incendiary weapon |
| *mizwada* | baggage tent |
| *moghrabi* | occidental, westerner |
| *muharrmat* | acts forbidden by Islamic law |
| *mutasarrif* | overlord, Turkish title |
| *nafud* | sand dunes |
| *nasrany* | Christian |
| *Pasha* | Lord |
| *Porte* | Ottoman government, abbreviation of 'Sublime Port', from satirical French *le porte sublime* in reference to *al bab al ali*, the high ingate of the Sultan's palace |
| *ras* | head, headland |
| *raudha* | garden |
| *rikat, ruka'at* | symbolic movements associated with prayer |
| *samn* | sheep's butter |
| *sharif* | noble |
| *shimal* | north wind |
| *shugduf* | ordinary camel litter |
| *suk, suq* | market place, bazaar |
| *sura* | verses of the Koran |
| *takbir* | symbolic gesture at beginning of prayer |
| *tair* | bird |
| *ukhlus!* | finish! |

| | |
|---|---|
| *ulema* | learned man |
| *um* | mother |
| *vilayet (Turkish)* | administrative region |
| *wadi* | valley, empty riverbed |
| *wakir al tair* | hawk's stand |
| *wasm* | tribal mark; used on cattle |

# INDEX

*Sub-headings are arranged in combined chronological and thematic order rather than alphabetical so as best to reflect the lives of the individuals.*